ON THE LEFT BANK
OF THE TIBER

Also by the author

A Midlife Journey

Visit www.gracewing.co.uk

ON THE LEFT BANK OF THE TIBER

By

Gerald O'Collins SJ

GRACEWING

Originally published in 2013 by Modotti Press,
an imprint of Connor Court Publishing Pty Ltd, Australia

This edition published in 2013 by
Gracewing
2 Southern Avenue
Leominster
Herefordshire HR6 0QF
www.gracewing.co.uk

ISBN 978 085244 835 9

CONTENTS

For Jürgen and Elisabeth Moltmann
De licentia superiorum ordinis

Preface

In March 1997 the production crew for an Australian television company came to Rome to shoot a film for 'Getaway', a programme designed to encourage and enlighten prospective tourists. They put me in front of the camera while I took a handsome, young actor around the main sights of Rome. We finished by sitting on the edge of the Trevi Fountain. Before David Reyne and I performed the usual ritual of throwing three coins over our shoulders into the fountain and making wishes, I stole some words from a famous Bengali poet, Rabindranath Tagore (1861-1941), and said: 'David, you came as a stranger; Rome received you as a guest; and now you're departing as a friend. Well, friend, what's your biggest impression of the city?' With a flamboyant gesture towards the exotic crowd around us, he replied: 'I feel that I'm on the stage all the time.'

I too felt that I had been acting in a living theatre that opened well over two thousand years ago and is still going strong. The Trevi Fountain, a mecca for millions of tourists who patrol the streets of Rome, was completed in the eighteenth century but is fed by the Acqua Vergine, an aqueduct constructed in the first century B.C. In a gleamingly modern ice cream shop at the Trevi, a green Roman column rises through the floor and goes up through the ceiling. Faces underline my sense of continuity. The soft beauty of an Italian face can bring to mind a Madonna painted by Raphael or some other Renaissance genius. At times I spotted square-jawed men and asked myself whether they have in fact stepped right off the Emperor Trajan's second-century AD column, shed their armor, put on modern clothes, crossed the Piazza Venezia, and joined those enjoying an evening stroll along the Via del Corso. If you yearn for a world with a history, Rome is the place

What better place could there be than the Eternal City for coping with the move into the third millennium? The Great Jubilee year of 2,000, which drew millions of pilgrims to Rome (and many tourists who became pilgrims), not only recalled the birth of Jesus Christ but also evoked God's provision of a jubilee year in Leviticus 25 to encourage freedom and holiness. Leviticus 25 made me hope that the visitors, who walk through our Jewish quarter down by the Tiber and eat in its fabulous 'trattorie', will recall that Jews have lived in Rome far longer than Christians. Jews came to Rome as part of a dispersion around the Middle East and the Mediterranean world which began even before the Babylonians captured Jerusalem in 587 BC. An Italian Jew, Giorgio Barzilai, claimed a family tree stretching back three thousand years and assured me that, despite the slight difference in spelling, he was descended from Barzillai the Gileadite who cared for King David and his troops when they were on the run during the revolt led by David's son, Absalom (2 Samuel 17: 27-29; 1 Kings 2: 7). Giorgio became one of the best friends I have ever known; more of him in a later chapter.

Autobiography is inevitably an act of self-justification. Will the overriding objective become an argument for Gerald O'Collins? At all events there is someone else to defend. I dedicate this book to Jürgen and Elisabeth Moltmann not only in deep gratitude for their friendship but also in order to justify Jürgen's advice when he was in Melbourne (Australia) for the 1973 Eucharistic Congress. The speakers at the congress included Mother Teresa of Calcutta and Cardinal Karol Wojtyla, soon to become Pope John Paul II. I was sitting in the back of a taxi between Moltmann and a European Catholic theologian when I told them that I had just been invited to teach in Rome. The Catholic theologian cut in sharply: 'Don't you go to that clerical ghetto!' By way of rebuttal Moltmann shook the lock of dark, silky hair that constantly hung over his forehead, and quoted a German proverb: 'Rome is worth a journey (Rom ist eine Reise wert).' I am happy to have followed Moltmann's advice, and he was to visit me several times in Rome.

How did I experience, serve, and fail students, colleagues and others over more than thirty years of teaching and writing theology on the banks of the Tiber? To help students who come from all over the world and cope with teaching them amid a sea of Italians may not quite be paradise on earth. 'How could you possibly survive there?' was a question that American and Australian friends and acquaintances put to me every now and then. Presumably if some expressed this doubt, more shared it. Almost always these worriers were Catholics and often enough professionally religious people.

Just before Christmas 1994 I went off to a charmingly exuberant party hosted by an Italian lawyer and his Irish wife. Happy, large-hearted people, they used to invite locals and visitors for gatherings in their Roman home.[1] As I walked towards their front door, I fell into step with a stranger who was obviously heading to the same party. When I introduced myself, she said: 'Yes, I've heard of you and read some of your work. Now, who's the latest victim in the witchhunt?' Among the strangest first words with which I have ever been greeted, they came from someone who apparently pictured Cardinal Joseph Ratzinger and his colleagues at the Congregation for the Doctrine of the Faith snooping around behind the Roman bushes and constantly searching for unorthodox professors to be penalized and dismissed.

---

1 One of their sons featured in international news in 2011 when he appeared as a lawyer for Amanda Knox (who had been convicted of the 2007 murder of Meredith Kercher) and had Knox's conviction overturned on appeal.

Later in this book I will have something to say about the shadow side of the Vatican and its officials. But I found Rome to be at least as free and happy an environment for teaching as any I have experienced in North America, the British Isles, Australia, and other parts of the world. At this point some readers may smile in disbelief and think to themselves: 'this is just another Jesuit who conceals the truth.' If so, I invite you to plunge into some of the books and articles I have published during my Roman years and ask yourselves: 'Does O'Collins write like someone looking fearfully over his shoulder all the time, as if he expected to catch sight of some staff member of the Vatican's truth police menacingly bearing down on him?'

One doctoral candidate, a priest from New Jersey, let his fears emerge at our very first meeting. A mature candidate, he had already successfully completed a doctorate in religious studies at an American university. Now he needed a doctorate in theology. We chatted about the thesis topic he had chosen and I felt very much at ease about the whole project; here was someone whose previous degrees and publications had already proved his academic expertise. His second doctoral thesis could be written very competently and would be happily defended in the minimum amount of time. Before he rose to leave my room, Frank nervously cleared his throat and asked: 'I presume my completed text will have to he submitted to the Congregation for the Doctrine of the Faith?' 'What a splendid idea!', I replied with a touch of irony. 'But why stop at doctoral dissertations? We could have a van come by every month to take all the license [= master's] theses along as well. The officials would wear themselves out reading all those texts, verifying the footnotes and checking the bibliographies. They could certainly free us from much of that work.' Frank was relieved to learn that no such control existed. But he left me a little sad. I pondered on the 'culture' (fostered by some elements in the media?) in which a mature, highly intelligent priest and academic could entertain such misapprehensions and fears.

Over the years it was often those who were not Catholics, like Moltmann, Reyne, and some of my Jewish friends, who regarded it as a wonderful privilege to work in Rome. Walking home with me from the Spanish Steps under a quiet and pleasant sky, one friend commented: 'People pay thousands of dollars to come and do what you can do any old evening.'

Some people imagine that the Gregorian University teaches Gregorian Chant and is even connected with Pope Gregory the Great who died in 604. In fact the name comes from Gregory XIII, a sixteenth-century pope who was an outstanding benefactor of the University in the early years after its foundation in 1551. With the help of a committee led by Clavius, a professor of mathematics and astronomy at the University, Gregory XIII (pope 1572-85) brought to fruition the correction of Julius Caesar's calendar, replacing it with the Gregorian calendar, now almost universally used.

Early in my Roman years I did a short interview for BBC Radio with Gerald Priestland for his programme 'The Case Against God'. A few weeks later a cheque arrived from London via Vatican City; apparently the BBC accountant thought the Gregorian University must be situated physically inside the Vatican.

'Of course, you teach in Latin' was a remark one could hear from visitors. In the spring of 1968, theology professors began switching from Latin to Italian as the usual language of instruction. The other faculties and institutes of the Gregorian followed suit. The Faculty of Canon Law was the last to run down the Latin flag. In 1993 they changed to teaching in Italian — much to the disappointment of some German high school students who studied Latin at home and liked to hear it spoken when they visited Rome during their term breaks.

The majority of the Gregorian's students live in such colleges as the Capranica (mainly for Italians), the French College, the German-Hungarian College, the Irish College, the North American College (normally known as 'NAC'), the Scots College, and the Venerable English College, so called because it is the oldest of these foundations. Hearing the word 'college', many fondly imagine that these establishments are also teaching institutions with a full academic faculty, along the lines of King's College (London) or such undergraduate colleges as Williams College (Massachusetts). In fact the Roman colleges fall into two categories: seminaries such as the North American College and the other colleges listed above (with only a small staff that attends to the spiritual and pastoral formation of their students who are preparing for the priesthood); or halls of residence for young priests where they can live together in a friendly, spiritual environment. Such are the Brazilian College, the Mexican College, the Portuguese College, and the Spanish College. The only college in Rome that boasts a full teaching staff is the Beda College, an independent, English-speaking seminary for 'delayed' vocations or mature students for the priesthood. Since its students can be in their fifties or even sixties, they have to endure such cracks as: 'the Beda students have given their flesh to the world, and now they want to give their bones to God.'

Students in all these colleges spend two to five years in Rome, some remaining longer for further degrees. Members of the teaching faculty of the Gregorian University, however, frequently stayed for twenty years or more, and they saw generations of students from the different colleges come and go. Most of the professors were non-Italian like me and hence living an expatriate existence. Back in the

1980s I had the opportunity to join a number of other 'Australian' Italians and comment on expatriate life for an Australian TV film, 'Postcards from Italy'. The director drew the title from a complaint sometimes heard in Australia: 'when you're in Italy, you only send us postcards.' She interviewed Australians from Milan to Palermo, people who were making their living as authors, painters, hairdressers, teachers, and journalists. A novelist who spent many years in Naples and on the Isle of Capri, Shirley Hazzard, summed up the sentiments of the majority of her fellow Australians: 'Italy brings out the best in you.' Many other foreigners would agree. We cherish our native land, with all the relatives and friends who live there. But Italy may have brought out the best in us.

This preface tried to give a flavour of things Roman and Italian. It is time to begin the book seriously. The theme for the opening chapter picks itself: the place where I lived and taught. But before moving to Chapter One, I want to thank Martin and Teresa de Bertodano for the many valuable corrections and changes they proposed when reading through the first version of this book. Martin also suggested that I should indicate briefly at this point my background. Let me do so.

Born in Melbourne (Australia) in 1931, I grew up on a farm almost thirty miles distant from the centre of the city. Until I went off to boarding school at the age of twelve, life with my three (older) sisters and two (younger) brothers seemed one long sabbatical. We were taught by a governess; when she left to marry, I read books in the library of classical literature my mother inherited from her father, dabbled in a correspondence course from a city college, and rode a horse to school for one year at a primary school. After a five year stint at boarding school and one year at the University of Melbourne, I joined the Society of Jesus in 1950 and was ordained a priest in 1963. Studies in Australia, Germany, and England closed with a Ph.D. at

Cambridge University in 1968. Then followed five years of teaching one semester each year for Weston School of Theology (within the Boston Theological Institute) and the other semester home in Melbourne for the Jesuit Theological College (within the United Faculty of Theology at the University of Melbourne). In 1973–74 I took a sabbatical as a visiting fellow back at Pembroke College, University of Cambridge and wrote volume one of my autobiography, *A Midlife Journey* (published in 2012 by Connor Court). This book picks up the story from August 1974 when I came to teach full time in Rome.

Since I arrived on the left bank of the Tiber in 1974, for better or worse I have published numerous articles in journals, chapters in books in collaboration, and over sixty books that I authored or co-authored. In the UK, Oxford University Press have published twelve of these books; in the USA, Paulist Press (Mahwah, New Jersey) have published thirty-one of them; several other publishing houses have put out further works I wrote or co-wrote. *On the Left Bank of the Tiber* will describe and explain the matrix that generated all that theological and spiritual writing.

Jesuit Theological College, Parkville (Australia)
Gerald O'Collins, SJ, AC
28 February 2013

Photographs

Gerald O'Collins SJ in Rome, 1995

1

The Gregorian

Moored like a large liner to the slopes of the Quirinal Hill, the Gregorian University rides at anchor just below the Quirinal Palace. That vast home for the Italian president stretches away flatly from a box-shaped tower and looks for all the world like a mammoth oil tanker. Among the Gregorian's most imposing features are the twenty-feet high portals of bronze. They open easily, since they are not hung from lateral columns but, as in Roman times, are hinged right into the stone floor and slotted into a groove at the top. To the left of the portals, down the Via della Pilotta, four charming stone bridges cross the sunken street and give the Colonna family access from their palace to a villa or summer residence. In this case the villa is only a few yards from the palace. Most of the old Roman families such as the Borgheses and the Dorias had villas at least a mile or two away, and sometimes well outside Rome, even up in the Castelli Romani or 'Roman Castles', a cluster of walled villages on volcanic hills to the south of the city. To the right of the Gregorian's monumental front entrance, the Trevi Fountain is three hundred yards down a narrow street. The square dominated by our pompous portals is called the Piazza della Pilotta.

'Pilotta' comes from 'pelotes', a game Spaniards used to play; 'Pelotz' is still played in the Basque parts of Spain. The name of our square has nothing to do with some Pilate family who had a legionary thug named Pontius among their ancestors. When you head down the Piazza della Pilotta and turn left at the bottom, you come to the Piazza Venezia, where traffic swirls around the Victor Emmanuel monument, a gigantic white wedding cake backing onto the Roman forum.

The Gregorian stands right in the heart of the historical centre of Rome, a mixture of buildings and streets whose origins stretch back to Roman times and where the living seem to co-exist with the heroic dead. Like most of the ecclesiastical places for study in Rome, the Gregorian University is on the left bank of the Tiber. The burial places of Saints Peter and Paul serve to symbolize the distinction (which is not the same thing as separation) between the official church of leadership over on the right bank of the river (Peter) and the charismatic church on the left bank, represented in part by those with personal gifts as teachers (Paul). To reach Peter's tomb under St Peter's Basilica you must cross the Tiber to the right bank. St Paul's Outside the Walls, which may still contain the apostle's remains, lies a couple of miles down stream and on the left bank. Paul the brilliant theologian died a martyr's death like Peter, the Galilean fisherman turned Christian leader. Faith and martyrdom united them. But their grave sites express differing functions within and for the one church community.

A View from the Roof

The view from the flat roof of the Gregorian shows Rome trimly articulated at your feet. To the immediate left you can peer down into the Colonna garden where the son of the prince and princess sometimes played with his friends and where once or twice a year torches illuminated a dazzling reception. A six-storeyed villa closes the far end of the Colonna garden; for years the top rooms provided a Roman home for Gianni Agnelli, the Fiat magnate from Turin.

When you look to the right of this villa, you can just spot St Peter mounted since the sixteenth century on top of Emperor Trajan's Column and gazing over Trajan's Forum. Looking further around to the right you will see the cupolas of the Church of the Gesù (or Holy Name Church), Sant'Andrea della Valle (where Giacomo Puccini set the opening act for 'Tosca'), and San Giovanni dei Fiorentini. Straight out in front one's eyes can rest on the unique majesty of the cupola of St Peter's. Female, bosom-like cupolas dot the scene; there is not a single phallic, Gothic spire in sight.

Looking further to the right you catch St Paul standing since the sixteenth century on top of Emperor Marcus Aurelius's column. Holding the sword of his martyrdom, the apostle keeps watch as a sentry over the Italian house of parliament. It's a shame that he's not alive among us today. Otherwise from his lofty perch he could have steadily castigated corrupt and criminal parliamentary deputies. Close by and even more to the north, you can make out the backdrop to the Trevi Fountain and above it the Church of Trinità dei Monti and the Villa Medici, which dominate the Spanish Steps.[1] Mount Soratte, which the Latin poet Horace celebrated, rises in the distance to the north.

To complete my guided tour from the roof of the Gregorian, I normally took visitors to the back of the building, where they can gaze down into the ruins of the Temple of the Sun or lift their eyes beyond the Roman bricks and take in the delightful Piazza Quirinale. Every afternoon band music accompanies the changing of the

---

1 An eighteenth-century baroque work, the Trevi Fountain features the god Neptune in a chariot drawn by two horses. Built also in the eighteenth century, the Spanish Steps, named after a palace that used to be occupied by the Spanish Embassy, lead up the Pincian Hill to the French church of Trinità dei Monti (the Trinity of the Moutains) and to the Villa Medici, which since the nineteenth century has housed the French Academy in Rome.

presidential guard and children always have space to play. For years
I hadn't visited the Piazza Quirinale by night. In 1995 after a dinner
with two friends I led them back that way to their hotel. It was a mild
autumn evening; every few yards the square was lined with couples in
passionate embraces.

Life on the Fourth Floor

During more than thirty years at the Gregorian I lived in the same
room (C451), on the fourth floor and just under the flat roof. As
the room faces inward and across the glass-roofed atrium, no traffic
noises are heard. The sight of the flag that tops the Quirinal Palace
and the sound of the distant chimes of its clock link me to the world
outside. Showers and toilets are located down the corridor which
leads to the back of the building. Until the early 1990s the small
washbasins tucked into the corners of the rooms offered only cold
water. The pipes that now bring hot water run along the ceiling of
the corridors outside the bedrooms. They call to mind the equipment
for submarines. One might imagine firing a torpedo through the glass
doors at the end of my corridor, out across the Roman rooftops, and
straight on to the Villa Lante high up on the Janiculum Hill. A slightly
curved shot to the left could bring the statue of Giuseppe Garibaldi
down from its pedestal on top of the Janiculum. He is 'defended' by
a cannon that is fired at twelve o'clock. The midday boom normally
drifted across the city into my room. 'Per inciso' or in parenthesis,
as the Italians say, the most dramatic view of Garibaldi (1807-82), a
fighter for Italian unity, has to be close up, from the botanical gardens
at the foot of the Janiculum. The huge pedestal is covered by the lush
leaves of the trees; so Garibaldi gives the illusion of riding through
the sky.

Until 1946 Italy was a monarchy; in that year the people in a

referendum voted in favour of a republic. Every year on the Feast of
the Republic, which recalls the referendum of 2 June 1946, several jet
aircraft thunder low over Rome and belch out red, white and green
smoke to form the Italian flag in the sky. As 2 June is my birthday, I
took the ceremony as a personal salute.

When I came to live at the Gregorian, my fourth-floor corridor
provided me with some impressive companions, each in his austere
room with a desk, a bed, some book shelves, a wash basin, a couple
of chairs and a modest closet for clothes. On one side, Antonio
Orbe rose before five o'clock but was the quietest and gentlest of
neighbours. This Spaniard, who loved music, soccer, and bull-fights,
dedicated his life to research and writing on St Irenaeus (d. about 200)
and the second-century Gnostics whom Irenaeus hammered. Orbe
never seemed concerned to negotiate English translations of his
works. The outstanding scholarship that made him a mouthpiece of
Irenaeus on earth has remained largely unknown outside the Spanish-
and Italian-speaking worlds.

Two doors away on the right Giacomo Martina spent twenty
years on an old-fashioned typewriter composing a three-volume, two
thousand page account of the pontificate of Pius IX (pope 1846-78),
remembered not least for being the longest 'reigning' pope since St
Peter. An indefatigable and scrupulously honest historian, Martina
set Pio Nono in the context of the world church and its nineteenth-
century expansion. He resisted the normal fascination with 'the
Roman question', that is to say, with the incorporation of the papal
states into the Italian nation brought by the 1870 unification of Italy.
Martina served on the commission which examined the suitability
of Pio Nono for beatification or official naming as 'blessed' —an
essential step towards 'canonization' or being declared a saint. While
the majority of the commission voted in favour of beatification,

Martina not only recorded his negative vote but also wrote a personal letter to Pope John Paul II and continued to argue the case against Pio Nono as a candidate for beatification and canonization.

For years the voice of Martina prevailed against those Vatican officials who aimed at having a pope canonized or beatified from each century. St Pius V (pope 1566-72) from the sixteenth century is followed by Blessed Innocent XI (pope 1676-89) from the seventeenth century. In 1954 St Pius X (pope 1903-14) was canonized to exemplify papal sanctity in the twentieth century. But there remained the yawning gap of the eighteenth and nineteenth centuries. Martina's scholarship could not check the rush to fill the gap with 'Blessed Pius IX'. On 3 September 2000 'Pio Nono' was beatified together with the much loved John XXIII (pope 1958-63); a crowd of one hundred thousand rapturously applauded the beatification of Pope John but reacted with sullen silence to the beatification of Pius IX. Martina's monumental life of Pio Nono remains untranslated and unavailable for those who do not read Italian. In his own way Martina, like the Irenaeus scholar Orbe, furnished me with the image of an absolutely dedicated, scrupulously fair, and utterly otherworldly scholar. Before I leave Orbe and Martina, let me add a story about each of them.

In March 1977 when my mother died in Australia, Orbe somehow learned the news very quickly. When I arose the following morning at 5.30, the letter box in my bedroom door already carried a note from him: 'My sincerest sympathy. I have said Mass for your dear mother this morning. Orbe.'

Some evenings during the concert season I used to receive a free ticket from an Italian family who had an extra place at the Santa Cecilia auditorium in the Via della Conciliazione. Often enough I found myself next to one of Martina's cousins, a leading Italian judge who eventually became the Chief Justice of the Supreme Court of Italy. A very discreet person, the judge would talk only about music and his two children. One evening I left the theatre with him and expected to find bodyguards waiting at the exit. At the time he was hearing appeals from some convicted members of the Mafia, and during the daytime the court and his nearby home seemed like military bunkers. But there was not a guard within sight. I walked with the judge part of the way to his home, but as quickly as politeness allowed I swung off to the right and crossed one of the bridges over the Tiber. The incident made me think that the Mafia, at least in Italy, don't do much killing after sunset. Years later, shortly before his retirement the judge publicly supported legalization of drugs as the best practical solution to a dreadful problem. 'Now we know where he stands', I told Martina teasingly.

Goenaga, Monachino, and Cappello

When I arrived at the Gregorian aged forty three, many of the Jesuits living there were a good deal older than me, including a wiry little Spaniard, José Goenaga, who had come to teach philosophy in the late 1930s. José would go to endless trouble to answer my enquiries about his early years in Rome during the Second World War and its aftermath. In 1945 the chief rabbi of Rome, Eugenio Zolli (1881-1956) became a Catholic and lived for a time at the Gregorian in room C311, as a guest of the then rector, Father Paolo Dezza, who was to become papal delegate for the Society of Jesus (1981-83) and be created a cardinal in 1991. Goenaga was full of reminiscences about the forties and the fifties, when the legendary Canadian philosopher-theologian, Bernard Lonergan, taught at the Gregorian and also occupied room C311. Years later Luis Ladaria, an outstanding theologian who did his doctorate with Orbe, took over what had been Lonergan's room — a happy academic succession of occupants.

An Italian scholar who for years served as dean of our church history faculty, Vincenzo Monachino kept me spellbound with his story of a trip north of Rome in January 1944, on the day after the American and British troops landed south of Rome at Anzio and Nettuno. Somehow Monachino had got the use of a truck and headed up the Via Flaminia to buy provisions for the hungry Jesuits in Rome. He filled his truck with produce from farmers, and then, to his dismay, saw that the highway back was one long line of German trucks and armored vehicles heading south through Rome to attack the allied troops at Anzio. As he had studied German for several years, Monachino was able to talk his way into the column. He found himself and his truck in the midst of soldiers fearful of being shot up by the dominant allied airforce. On that sunny day they would have been sitting ducks, without any significant air cover of their own. But down at the beachhead the allied commanders, who had so far met very little resistance from German infantry and tanks, feared that they would be hit from the air. They kept their fighters covering the beachhead against raids which came only some days later. What if they had sent their fighters north of Rome to attack the approaching German columns? This was one of those tantalizing 'ifs' of the Italian campaign. At all events Monachino brought his truck safely home to the centre of Rome, even being escorted by a German officer down the Via del Corso and right to the Gregorian after the curfew.

One Jesuit whom I could not meet at the Gregorian, since he had died a decade before I arrived, was Felice Cappello (1879-1962), a canon lawyer of outstanding holiness. The room he had occupied (C454) was right across the corridor from mine. The Roman public remembers him as a confessor to whom thousands went to receive absolution and help in a confessional on the left hand side as you walk up the Church of Sant' Ignazio. Day after day Cappello would be escorted by a policeman to protect him from importunate well-wishers as he made his way from the Gregorian across the Via del Corso and down a line of penitents in the church to spend hours listening to them in his 'box'. Confessor to Rome, he was also the priest to whom the Jesuits of the Gregorian flocked for confession.

'What was so special about him?', I asked several of the old timers. 'He was always so patient', was their usual answer. They fascinated me with their stories about him. One day a stranger happened to run into Cappello himself and asked: 'Where do I find that saint, Father Cappello?' 'Cappello sì, santo no (I'm Cappello but I am not a saint)', he was told. Another story concerns Father Wladimir Ledochowski (1866–1942), the awesomely autocratic superior general from 1915 until his death in 1942. Like later Jesuit generals he lived up near the Vatican and nowhere near the Gregorian University, but in the late 1920s he had personally overseen the construction of what is still the main building at the Gregorian. After its completion he continued to drop in unannounced like a property owner visiting his buildings. One day Father Ledochowski knocked on Cappello's door, without heeding a notice showing that Cappello was 'occupato' (engaged). From inside Cappello called out, 'I'm engaged.' From the corridor Ledochowski replied, 'It's Fr General here.' 'I'm still engaged (sono occupato lo stesso)', Cappello insisted. He could have been under pressure to complete some research for Pius XI or Pius XII. He used to advise these popes until the day came when his opinion did not coincide with what Pope Pius XII expected. 'This is a matter of church law (*de iure ecclesiastico*)', Cappello told him. 'But surely it's a matter of divine law (*de iure divino*)?', Pius XII insisted. Cappello would not budge; his knowledge of canon law had led him to a different, more liberal, conclusion. That was the last time, so I was told, that the Pius XII asked Cappello for an opinion. After the election of John XXIII, Cappello was called back again as a papal advisor.

When Cappello died, his casket remained open for at least a day in the student chapel on the ground floor near the Gregorian's main entrance. Princess Orietta Doria Pamphilj was among those who came along to say goodbye. 'Everyone from cardinals to garbage collectors', she told me, 'lined up to pay their respects, pray, and touch the corpse.' One relative of Cappello who came was Albino Luciani, then bishop of Vittorio Veneto and later to become Pope John Paul I. Luciani came south for the requiem Mass in the Church of Sant' Ignazio and stayed overnight in a spare room in the Gregorian infirmary. He knew us well, because he had written a thesis for the Gregorian's theology faculty during the 1940s, on Antonio Rosmini-Serbati (1797–1855), a philosopher, priest, and founder of the Institute of Charity (Rosminians).

Like many of his predecessors at the Gregorian, Cappello was buried out at Campo Verano, the giant Roman cemetery not far from the main railway station. Later the metal casket was shifted to the Church of Sant' Ignazio where Cappello's confessional box still stands. In November 1996 as part of the official procedure for the process that could lead to his beatification and eventual canonization, the casket was opened so that his remains could be verified. City representatives, Vatican officials, and some Jesuits (including one or two who had known him) were astonished to see Cappello lying there seemingly perfectly preserved thirty four years after his death, the only difference being a red spot on the tip of his white nose. Thoughts ran instantly to the possibility of an incorrupt body, as has sometimes been observed with saints from the past. Within days, however, Cappello's remains had collapsed. In death as in life much about him was so ordinary, and he now has a tomb in the place where he heard thousands of confessions. I was in no hurry to see Cappello beatified, as that would have turned his room across the passage from mine into a shrine. Life would no longer have been so gloriously peaceful up there on the fourth floor.

Alfaro, Boyer, Tromp, and Dhanis

It was on a late August evening in 1974 that I arrived to begin my new life at the Gregorian. The following morning I came down to find those few of the community who had already returned from summer holidays or other commitments sitting in prayerful silence drinking their coffee and eating rolls in our breakfast room. I thought of shouting out Lytton's Strachey's parting shot to some of the Bloomsbury Group: 'You are doomed, all of you doomed!' I was stopped by the arrival of a dapper little man with a moustache and wearing a white jacket. 'He has come to take one or two of them away to the clinic', I thought. But this was Vittorio, the assistant infirmarian, who was picking up some breakfast for one or two sick or aged members of the community. The situation was saved for me by the arrival of Juan Alfaro, a small, bright-eyed Spaniard whose work I had read and admired. 'You are most welcome', he told me in Italian and gave me a big hug before starting his breakfast.

Alfaro was a longtime colleague of the German Jesuit theologian Karl Rahner, with whom he collaborated on a six-volume theological dictionary that appeared in four or five languages, *Sacramentum Mundi*. Alfaro knew the Scriptures much better than his German friend, and had done excellent work on the Gospel of John. When Pope John Paul II's first encyclical, *Redemptor Hominis* ('the Redeemer of human beings'), appeared in 1979, I counted over forty quotations from or references to John's Gospel; Paul's Letter to the Romans came in a distant second with around twenty quotations or references. 'Did you have a hand in that encyclical?', I asked Alfaro. He smilingly admitted that the Pope had consulted him about the text. Some years later he also admitted having prepared an address to theologians which the Pope delivered during a visit to Spain in late 1982. The only change was a final paragraph which the Pope added — about theologians finding inspiration from the Blessed Virgin Mary. It grieved me when Alfaro fell victim to Alzheimer's disease shortly after he became emeritus and retired as a full professor on the Gregorian's theology faculty at the age of seventy.

I had been prepared for some of my colleagues at the Gregorian by the amusing descriptions of an American friend, who had taught there and finished his teaching career in New England. Phil Donnelly was a devastating mimic, doubtless including me and my Australian accent in his repertoire. When he lived at the Gregorian, Phil had known a grand old man of the philosophy faculty, Charles Boyer. A tiny Frenchman, Boyer was a pioneer in initiating ecumenical relations with other Christian churches. When Phil learned that Boyer would be travelling to the United States, he alerted the New York media that the great Charles Boyer would arrive on such and such a ship. The minuscule Jesuit was amazed to find journalists waiting to catch him when his ship docked and he went ashore. They found a bird-like intellectual in priestly dress instead of the French actor they had been expecting.

Boyer lived to see John Paul II visit the Gregorian in late 1979 and lunch with the community. As the Pope was leaving our dining-room, he bent down and huddled over Boyer in order to allow him talk straight into his ear. The scene still gleams in my mind. I wanted to ask Boyer: 'What advice did you give him?' I regret that I did not do so at once. Boyer, seemingly in good health for a man of 95 years, died shortly afterwards. His longevity undoubtedly owed something to a remarkably placid disposition and his capacity to fall asleep on any occasion. The story goes that on one occasion he took his place to preside at a meeting and managed to doze off even while a colleague was introducing the speaker. The applause that welcomed the speaker at the end of the introduction woke Boyer up. To everyone's astonishment, he rose to his feet and delivered a vote of thanks for a speech that had not yet been given!

Another older and most affable companion at the Gregorian was the Dutch theologian, Sebastian Tromp (1889-1975). In 1943 he wrote for Pius XII an encyclical letter on the church, *Mystici Corporis* ('the Mystical Body'). When Pope John called the Second Vatican Council, Tromp became the secretary of the theological commission and played a major role in preparing the initial drafts that the bishops were to reject or at least to modify drastically. Tromp, Cardinal Alfredo Ottaviani (1890–1979), and others, who had trusted the bishops to vote for the texts presented to them, were dismayed to discover shortly after the Council opened in late 1962 that the majority of the bishops refused to perpetuate the old formulas and wanted instead a fresh, biblical and pastoral approach to teaching. Tromp remained secretary of the theological commission and, to his lasting credit, never or hardly ever meddled with the new drafts.[2] He was remembered rather as saying, 'After a good drink I'm ready for any heresy.' In any case, he was 73 years of age when the Council opened; he had to rely on Gérard Philips (1898-1972), a younger professor from Louvain who as its undersecretary became the real workhorse of the theological commission.

I was much closer to another aging theologian from the Low Countries, Édouard Dhanis of Belgium (1902-78). We were linked by our common specialty, fundamental theology, which deals with

---

2 One apparent case, however, of Tromp's unilaterally meddling with a text is recorded by Yves Congar, *My Journal of the Council*, trans. M. J. Ronayne and M. C. Boulding (Collegeville, Minn.: Liturgical Press, 2012), pp. 640-41.

such basic issues as the resurrection of Christ. In 1970 Dhanis had rounded up a remarkable team of biblical scholars (such as Raymond Brown, Joachim Jeremias, Carlo Maria Martini, Xavier Léon-Dufour, and other stars) for an international, inter-church symposium on the resurrection. For years I wanted to follow suit but do something broader — by bringing a range of philosophers, theologians, and specialists in other fields together with the scriptural experts. Dhanis was long dead by the time Stephen Davis of Claremont (California) and I co-chaired the Resurrection Summit in New York at Easter 1996. With the untiring help of Dan Kendall, an American Jesuit who had been my first doctoral student, we managed to have the proceedings published by Oxford University Press in May 1997. I was determined to achieve speedy publication, as I knew how quickly the public forgets even a sensationally successful meeting and the symposiasts can themselves lose interest in what they said and wrote. Dhanis's edition of his 1970 symposium took five years to be published as *Resurrexit* by the Vatican Press. The book never had the impact that it greatly deserved.

Several times in my early years of teaching a course on God's self-revelation in and through Jesus Christ, Dhanis came along to give a guest lecture to the 160 or so students in the first-year theology hall. I enjoyed introducing him as a 'consultor for the Congregation for the Doctrine of the Faith, what used to be called the Holy Office'. The whiff of the old inquisition woke the students up. After one such appearance Dhanis had something else on his mind, however. He asked me a little apprehensively: 'Were those students in black suits along the back row members of Opus Dei?' 'Not as far as I know', I assured him. Most of our students dressed casually, although the majority of those already ordained wore a clerical collar or a cross to indicate their identity. An organization of laypersons and clergy, the members of Opus Dei have often been criticized for secretive behavior, theological conservatism, and rigid spirituality. One can be in the company of members of Opus Dei without knowing it. A later chapter will return to them.

Dhanis is often recalled as a disastrous rector of the Gregorian, a mistaken appointment made by his fellow Belgian, the Jesuit General, John Baptist Janssens. As rector Dhanis found himself unable to cope with the changes triggered at the Gregorian by the Second Vatican Council (1962-65). He was replaced in 1966 by Hervé Carrier, an affable Canadian sociologist who carried the University forward for twelve years. Dhanis may not have commanded universal respect, but that chunky, slightly awkward man won my lasting affection.

One memorable evening in late 1974, Dhanis came to my room for a conversation with one of Hans Küng's former assistants, a friend of mine who had every reason to be angry over the treatment had received from his ex-boss.[3] At that point Küng's disputes were still going on with the Congregation for the Doctrine of the Faith (the CDF) over such matters as papal infallibility and the possibility of the Eucharist being celebrated by those not ordained. In our chat with Dhanis my German friend surprised me by also urging Dhanis to persuade the others at the CDF to leave Küng alone. 'If you don't, you will only sell more copies of his books, and it won't help the ecumenical movement.' Küng had many friends and supporters among Anglicans and other non-Roman Catholics. Dhanis' response amazed me. He spoke of Küng with touching courtesy and also gave the impression of wanting the whole affair brought to some kind of peaceful public closure. A month or two later the CDF published what has to be the mildest rebuke in its long and shadowed history. Küng

---

3 I wrote of the difficulties which Josef Nolte had with Küng in *A Midlife Journey* (Ballan, Vic.: Connor Court, 2012), pp. 306-07.

was not required to retract anything that he had written against papal infallibility nor to abandon publicly his support for wider eucharistic celebrants (at least in emergency situations). He was asked only to refrain from repeating those views. I recognized the moderation of Dhanis in that statement, especially after he had laughed away the lip-service my German friend and I paid to the power of the CDF. 'We're just a toothless tiger', he assured us. In those days the mild Cardinal Franjo Seper still headed the CDF.

Four years later, however, in 1979 Küng disregarded the injunction to refrain from questioning papal infallibility and wrote an introduction for an angry and one-sided study by August Bernhard Hasler, *How the Pope Became Infallible*. Küng gave as his excuse: 'I couldn't turn down the request of my fellow countryman for a word of introduction.' Hasler was a disillusioned and dying man, whose historical and theological research did not stand the scrutiny of recognized scholars like Martina, who was still in the throes of his research into the life of Pius IX. Dhanis was now dead and the CDF responded to Küng's introduction by removing his right to teach as a member of the Catholic faculty of theology at the University of Tübingen. He remained a fully paid professor with his own institute, but he was now freed from the ordinary lecturing and examining duties of his colleagues!

In the last years of his life, Paul VI gave Dhanis the painful task of trying to deal with the charming but rigidly stubborn dissident, Archbishop Marcel Lefebvre, who, after leading a number of right-wing Catholics in a breakaway movement after Vatican II, intended to ordain some bishops and priests for his movement. Presumably the Pope chose Dhanis because he spoke French, was about the same age as Lefebvre and, most significantly, represented a conservative (but not dissident) point of view. Dhanis met Lefebvre at least once but could not dissuade him from ordaining priests and bishops for his schismatic movement. To thank Dhanis, the Pope gave him a cross as a present, even though the mission had failed. The gift symbolized the pain felt by the Pope and by Dhanis, who, nevertheless, gave me a somewhat humorous version of the charm and intransigence he met in Lefebvre.

Schneider, Alszeghy, and Flick

One professor at the Gregorian saddened us all by failing to return after what should have been a normal summer break with his widowed mother; this was Burkhart Schneider (1917-76). He was much younger than three other Germans at the Gregorian, who had passed off the scene by the time I arrived. Robert Leiber (1887-1967) went daily by public transport across the Tiber to serve Pius XII as private secretary. One of the Gregorian's 'brothers' (of whom more later) remembered the asthmatic Leiber frequently coming home tired and stopping to puff on his inhaler before he climbed the last stretch up the Piazza della Pilotta to the Gregorian. Gustav Gundlach (1892-1963) and Heinrich Lennerz (1880-1961) normally stayed at home when they had speeches or documents to prepare for the Pope — 'publishing under a nom-de-plume', one of them called it. Mother Pasqualina, Pius XII's housekeeper and perceived *éminence grise*, used to arrive in a black Vatican car at the Gregorian to pick up the completed texts from the Germans and pass on to them fresh requests. Gundlach, in particular, wrote text after text for the Pope.

Burkhart Schneider, nicknamed the 'carro armato' (the tank) by the students, began teaching at the Gregorian in 1965, almost a decade after the death of Pius XII in 1958. He was a member of the team publishing the twelve volumes of documents issued by the Holy See during the Second World War. Paul VI asked them to do this, after Rolf Hochhuth's play *The Deputy* charged Pius XII with failing to save Jews during World War II. When the American member of the team, Robert Graham, died in 1997, the Vatican's *L'Osservatore Romano* announced that the team had now all passed away. This mightily amused the surviving (French) member of the team, Pierre Blet, who wrote an obituary of Graham for the London *Tablet* in which he mentioned that reports of his own death were premature. He declined, however, to name the Italian newspaper which had consigned him to the grave.

During my first year at the University, 1974–75, Schneider in his role as editor of an historical journal published by the Gregorian occasionally invited me to his room and asked me to check the impeccable English he used to answer some correspondent or contributor. It was all a pretext to share a little of the excellent schnapps, which a farmer in the Black Forest had given him, and to make sure that I felt happy to be working in Rome. 'Time passes quickly here', he promised me. Schneider's mother lived in a slightly isolated place, and he would mail a postcard to her every day in order to guarantee that at least the postman would call on a daily basis. He always spent his holidays with her, but during the summer holidays of 1975 he fell ill with a previously unsuspected cancer and never returned to us. I wrote a letter to tell him how much I would miss his company but how much I looked forward to being with him in heaven. That is something I have not always had the courage to say to other friends or relatives, when I have learned that they were dying at a long distance from Rome. Through a mutual friend Schneider let me know that he had been greatly touched by the letter, and I appreciated how important it could be to do this more often.

In my early years at the Gregorian there were an intriguing pair of theology professors, Zoltán Alszeghy (1915–91) from Hungary and

Maurizio Flick (1909-79) from northern Italy. They took daily walks together and jointly published books on such themes as the cross and the human condition, one of which won the Malipiero Prize, a theology award worth about 2,500 euros and given every year or two by the Malipiero family of Bologna. Perhaps the most closely guarded secret at the Gregorian was the nature of their collaboration. Who wrote what? I suspect that Alszeghy did much of the research and that, after they had thrashed out their position and approach, Flick did more of the actual composition. The value and joy of such collaboration finally dawned on me, and I began publishing articles and then books with Daniel Kendall. The miracle of modern communication offset the obvious difficulty created by Dan living in San Francisco. When Flick fell ill in his late sixties, Alszeghy cared for him with moving devotion and was there to read to his dying friend the last letter he received. It came from a former student, a young American priest who wanted to thank Flick for his course and his personal example: 'You spoke well in your words and actions. Thank you again.' When Alszeghy read out the letter, Flick rallied for a moment to comment: 'Let's hope "They" think that way up there.' These were his last words before losing consciousness and dying.

In Rome, Flick was the only person I knew to predict the election of Albino Luciani after Paul VI died on 6 August 1978. The cardinals met later that same month when many of the professors were still away for the summer. Over supper in the Gregorian dining room, Flick shared his prediction with me. After John Paul I was elected on the first full day of the conclave, I asked: 'Father Flick, why did you think Luciani would be chosen?' 'He was the only clean (*pulito*) Italian cardinal', was the frank reply from someone who knew the Italian church well — not least from giving a Lent retreat to Paul VI and many cardinals in the Vatican.

When I arrived at the Gregorian in 1974, Flick suggested a roundtable discussion of my recently published *Has Dogma a Future?* At the time I thought it prudent to avoid unnecessary publicity, at least in Rome. Some people had already attacked me, because they failed to understand that the book concerned the terminology of dogma, and not the content of Catholic teaching. After the Protestant theologian Jürgen Moltmann had initiated fresh debate about the theology of the cross in a 1973 book that was read around the world, *The Crucified God*, I persuaded Flick to contribute a chapter to a joint work which appeared in English on both sides of the Atlantic, *The Cross Today*. Sir Anthony Kenny singled Flick out for extraordinary praise in his 1985 autobiography, *A Path from Rome*. This former priest turned Oxford philosopher recalled Flick as 'the best lecturer I have heard in a lifetime of lecture-going: every sentence vibrated with curiosity, energy and decision'.

Shadows and Lights

Some of my companions seemed to belong to another world. When one of them heard the news that six Jesuits in San Salvador, with their housekeeper and her daughter, had been murdered on 16 November 1989 (by the military as it quickly emerged), this Jesuit commented: 'they had it coming to them.' He had himself suffered from the Communists and had no time whatsoever for those who espoused liberation theology and sought to promote justice for the poor of this earth. Anything and anyone on what he considered the left could not be tolerated. Another companion, in a perfectly matter of fact tone, shocked me by announcing one evening over supper: 'I find it hard to decide whether Karl Rahner or Father Arrupe did more to harm the church and destroy the Society of Jesus. We will have to leave the verdict to history.' The innovations in theology partly prompted by Rahner and the changes in religious life encouraged by Arrupe, the

General of the Jesuits (1965-83), were anathema to him. He also came from a country which had been oppressed by Communism.

Among all the Jesuits from central and eastern Europe who lived at the Gregorian, the Poles surprised me with their dry humour. 'The Russians are our brothers,' one of them insisted with me. 'Why's that?,' I asked. 'You can't choose your brothers!' He also told me of the advice he had heard when home for holidays in Poland before freedom came in 1989. 'If you think, don't speak. If you think and speak, don't write. If you think, speak and write, don't sign. If you think, speak, write and sign, don't be surprised.' He had a story to tell about three young men who applied for a job with the police and had to take a simple arithmetic test. The question was: what is three by three? The first replied, 'six'. 'That's o.k.,' he was told. 'But please think about it a bit more.' 'Seven', he blurted out. Eventually he made it to nine and was sent out of the room. The second candidate entered. His answer to the question was 'six'. Further efforts failed to make him change his reply, and he was sent out of the room. The third candidate entered and replied 'nine' at the first attempt. The police official then filled in the reports. 'The first candidate,' he wrote, 'is stupid but is open to being corrected. The second candidate is stupid and stubborn. The third is intelligent and a danger to the state.'

The Pole in the Gregorian community who stood out for his calm goodness was Father Anton Mruk. Arrested in November 1939, this Jesuit was among the first prisoners in what was to become the extermination camp of Auschwitz. One of his prison duties was to clean the commandment's office. He took the opportunity to switch on the radio and catch the BBC news. The German officer could be relied on to return exactly at the usual time: so listening to the radio was not unduly risky. What took courage was sharing the news with other prisoners. One Judas could have sent Mruk to his death. In the end what probably saved his life was being transferred from Poland to Germany and the concentration camp in Dachau, where the killing of inmates was incidental, although widespread. Mruk saw out the rest of the war there, and emerged starving but remarkably intact as a human being and a Jesuit. In November to mark the anniversary of the day on which he was first arrested, I would invite him to my room and drink to his good health. 'When General George Patton liberated me from Dachau and I returned to a Jesuit community in May 1945,' he told me with grim humor, 'I noticed one difference at once. They rang bells throughout the day. In the camps the guards blew whistles and shouted at us.'

Occasionally he asked me to help him with letters to the British consular authorities requesting visas for Jesuit students from Poland who wanted to spend a summer studying English in Oxford. Mruk was always ready to give a hand to anyone, and anyone included a Polish bishop and then cardinal, Karol Wojtyla. Over the years Mruk's jobs for him included some advice in buying shoes on his visits to Rome. After this friend became Pope John Paul II in October 1978, Mruk went up to the papal apartments for the first Christmas party of the pontificate. The other Poles present included priests, seminarians and nuns. When the sing-song reached a number where in his old days as student chaplain Karol Wojtyla would join hands in a circle, he invited his Roman guests to do the same. After Mruk hesitated to take the hand of the nun next to him, the Pope quipped: 'I see Father Mruk isn't quite used to this.' Towards the end of his life, John Paul II asked Mruk to become his confessor. Every Saturday Mruk would go across Rome from the Gregorian and hear the Pope's confession. He was there in the papal apartments on Saturday, 2 April 2005, a few hours before John Paul II died.

Gregorian life brought much laughter but occasionally tears. An event that remains always sadly and vividly in my memory was the death one Christmas of a doctoral student. This Australian priest came to Rome in his forties, after working for a time as a missionary in an Asian country. He tried his luck with one supervisor who moved him on to another director, a somewhat forgetful and chaotic person. The student handed in his first chapter to that professor shortly before Christmas and asked: 'Will I see you in January when we all return?' 'No,' he was told, 'I work over the break and would like to see you at the end of December.' The student faithfully turned up, only to find that the professor had misplaced the chapter in the chaos of his room and couldn't locate it. The student returned home very upset and died in his sleep that night. He was a tense person and a great worrier. Others might have handled the situation with a laugh, but in this case stress undoubtedly helped to trigger a heart attack. The saddest aspect of it all was that the Australian student's body was not found for several days. The others in his community did not see him, but thought that he had gone away for the Christmas holidays.

Students did not live at the Gregorian nor did all the professors who taught there. Some Jesuits and other faculty members had their homes elsewhere. The most unforgettable of all the non-Jesuit teachers was Father Reginald Foster, a Milwaukee Carmelite who worked at the Vatican in the morning and then taught Latin for us — often six afternoons a week. In his jeans and often with a bottle of beer to hand, Reggie relished his mission of putting Latin back on the Catholic map. He came to appreciate his nickname, 'the Latin Lover'. His job at the Vatican entailed rendering into Latin encyclicals (authoritative letters on important themes addressed to the whole church) and other major documents issued by the Pope in Italian. On one occasion, early in the pontificate of John Paul II, Reggie sent back his translation and added the offer: 'If you like, I can shorten your text.' It was an offer not without justification, as some of the papal documents circled their topics at excessive length before coming in for a landing. The Pope wrote to thank Reggie and responded to his offer by quoting in Latin the notorious words of Pontius Pilate (John 19:22): 'quod scripsi scripsi (what I have written I have written).'

John Paul II's second encyclical, which appeared in November 1980, *Dives in Misericordia* ('Rich in mercy'), intrigued me because it dealt repeatedly with God's revelation, one of the topics of my lectures. Then I noticed that the English and Italian versions and, so my Polish friends assured me, the Polish version spoke in the normal way of God's 'revealing', 'making known', and 'manifesting' the divine reality and will, whereas the Latin version employed all kinds of elegant variations for these basic verbs. One day I met Reggie in the lift and confronted him: 'It was you who put *Dives in Misericordia* into Latin.' 'How did you guess?,' Reggie responded. 'It wasn't a matter of guessing,' I retorted. 'No one else would have dared to ring the changes on the standard vocabulary for God's revelation. In a hundred years time someone might well write a thesis on the development in the doctrine of revelation instigated by John Paul II, without realizing that you were the culprit.'

The Brothers and the Italians

Though some of our professors lived outside, not all of those who lived inside the Gregorian taught for one of our faculties or institutes. The non-teachers included a remarkable group of Jesuit brothers, men who belonged fully to the Society of Jesus but had not studied to be ordained priests. They included brothers from Spain such as Simon Eizaguirre, a Basque male nurse who for nearly fifty years worked in our infirmary. In 1962, before I reached the Gregorian he had cared for the dying Felice Cappello, laid out the dead body of that saintly canon lawyer, and helped to carry his casket out of the Church of Sant' Ignazio at the end of the funeral service. I had hoped that Simon might do the same for me, but he retired and went home in 1998. When I arrived at the Gregorian in August 1974, I was inclined to identify as skin cancer a lump that two months of sun over Florence had encouraged to grow on my forehead. Simon gave me some ointment, but when the growth hadn't surrendered after several weeks, he sent me off to a skin specialist and didn't seem penitent when I arrived home with several stitches and a huge patch where a surgeon had removed some skin cancer. Later I learned to cherish Simon for instantly providing me with just the right pills or ointments to fix bladder infections, cold sores, and lumbago.

Simon cared for us with indefatigable patience, as did José Mediavilla (1911–89), a transparently holy brother who was in charge of the dining room and the scullery. He saw his work at the Gregorian as a one-way mission, and never returned to his native Spain. He got up well before five o'clock and spent his days washing dishes, cleaning our breakfast room, preparing coffee at an unbelievably early hour, and caring for the dining room. In my first years at the Gregorian I loved serving at the one o'clock meal on Sundays, as it meant the chance of chatting with Mediavilla and hearing his stories about life at the Gregorian during and after World War II. 'In the early months of 1944,' he told me, 'you could often hear the bombing and shelling from Anzio and Nettuno.' 'The year before,' he added, 'when Italy changed sides in the war and the Germans captured Rome, a shell landed right outside the Gregorian and blew in some windows. You can still see some gashes on the bannisters of the main stairs.' I looked and found one or two. On Sundays Brother Mediavilla was regularly up at St Peter's for a Mass or for the papal benediction at noon. Then this wiry little man in his black robe would dash home on foot to see that we were all cared for at lunch. At the age of 78 a stomach cancer was diagnosed, and he died quickly. In death as in life this self-effacing servant of his fellow Jesuits never wanted to be a burden to anybody.

Our Jesuit brothers set a amazing standard of devotion, and —
one must add — of patience at the crude Italian (Gregorianesco
it was sometimes called) that we foreigners spoke. I also marvelled
at some of the Italian priests for also tolerating the way that I and
others massacred their delightful language. Ugo Vanni, a world class
commentator on the Book of Revelation, was a stylish Italian speaker
and writer. Always in service for the meetings of the council of the
theology faculty, he wrote the most exquisite minutes I have read in
any language. His prose was vivid, ironical at times, and utterly free
of the longwindedness to which Italians (and others) can be prone.
In my early years Ugo could see that I needed encouragement, and
would sometimes take me up to his room after lunch for a glass of the
strongest liqueur I have ever tackled: 'il latte della suocera (mother-in-
law's milk)'. No wonder that the bottle was labelled with a skull and
crossbones!

An even heartier Italian was Giuseppe Bernini (1916-77), a
professor of Old Testament who lived opposite me on the fourth
floor. I delighted to meet him on the street, so that I could cry out:
'Buon giorno, Padre Bernini.' With Rome filled with the works of the
incomparable artist, Gian Lorenzo Bernini (1598–1680), it gave me a
thrill to be able to call out the name along a crowded street. Bernini
died quite unexpectedly after a hernia operation.

But I was able to continue my practice whenever I ran into Father
Pietro Boccaccio, a retired professor who did not live at the Gregorian
but just across the square at the Biblical Institute. It had a ribald
flavour when we met on the Piazza della Pilotta or a nearby street,
and I could cheerfully greet him: 'Buon giorno, Padre Boccaccio.'
Totally unlike the author of the racy *Decameron*, Padre Boccaccio was
kindness personified. One Christmas it happened that my sister Maev
was staying in Rome. In those days it would have been inconceivable

At the Biblical Institute with Edward Farrugia in 1990

to invite her to share our Christmas dinner at the Gregorian. As I dreaded the thought of our eating together alone in some 'trattoria', I phoned Boccaccio. I hardly managed to say, 'my sister is in town,' before he said: 'Please bring her here to the Biblicum for lunch on Christmas Day. You are both most welcome.'

Some of the lay Italians who have worked at the Gregorian had the Boccaccio touch. Bilingual in French and Italian, Hilva Martorana served as secretary to at least six deans and one pro-dean of theology. Few professors and even fewer students realized how much she did through her administration, secretarial work (including brilliantly innovative letters in Italian and French), and wise advice to deans to keep the theological ship sailing ahead. She brushed aside my comment with embarrassment, when I told her one day: 'You are the mother of Catholic theology. Your impact goes out through our professors and students into the whole world.'

There were other Italian workers like her, but we also had some villains. One of them used to release at a price confidential information about boards for examinations and to do a little trade in Gregorian dissertations. On one occasion a text that had been accepted for our licence (or master's) degree turned up as a doctoral dissertation at another Roman university. The secretary general (or registrar) saw an amusing side to that sordid incident: 'Our licence dissertations must be good if they can get you a doctoral degree elsewhere.' Such cases involved students and institutes that had abandoned even rudimentary standards of scholarly and intellectual integrity. During my term as dean of theology, the two examiners turned down one doctoral thesis and their detailed reports made it utterly clear that they had done so rightly. The student, interpreting this failure as a moral mistake on the part of our examiners, declared that he forgave us all, and then successfully presented the same thesis for a doctorate at a university in a central European country.

Four Visitors to the Gregorian

And then there were the visitors. Pope John Paul II came twice, the second time in 1982 for an international meeting co-sponsored by the University of Macerata (a medieval town near the Adriatic coast) and the Gregorian to recall the Jesuit Matteo Ricci (1552–1610) and the fourth centenary of his arrival in China. Studies at the Gregorian, then called the Roman College, prepared Ricci for his mission to the powerful elite at the imperial court in what is now Beijing. The Pope's speech was remarkably open to the Chinese, their history, and their culture. But he held out an olive branch in vain; representatives of the Chinese government, after attending the first part of the Ricci celebration in Macerata (where the great missionary had been born) were pointedly absent from the second part held at the Gregorian.

The first visit of the Pope in 1979 was part of his early programme of going around the ecclesiastical universities and colleges of Rome. In speaking to our student body he urged them to cross the cultural divides and draw everything they could from the unique intercultural experience their Roman years offered them. Carlo Maria Martini, then in his second year as rector, welcomed the Pope and guided proceedings through the morning and over lunch with the community. Looking at Martini shepherding the Pope around with the ease of a born leader, I thought: 'You are finished now at the Gregorian.' Within weeks he was appointed Archbishop of Milan, and we lost a rector whose life had persistently drawn its inspiration and strength from daily contact with the Bible.[4]

Visitors from Asia included a Chinese Jesuit who had studied in Rome before going home in the 1940s to China, where he was

---

4 After Martini died on 31 August 2012, I published obituaries of him for the (Melbourne) *Age* and *Eureka Street* and co-authored the obituary published in the London *Times*.

condemned to spend years in solitary confinement. Alone in his cell he maintained his sanity by a strict regime of prayer and by visiting in his mind various churches in Rome. He imagined entering those churches, kneeling to pray for a while, and then rising to his feet and walking around to admire the frescoes, sculptures, and architectural triumphs. 'I was that busy,' he observed with a smile, 'I didn't have time to take a siesta.'

When another Chinese Jesuit, a bishop who had likewise endured years of imprisonment in his homeland, arrived one day for lunch, I couldn't believe that the community offered no applause as he walked down our dining room to the rector's table. 'What do you have to do or suffer to be applauded?,' I asked René Latourelle who was standing next to me. 'Only popes get applause here,' Latourelle responded. In the recreation room after lunch one theology professor, whom even the most charitable would have to say was a little out of touch with the practicalities of life, asked the bishop: 'What do you think of *Lumen Gentium* [the Second Vatican Council's dogmatic constitution on the Church] and its application to the Chinese situation?' The bishop laughed: 'I was in gaol during the Council and the years that followed. I haven't even seen the text yet.'

A visitor who brought tears to my eyes was a Vietnamese Jesuit, Joseph Nguyên. I got to know him when he was studying at the Biblical Institute. As the war drew to its close in Vietnam, he took early examinations and hurried home only to experience the fall of Saigon and years of work as a prisoner. When he left Rome in 1975, the Jesuit General, Father Pedro Arrupe, went out to the airport to see him off. He returned twenty years later as the Jesuit provincial of Vietnam and a delegate for our 1995 general congregation, a meeting which drew representatives from all the Jesuit provinces around the world and which other religious orders would call their general chapter. I can still hear the quiet voice of my Vietnamese friend as he told me the story of those twenty years and the incredible joy he felt on his arrival at Rome's main airport, where he was welcomed by Father Peter-Hans Kolvenbach, who had succeeded Father Arrupe as the Jesuit general.

René Latourelle

On the academic front, visiting professors were constantly invited by the French Canadian René Latourelle (b. 1918), a dynamic dean of theology who ran up twelve years at that job (1961-64, 1970-76 and 1982-85). His doctoral thesis, on the theology of divine revelation, sold, in all, over 100,000 copies in the original French and the translations into English and other languages. I have never heard of a doctoral dissertation in theology or any other discipline that enjoyed sales even approaching such a success.

Latourelle appreciated the value of contact with great outsiders for our students, above all for those doing the two-year licentiate programme and specializing in particular areas of theology. He secured courses of six weeks or even a whole semester from top American theologians such as Avery Dulles and David Tracy, the Greek Orthodox scholar John Zizioulas, Owen Chadwick from Cambridge University, Jürgen Moltmann from the University of Tübingen, and other stars. Thanks to the generosity of the McCarthy Family Foundation, we continued Latourelle's practice and enriched our academic offerings with visitors from famous universities. James Charlesworth came from Princeton, Gavin D'Costa from Bristol, Eamon Duffy and Janet Martin Soskice from Cambridge, James Dunn from Durham (England), George Lindbeck from Yale, Bishop Eduard Lohse from Göttingen, Dietrich Ritschl from Heidelberg, Geoffrey Wainwright from Duke, Metropolitan Kallistos Ware from Oxford,

Robert Wilken from the University of Virginia, Sergei Averintsev from the Russian Academy of Science in Moscow, and Tom Wright from Westminster Abbey. Through the McCarthy Visiting Professors. Latourelle's legacy of a broad theological exposure lived on.

He valued cultural achievements of all kinds and welcomed interdisciplinary dissertations that explored the theological relevance of Fyodor Dostoevsky (1821-81), Gerard Manley Hopkins (1844-89), and Flannery O'Connor (1925-64). After sitting with him on boards for comprehensive examinations which concluded the licentiate programs, I repeatedly heard him comment on students who had performed well: 'You could feel their broad culture in theology and other disciplines coming through.'

Latourelle also gave reality to my dreams of collaborative projects. We worked together as co-editors of *Problems and Perspectives of Fundamental Theology*, which appeared in English, French, German, Italian and Spanish. 'Get Karl Rahner to contribute,' he told me. 'Once we have the really big fish, then the others we ask will all agree.' Rahner cheerfully agreed to write for us, and dropping his name into our letters to the others naturally helped our cause. The failure of Johann Baptist Metz, an expert in fundamental theology from Münster, to deliver his chapter left us, however, with no representative of a practical style of fundamental or foundational theology that would suit exponents of liberation theology. Metz's excuse was the struggle he was going through over a call to a chair at the University of Munich, which would have brought him back to his native Bavaria. Joseph Ratzinger, then Archbishop of Munich, vetoed the appointment.

Even without Metz, *Problems and Perspectives of Fundamental Theology* proved a notable success; so Latourelle pressed ahead with a much more ambitious plan: a multi-volume work on the documents of the Second Vatican Council which would be timed to appear in 1987, a little over twenty years after the Council had ended in 1965. He gathered a large international team of experts and produced the work in English, French, Italian and Spanish. With this project completed, Latourelle turned up one evening in my room to discuss an idea that he had floated with me years before: a summer symposium of specialists in fundamental theology who would meet, perhaps at a lake in Canada, and produce a kind of manifesto about the present and future state of their discipline. I listened to him, and then another thought flashed through my mind: 'Why not prepare with others a dictionary of fundamental theology?'

Latourelle returned the following morning and said, 'Let's do it.' I gave him as much help as I could, and that couldn't be very much, as I had replaced him as dean of theology. I encouraged him to include women scholars in his team of contributors, and supported strongly a criterion of choice proposed by an American Jesuit colleague and in 1991 my successor as dean of theology, Jared Wicks: 'For the entry on Anglican views of fundamental theology, you should ask an Anglican to do it. And the same goes for a Lutheran view of fundamental theology, and so forth.' In 1990 *The Dictionary of Fundamental Theology* began appearing in various languages: English, French, Italian, Portuguese, and Spanish. The contributors wrote in their mother tongue, and their entries were translated when necessary. Thus for the English edition the ten or so pieces written by Wicks and myself went straight in, whereas our entries had to be translated for the other language editions. In that sense there was no original edition, *composed* and then published in one language, from which all the other editions derived. That dictionary proved to be Latourelle's last great hurrah for fundamental theology — at least in Rome. After he retired home to Montreal in 1990, he published at least six books, exemplifying a Gregorian's professor drive to communicate.

Although Latourelle had departed the Gregorian, his innovative ideas left their mark on me: not least in my ongoing collaboration in co-authoring articles and then books with Daniel Kendall of the University of San Francisco. Working together has shown me over and over again that in such cases the result is greater than the sum of the two parts. From writing with Dan, it was a small step to collaborating with him, Stephen Davis, and others in the 'Summit' meetings in New York (1996, 1998, 2000, and 2003) and in the books on the resurrection, the Trinity, the incarnation, and redemption that emerged from them. Of those enterprises I will write more in a later chapter. Looking back now, I can see the big part that an apprenticeship with Latourelle, as well as the example of Alszeghy and Flick, played in those joint ventures.

The Daily Schedule

This chapter aims to give a preliminary sense of what life was like at the Gregorian. By providing some idea of my daily schedule from October to June I can round off this opening sketch. Generally I would rise at 5.30 and in my early years would take a walk down to the Colosseum and back to the Gregorian by way of the Circus Maximus. A few police guarding public buildings would expect me and others to come by at a certain hour. 'Where were you yesterday morning?,' they once asked a fellow Jesuit who normally went jogging even earlier than I went walking. After some praying I would join Martina, the biographer of Pius IX, and several others in concelebrating a Mass around 6.50. A quick breakfast followed, at which, year by passing year, I would draw encouragement for the day from the wit of, successively, a Pole, a Spaniard, an Italian, and a Frenchman. They worked on the rest of us the way cheerful radio announcers do for a wider public through breakfast broadcasts.

I usually had class at 8.30, the dawn patrol hour when some students would still need a little waking up and a few would arrive late. On the way down to class I would stop for a quick cup of strong coffee in our recreation room on the third floor. Gulping it down I normally let my eyes cross the city to Michelangelo's masterpiece, the dome of St Peter's. It always fills me with a feeling of its power and perfection. Full of coffee and inspiration, I would hurry down to the large hall on the second floor where three or four times a week I tried to open the minds of one hundred and fifty or two hundred first-year theological students to new thoughts and fresh connections. For years I taught fundamental theology, covering such themes as God's self-revelation, the transmission of that basic revelation through the great tradition and the inspired scriptures, and the case for believing in Jesus as personally risen from the dead. Then from the spring of 1992 I switched to teaching the same first-year students Christology, or the doctrines of Christ's person, natures, and saving work for the world.

The theology faculty provides basic courses for students in what is called the first cycle. These are students who already have a B.A. (with an appropriate number of credits in philosophy). Their three-year programme at the Gregorian covers essential courses which centre on Christ in the first year, on the church in the second, on the individual in need of God's grace in the third. The programme corresponds fairly closely to that of the Master of Divinity degree in the United States. In the semester when a professor did not teach a first-cycle course, he was expected to take a second-cycle course for those specializing in fundamental theology, systematic theology, moral theology, biblical theology, or patristics (the study of early Christian writers) and the history of theology. Those courses met once a week for two hours. Over the years I taught second-cycle courses on issues in fundamental theology, on Christ's death and resurrection, and on the use of the Scriptures in theology. As professors both in the first and the second cycle could repeat and modify year after year the same course, the system provided a marvellous chance for deepening one's grasp of a particular field and publishing in it.

Community prayer at 12.50 usually precedes the main meal at one. After a thirty-minute siesta I would be back at my desk at three. Some afternoons there were seminar sessions (in Italian or English) for a dozen or so students from the first or the second cycle. The evening meal was a self-service affair that ran from 6.30 to 8.30. I rarely joined others for the evening news on television, preferring to get my information from the *Herald Tribune* and the *Frankfurter Allgemeine*. Some evenings I went up to our flat roof, which feels so liberating with the great sky above and to the north planes turning and cutting across the horizon towards Fiumicino airport. In September and April the sunset flares around the cupola of St Peter's. Later the moon may rise behind the Gregorian and come majestically up over the Colonna villa. I was frequently more or less alone up on the roof. The only time that I remember the community packing the terrace at night was in the spring of 1997, when they all decided to see the Hale Bopp comet gleaming through the dark sky out to the north.

The quiet hum of traffic from the Rome's central streets crept up to our roof and created a soothing atmosphere before or after my night prayers. For me it has always been lights out by ten o'clock at the latest. I have lived by what a crocodile hunter told me back in Australia in the fifties. 'Every hour of sleep before midnight,' she assured me, 'is worth two after midnight.'

2

Visitors

'All roads lead to Rome' — so the proverb tells us. At the beginning of the third millennium one must add: 'The air-lines and railways bring all types to Rome.' An extravagant parade of passing visitors have filled my years in the eternal city. Let me start with nephews, nieces, and other young folk, who began arriving from the late 1970s.

The Peters Connection

Fresh from a stint as a veterinarian at the Melbourne zoo, red-haired Bronwen Peters, a niece who has always reminded me of the actress Lynn Redgrave, kept our company helpless with laughter one evening in a Roman 'trattoria'. In startling detail she began to describe how she had removed a plastic bucket which an elephant had swallowed along with its food. 'I slipped a huge glove over one hand and stood on some steps behind it,' she began. We rushed her on to other animals! 'When operating on a giraffe, you *must* keep its head up; otherwise it may choke itself to death,' she insisted.

Her brother Mark joined Bronwen on that visit; her other four brothers came on various occasions. James turned up one day via Casablanca and just in time for a birthday dinner-party which some Irish friends gave for me in a restaurant next door to the palace where Lucretia Borgia lived for a time. One of the dishes on the menu hinted at a Borgia readiness to add a little poison! A couple of days later a young friend with hair like honey and a name to match, Daniela

Bellardinelli, drove James and me in her tiny Fiat 500 (a 'Cinquecento' as we call it) down the Via Appia to enjoy the strawberry festival in Nemi, the place of Diana's Temple and the opening for Sir James Frazer's *The Golden Bough* (1890). With his bright hair and blue eyes, James looked like a latter-day Ulysses on his way to the Trojan War. And he had and still has a passion for the Greek and Latin classics. On the drive back along the Via Appia or 'queen of all roads'. a police patrol car flagged Daniela down. 'Let me deal with this,' she said as she walked back alone from her battered car which could no longer produce the appropriate stop and turning signals. Daniela was so sweet and pretty that the traffic police couldn't bring themselves to book her. 'But please, before you take the car out again, get it fixed,' they begged her.

The youngest of the Peters boys, Stephen, arrived on his second visit after some days in Greece. I took him to a 'pensione' which offered only basic services. From his second-story window he leaned out to make arrangements for our evening rendezvous, and I enquired about his laundry. 'I was hoping you would ask that,' he replied. A large bag thumped down on the sidewalk next to me. Back at the Gregorian I crammed the lot into a laundry machine, but there was a problem about getting the clothes dry. In those days we didn't have dryers, and used lines at the back of the roof. Stephen's football shirts and underwear that displayed ants and other flora and fauna had no counterpart in the laundry which the Gregorian community hung out to dry. I hid his gear on the very back lines to reduce the chances of older fathers and brothers jumping to the startling conclusion that they had a youthful alien among them.

My Italian friend Leonardo was slightly older than Stephen but also an engineer. Leonardo looked like the right one to guide Stephen through the Roman night life and some of the discotheques. Leonardo wanted to give Stephen a little coaching in Italian before they went out. First question: 'Hai un amico? (do you have a boyfriend)?' Hopefully the answer would be negative, and then came the second question: 'Ti piacerebbe guardare la luna con me (would you like to look at the moon with me)?' Leonardo's lesson brought tears of laughter to the eyes of the older people with whom we were taking an early meal before releasing the two youngsters onto the Roman piazzas. Their proposed questions recalled some of the expressions found in legendary books for English-speaking tourists in Italy: 'Lightning has struck my grandmother's ear trumpet.' As if that wasn't enough, you were told how to say in Italian: 'the left, rear wheel has just fallen off our carriage.'

My sister Moira and her surgeon husband Jim Peters, the parents of Bronwen and her brothers, turned up one early June in the late 1970s. Lecturing at the Gregorian had just finished, an examination period (leisurely for the faculty) was starting, and the academic year was closing down. In June long days shine down on the city, brilliant light fills the churches (you need it, as the ubiquitous baroque is short on windows), and the temperature has not yet risen to the sweltering heat of July and August. Moira and Jim timed their visit to coincide with my birthday, 2 June. Jim proposed an evening meal in the 'Domus Aurea', a grand restaurant set above Nero's palace (of the same name) on the Colle Oppio and overlooking the Colosseum. Since it was after all my birthday we were celebrating, Jim settled for my suggestion: the 'Vecchia Roma', a less expensive restaurant tucked away in maze of narrow streets under the Capitol hill and on the edge of the old Jewish quarter. Jim's virtue was quickly rewarded. We had scarcely been seated outside under the sky of a pleasantly warm evening when Anthony Quinn turned up with a party of six or seven. They took a table right behind me. Seated opposite me, Jim spent the meal discreetly observing the great actor who sat facing him across my shoulders. 'Remarkably small hands for such a big man,' Jim remarked as we left the 'Vecchia Roma' just before midnight. Quinn and his party were the only others still there as we walked off down a tiny street. We had only gone a few yards into the night, when we heard the sound of glasses being broken against a wall of the restaurant. Quinn and his party were repeating what he did in the film 'Zorba the Greek'.

Gadamer, Lohse, and Heaney

Sooner or later most of the great, the good, and the ugly fetch up in Rome. Three of the great who freshened my outlook over the years were Hans-Georg Gadamer (1900-2002), Eduard Lohse (1924-97), and Seamus Heaney (b. 1939). Gadamer, a giant among German philosophers of his generation, returned to Italy over and over again. On one visit to Rome in 1975, he spoke at the local branch of the Goethe Institute on the long history of the tense but fruitful relationship between poets and philosophers. An Italian professor of philosophy, instead of briefly introducing Gadamer, annoyed the large audience by spending twenty minutes telling us about his own contacts with German philosophy and German philosophers. But Gadamer dazzled us with a forty-five minute account of what western philosophers from the time of Plato have made of poetry. This tour-de-force set me thinking furiously about whether Jesus can in any proper sense be called either a poet or a philosopher. The result was an article, 'Jesus between Poetry and Philosophy', which I published first with *New Blackfriars* in 1976 and then reprinted in a book I co-authored with Dan Kendall, *Focus on Jesus* (1996).

A New Testament scholar and retired Lutheran bishop, Lohse came to us in 1991 as a visiting McCarthy Professor. (I will explain the origins of that chair later.) When he was presiding Lutheran bishop in Germany, Lohse led the way in inter-church relations with Roman Catholics and welcomed John Paul II to Germany in 1980. In October 1991 I collected Bishop Lohse and his wife at the airport and took them to a 'pensione' just off the Piazza Farnese that is run by Rome's most picturesque group of nuns, the Sisters of St Bridget of Sweden (d. 1373). They still wear a distinctively Scandinavian headgear. My imagination adds a spear in their right hand to complete the Nordic look. When I walked in that day with the Lohses and their luggage, we ran into the Catholic Bishop of Stockholm, a German with a name that trips off the tongue, Hubertus Brandenburg. Lohse and Brandenburg fell into each other's arms, the first and only time I have ever seen two German bishops giving each other a hug. Their friendship went back to World War II when they served together in the German navy.

In his six-week course at the Gregorian Lohse examined major themes from St Paul's Letter to the Romans, a choice I had encouraged him to make. Where better to discuss that letter than in Rome itself? In his public lecture Lohse dealt with Paul's view of the Petrine ministry. Before a huge audience, which included in the front row a weary Cardinal Joseph Ratzinger who occasionally nodded off, Lohse analyzed passages from the First Letter to the Corinthians and from the Letter to the Galatians in which Paul explicitly refers to Peter and to his ministry. It was a superb and balanced analysis which kept its distance from the implicit references to Peter that self-indulgent scholars optimistically detect elsewhere in the Pauline correspondence. In the discussion period that followed the lecture the last question summed up the drift of the lecturer's argument: 'Bishop Lohse, your interpretation seems to mean that Paul contributed in a major way to the emerging view of Peter's ministry. Would you call

Paul the principal architect of the Petrine office?' Time had run out, and all Lohse could say was simply 'yes'.

In 1989 Seamus Heaney came to Rome and I attended one of his lectures: at the Irish College and on W. B. Yeats. Yeats had died fifty years previously on 28 January 1939. Heaney was born some weeks later, on 13 April of the same year. Did the poetic spirit of Yeats pass into Heaney — a little like Elisha inheriting the prophetic spirit when Elijah was taken up to heaven by a chariot of fire (2 Kings 2:1-15)? At times biblical scholars and theologians disparage each other in a display of what is known as *odium theologicum,* an attempt to improve the speaker's own rating by putting others down. Heaney, while observing that 'Yeats felt himself to be God's vicar of poetry on earth,' never gave a hint of what might be called *odium poeticum.* Heaney expressed himself in a brilliant, modest, and witty manner which won him even more admirers.

A general hope was fulfilled when shortly afterwards Heaney was elected Professor of Poetry at Oxford University. He also occupied a chair at Harvard University, first as Visiting Professor and then as Boylston Professor of Rhetoric and Oratory (1985-97). His five-year term at Oxford (1989-94) had hardly ended, when he was awarded the Nobel Prize for Literature in 1995. When I heard that news, I wondered what on earth Heaney would do with the rest of his life. He was not yet sixty. But he continued to go from strength to strength. In 1999 his translation of *Beowulf* was awarded the Whitbread Prize.

Anglican Leaders

Anglican leaders have been constant visitors to Rome even before 1966 when the Archbishop of Canterbury set up a representation in the city. The Anglican Communion is still the only non-Roman Catholic Christian community to have a permanent office in Rome.

Groups of Anglicans (often with others joining them) came for 'Romess', as they used to call the summer programmes that took them around the principal Christian sights and also featured several local speakers. Whenever I was still in town and had not yet departed to lecture elsewhere, I was recruited to speak, above all, on 'Peter in Rome': that is to say, on the ministry of St Peter and his successors, the Bishops of Rome.

Over the years the Anglican Centre co-ordinated visits by Anglican bishops from around the world; on such occasions I was asked to tell them about theological education in Rome. Discussion frequently moved towards the spiritual and pastoral formation of seminarians and young priests who lived in the national colleges and the role of Gregorian professors in that formation. I would tell them of our availability as spiritual directors, retreat givers, and confessors. This brings me to a parenthesis.

From the autumn of 1981 to the summer of 2001, I was the house confessor for the young priests in the graduate section of the North American College, the Casa Santa Maria. This involved going to the Casa on Mondays for the 7.30 meal, often giving advice at table on academic problems about which the years in Rome have made me street wise, and then hearing confessions downstairs in the sacristy. I loved to pray afterwards in their grotto-like chapel, a spectacularly rich gem of eighteenth-century art, dedicated to Our Lady of Humility and arguably the most beautiful small chapel in Rome. The Americans acquired it along with the whole building in the mid-nineteenth century. It had previously been a convent for contemplative nuns: that is to say, for nuns who give their lives to prayer rather than to active ministry in areas like education and health care. Two thousand years ago Roman firemen occupied the site, which today stretches from the Piazza della Pilotta to the Via dell'Umiltà (the Street of Humility).

That name prompted Orietta and Frank Doria to dub the student priests 'the Humility Street boys'. It was meant in fun as the Dorias showed themselves good friends to the American students. Those young priests normally called their college 'the Casa', almost as if there were no other 'casa' or house around. They strongly reminded me of the way Christchurch students in Oxford used to speak of their college as 'the House'. (End of parenthesis.)

The Anglican Centre is housed in the Doria Palace and the family repeatedly entertained Anglican visitors, high and low. In 1989 they put on a big reception for Archbishop Robert Runcie, who had come on an official visit to Rome as Archbishop of Canterbury. The visit outraged the Reverend Ian Paisley who descended on the city and on the evening of the reception stood across the Via del Corso from the Palazzo Doria holding up a hostile placard. An enterprising middle-aged guest spotted him on her way into the reception. She darted over the road through the traffic, held out her hand, and said with a smile: 'I've always wanted to shake the hand of a totally dedicated bigot.' To his credit Paisley laughed. But he had been at his antics since early morning, when he had taken a friend with him to protest at the Holy Communion service which Archbishop Runcie celebrated in the Anglican church of All Saints close to the Spanish Steps. Worship had hardly begun before the two protesters rose to their feet and denounced Runcie for betraying the martyred Archbishop Thomas Cranmer and all that the sixteenth-century Reformation stood for. Church wardens ushered Paisley and his friend out; then Runcie resumed with the words: 'Let us now continue with the words of Cranmer as found in the Book of Common Prayer.'

Bevan Wardrobe was the priest in charge of All Saints when Runcie came. I had ongoing contacts with the incumbents of that church as well as with the American Episcopal Church, St Paul's

Within the Walls. The story goes that, when Bevan was short listed as an incumbent for All Saints, the other prominent name on the list was that of a Reverend Mr. Pope. The appointments committee at once saw that they couldn't be responsible for nominating a second Pope in Rome; so Bevan got the job.

Rome saw the start of a warm friendship with George Carey. As a parish priest he first came to Rome for a course, and later attended another course organized by the Anglican Centre shortly after his consecration in 1987 as Bishop of Bath and Wells. I contributed to both courses, and on the second occasion got to know Carey even more when he stayed on for a few days after the other bishops had left. It seemed only a short time before he was back in Rome in 1992 as Archbishop of Canterbury and invited me to take part in a theological conversation in the Anglican Centre. That was the day on which I celebrated Gesine Doria's wedding in the old family church (Saint Agnes in the Piazza Navona) with another priest and

George and Eileen Carey in Rome with Gerald O'Collins, 2001

a charming Italian bishop, Don Luigi del Gallo Roccagiovine. I returned to the Doria Palace for one quick course of a mega-meal, and then disappeared upstairs to share local theological views with Archbishop Carey in the part of the palace given over to the Anglican Centre. Later there was to be a magic Sunday at Canterbury where the Archbishop had invited Cardinal Carlo Maria Martini to come and preach. In the cathedral everything was done with Anglican precision and style, and lunch was a delightful family affair prepared by the Careys' daughter Rachel and her husband Andy Day. Subsequently the Careys and I spent a memorable week together teaching in the USA during the summer programme of 1996 at the University of Notre Dame. One day I will tell Archbishop Carey about a major disappointment concerning one of his predecessors at Canterbury, Archbishop Michael Ramsey. In late 1975 I encouraged the then dean of theology at the Gregorian, René Latourelle, to invite Ramsey (who was now retired) as a visiting professor for six weeks or so. Pope Paul VI's right hand man, Archbishop Giovanni Benelli (1921–82), unfortunately vetoed the invitation as 'inopportune'. It would have been splendid to have heard the results of all Ramsey's experiences in ecumenical affairs, but instead we had Eric Mascall, a neo-Thomist, Anglican theologian who had just retired from teaching at the University of London.

Worse was to happen a few months later, and not simply on the Anglican front. In 1976 Pope Paul VI issued a ukase against any non-Catholics teaching at the Gregorian and at other Catholic universities and colleges in Rome. Highly embarrassing, as non-Catholic theologians had been coming as visiting professors for eight years! Of course, one was never *sure* from what level such decisions came. But in this case Vatican officials like Cardinal Garonne, who as prefect of the Congregation for Catholic Education was the ex-officio Grand Chancellor of the Gregorian University, denied that it was his decision and pointed to the man at the top.

On the night I heard the news about the ukase against non-Catholics teaching at the Gregorian, I had dinner with Dr Harry Smythe, the head of the Anglican Centre in Rome and former vicar of an Anglican church in St Kilda (Melbourne, Australia). Harry had just come from a visit to the 'Holy Father', as he always called him. It was a private visit during which the Pope kept a cardinal waiting. Harry had brought a letter to the Pope from Dr Michael Ramsey who recalled with gratitude the 1966 meeting between Ramsey and Paul VI. The Pope laughed at Harry's joke about having just read a sign scrawled on a Roman wall, 'Viva Paolo Sesto (long live, Paul VI),' and himself added: 'I don't think there are too many of those signs around. But I can't get out to see for myself.' And yet Paul VI had just issued a document forbidding the likes of Harry to teach at the Gregorian. In fact, Harry had *already* been invited to teach a course for 1976/77. So our rector insisted that 'odiosa sunt restringenda (odious things should be limited),' and that the ukase should apply *only* to future invitations. The ban, of course, led to a furor at the Secretariat for Christian Unity. Its prefect or head, Cardinal Willebrands of Utrecht, quickly came to Rome, had an audience with the Pope and wrung a reluctant concession out of him to the effect that instances of non-Roman Catholics teaching at the Gregorian should be examined individually, as had always been the case. But, in the event, it took years before other Christian theologians returned as visiting professors.

I concluded that we must be getting into the last days of Pope Paul's reign. All the panicky little fears were coming out, and a veteran of the last days of Pius XII and John XXIII assured me that the signs were running true to form.

Continuing Education

I always liked to give a hand with the courses laid on in Rome for
Catholic bishops. My first experience of that kind of audience came
only a few weeks after my arrival in August 1974, when the Casa
Santa Maria hosted a group of fifty or sixty bishops from the United
States. I was invited to present something on the resurrection of
Jesus Christ. After the lecture one archbishop summed up his view of
resurrection as 'the soul leaving the body and the soul coming back
into the body'. 'There's more to it than that,' I replied. 'St Paul stresses
the glorious transformation brought about by resurrection from the
dead. It involves a new way of living.' When the archbishop persisted
with his simple model of a soul's exit and return, David Stanley, a
Canadian scriptural scholar who was present, cut in: 'Archbishop,
that's just heresy.' One of the episcopal participants, gentle Cardinal
Terence Cooke from New York (1921-83), tried in vain to correct the
archbishop. Some months later the archbishop died at home in the
United States. Shortly afterwards I ran into Cardinal Cooke, who said
with a smile: 'Well, he knows the truth now.'

Once or twice the committee responsible for what were
euphemistically called the Bishops' Theological Consultations put
together a predominantly conservative team of lecturers. The bishops
took a dim view of such consultations, since they hardly wanted to fly
over for a month in Rome to hear material they had been given thirty
years previously during their seminary training. They were looking
for fresh insights and new ways of putting things, and they wanted to
discuss matters among themselves in a very relaxed way. In short, they
expected an in-service training programme that would update them.

Sometimes theological gatherings with bishops took an informal
shape and involved non-Roman Catholic professors. On one such
occasion the Protestant theologian Moltmann flew down to Rome

from Stuttgart to speak at a conference arranged by the Passionists in October 1975; I persuaded him to give a talk one evening at the North American College. I described the evening in a letter to an American friend:

We had dinner first with Archbishop Bernardin [still at Cincinnati and not yet Cardinal Archbishop of Chicago] and Cardinal Medeiros [of Boston]. It happened that the teams of their respective cities were meeting that evening in the World Series. But Moltmann managed to steer the conversation away from sport to the problem of the seeming ineffectiveness of so much preaching. It was the first time I had met Bernardin. He seems frank, open, and altogether a good thing. Medeiros came to Moltmann's after dinner talk, more or less an introduction to his new book on the Church. Then we had a chat and a drink till nearly midnight, discussing the Eucharist and inter-communion. Medeiros looked surprised to hear some of the points made. But he gave Moltmann a great hug at the end, and invited him to come and stay with him in Boston. Moltmann told me afterwards how pleased he was to meet such a human cardinal. I told Moltmann how glad I was to be able to run an informal seminar for a cardinal and an archbishop by enlisting good Protestant support.

The bishops came every few years, and for only a month's course. A three-month course held twice a year for priests and called the Institute for Continuing Theological Education had been launched in the 1970s. This programme in the autumn and the spring normally opened with Ambrose McNicholl, a warm-hearted giant of a priest, taking his audience through the philosophical currents of our day. This lovable Irish Dominican opened minds up to modern debates and made them more receptive to what followed; other speakers then lectured on biblical studies, systematic theology, moral theology, canon law, and the rest. When stomach cancer struck Ambrose down in 1981, I visited him in a hospital run by the Blue Sisters, a congregation of nuns who wore blue dress. Then I walked along the road in the spring sunshine to some botanical gardens. Young Italians were locked in embraces among the beauty of all those trees and shrubs in full flower. Life was bursting out, while Ambrose lay dying like a Celtic warrior cut down in battle. He led our team that the organizers drew from the Angelicum, the Gregorian, and other Roman academic institutions. By the mid-1990s I was the only survivor of that original group who from the 1970s serviced a healthy Roman industry, updating courses for clergy and religious. Most had retired and returned to their countries of origin; Ambrose and another affable Irish priest, the Redemptorist Sean O'Riordan, had gone home to God. I cherished teaching on that team and meeting the priests and bishops; their questions and interests took us towards the actual struggles and challenges being faced by Catholic leaders. Some popular books I published emerged from those encounters, the first being *What are they saying about Jesus?* (1977), which initiated the Paulist Press' long series of *What are they saying about...?* (WATSA) books. By October 2002 they had published well over fifty of these.

Roman Synods

Normally every three years synods or assemblies of bishops take place in Rome during October. Each national conference of bishops sends representatives. Archbishop Angelo Fernandes of New Delhi sometimes called me round to his 'pensione' when he flew in from Delhi and wanted to chat about the *instrumentum laboris* (instrument of work) or paper prepared as a basis of discussion for the synod. I remember one such paper (for the synod on the sacrament of reconciliation), which seemed to me utterly below standard. As I said to the Archbishop, 'it's an insult to you bishops who have come all this way for the synod.' But in a charitable way he always tried to find the best in what he read. Once or twice Archbishop Frank Rush of Brisbane represented the Australian bishops at those synods. He arrived with his breviary or book for daily prayer, a copy of the Vatican II documents, and a book of poetry. On one occasion he carried with him a volume of Bruce Dawe's verse, and sat reading to me into the night. When he had finished reciting a poem on Christ's death, 'And a Good Friday was had by all', and saw how fascinated I was by the writer's ear for ordinary Australian speech, he pressed the book into my hand, saying: 'I can easily get another copy.'

Another Australian bishop whom I met at one synod was Archbishop Guilford Young of Hobart in Tasmania, who was a pioneer of liturgical reform nationally and internationally. Over lunch one day he lectured me on the need for theologians to take the liturgy or public worship of the Church much more seriously. The point is worth making again at a time when many theologians continue to ignore the liturgical texts in their teaching and writing.

Guilford had been kept in Rome during World War II and returned to Australia to become the auxiliary bishop for the Archdiocese of Canberra-Goulburn. He was not quite thirty-two when consecrated in September 1948 and reputedly the youngest Catholic bishop in the world.[5] Teenage girls swooned over the tall and handsome Guilford when he went around the archdiocese to confirm batches of adolescents. One of them is supposed to have been Colleen McCullough, who grew up in rural New South Wales. Guilford could well have supplied her with the image of a fascinating churchman from Rome, who grew into Ralph de Bricassart, the hero of *The Thorn Birds*. I should have asked Guilford if he had confirmed Colleen.

---

5 Archbishop Denis Hurley of South Africa, who turns up in the next chapter, was also thirty-one but six months younger when first consecrated an auxiliary bishop in 1947.

Sometimes lobbyists and speakers who are not officially invited turn up in Rome for the synods. In the evenings the bishops can attend presentations and tap into some of this freely offered expertise. A woman from New Mexico, whom I had met at the University of San Francisco, came for a synod which was to make recommendations to the Pope about the life and role of the laity. Catherine worked in an institution for the criminally insane and aspired to be ordained a deacon in the Catholic Church. She was also a juggler. Over a meal in a pleasant trattoria near the Piazza Navona, she told me that she had whiled away the hour or so after lunch and before the synod resumed by putting on her costume, painting her face, and doing some juggling in St Peter's Square. Italian women frowned at her and, to her astonishment, claimed: 'You're disturbing the Pope's siesta.' She pretended not to understand Italian and continued juggling. Catherine liked the people she saw in the Piazza Navona, 'in touch with their sexuality and not like those buttoned-up monsignors at the Vatican'. I hoped that remark had not reached the next table. An unscrupulous divine providence had arranged for my American confessor, Jack Carroll, to be sitting right next to us as the guest of a party of Filipinos. But he didn't even appear to notice that I was there.

Romero, Gutiérrez, Cox, and McIntyre

In 1980 Archbishop Oscar Romero of El Salvador came to visit a Spanish professor in our faculty of missiology. On the occasion of his visit, he stopped in the huge Franciscan basilica at the foot of our square. It is named after the twelve apostles, and was an appropriate place for him to pray not to lose apostolic courage in the face of the murderous situation in his own country. The prayer was answered as Romero was all too soon to die a martyr's death at the hands of a fellow countryman.

Gustavo Gutiérrez, the Peruvian liberation theologian, came by on visits to a Mexican professor at the Gregorian and later to Jacques Dupuis (of whom more in Chapter 8). Gutiérrez had interrupted his studies at the Gregorian and returned home to launch liberation theology with a 1971 book. After some severe statements from the Congregation for the Doctrine of the Faith (hereafter CDF) on what they feared was his reduction to politics of the Christian message, Gutiérrez made his peace with Cardinal Ratzinger, the prefect of the CDF. This did not prevent the head of the Congregation for Education, who was ex-officio our chancellor, from personally intervening to force the cancellation of a lecture which Gutiérrez had been scheduled to deliver at the Gregorian late in 1994. This intervention seemed all the more puzzling, as Pio Laghi, the cardinal in question, had recently been interviewed for a Sunday edition of the *New York Times* and had supported freedom of theological speech. In the event Gutiérrez' lecture took place at the Brazilian College and was open to any who wished to come and hear him.

A Harvard theologian, Harvey Cox of *Secular City* and *Feast of Fools* fame, spent several days in Rome in 1978 to research the peace appeals made by Paul VI during the Vietnam War. Cox had also been in the city at the time of the Vietnam War, and with a delegation from the United States had tried to meet Pope Paul. Only later did they discover why they could not then meet the Pope. The US State Department, through the American Embassy in Rome, had intervened to block the proposed meeting for Harvey and his party. On a delightful walk together, Cox and I paused at the corner of the Via del Seminario to enjoy a lively conversation as our eyes dwelt on the majesty of the Pantheon. Without a break in what he was saying, Harvey suddenly bent down to help a woman to her feet. Like many others she had tripped on one of the metal stanchions that protect the buildings at the entrance to the Via del Seminario. On the same European visit Harvey travelled to Spain to check out what was happening three years after General Franco's death. That visit posed no risk, unlike Harvey's stop in Teheran on his flight home to the United States. That stop coincided with the last days of the Shah's regime and the coming to power of Ayatollah Khomeini in January 1979. But Harvey's luck held and he was able to escape Teheran. Home in Cambridge, Massachusetts, Harvey did something that not all visitors found time to do. In January 1979 he wrote to thank me for a meeting with some theologians and for the lunches I had arranged for him at the Gregorian and the Biblical Institute: 'your generosity and your friendship made my brief visit to Rome one I will never forget.'

Another delightful visitor was Professor John McIntyre, then Moderator of the Church of Scotland. This outstanding Presbyterian theologian had welcomed John Paul II when the Pope visited Edinburgh in 1982. On that occasion they sat side by side on two dignified chairs especially provided for the occasion. A day or so later a van turned up and two respectable looking men in overalls carried the chairs away as if they had every right to do so; it was in fact a cool theft, perhaps on contract for some specialist collector. McIntyre had come to Rome to return the Pope's visit to Edinburgh. On the day he visited the Pope, he also came to the Gregorian and attended my seminar for licentiate students. Before and after that session I took him everywhere I could in our building, wanting to show him off to anyone we met. Even by Roman standards he looked unusual, wearing black breeches that clung tightly to his stockings and ended well above his silver-buckled shoes. A white lace jabot covered his throat above a somber jacket. The Roman public is long ago accustomed to a wide range of clerical dress, both official and dishevelled. But McIntyre held their attention that day in his official Moderator's attire, reminiscent of Rembrandt's portrayal of some Dutch Calvinists.

The Media

Rome attracts journalists as honey does wasps. Most of them are wonderfully interesting, hard-working people like David Smith of London's ITV. On a sunny winter's day, 2 January 1982, he interviewed me on top of the Pincian Hill, the largest public garden in Rome. St Peter's basilica formed the distant backdrop; below us thousands of brightly colored marathon runners passed through the Piazza del Popolo. David appreciated Pope John Paul II's appeal for civil and religious liberty in central and eastern Europe. Picking up on Joseph Stalin's question about Pius XII ('The Pope! How many divisions has he got?'), David insisted: 'John Paul II doesn't have any army or group of parliamentary representatives to implement that policy.' 'Look, David,' I responded, 'you and I want to speak up for the truth in our world. As a journalist and a teacher we care about justice, and hope that what we say or write will have an impact. It is certainly worthwhile for the Pope to raise his voice. Something may very well happen.' And indeed it did.

I was unaware at the time that John Paul II had also been raising his voice privately with Andrei Gromyko, the Soviet foreign minister since 1957. Years later a friend of mine who spoke fluent Russian and at times acted as interpreter for popes, remarked on the difference between Gromkyo's reception by Paul VI (pope 1963-78) and John Paul II. On at least one occasion Paul VI pulled out some papers and quietly said to Gromyko: 'I have some reports here which show that civil and religious liberties are not being respected in your country.' When Gromyko assured him that 'these reports must be misinformed,' Paul VI passed to another topic. When John Paul II raised the same issue and Gromyko made a similar reply, the Pope slammed his fist on the table and shouted: 'That's untrue, and you know it's untrue.'

One chilly morning in December 1989 David Smith returned with

London ITV and put me in front of a camera at the Trevi Fountain, an hour or two before Mikhail and Raisa Gorbachev were to be received by the Pope on 1 December 1989. All David wanted me to say was: 'This encounter is truly an historic moment' — a normal enough platitude in a year crammed with historic moments as communist regimes collapsed one after another. I uttered my banalities and decided that this was neither the time nor the place to add, 'I told you so.' Garbage collectors were busily working their way around the fountain, and it was hard enough to get something audible on tape anyway.

Early in the pontificate of John Paul II, I was happily taking an afternoon siesta when the phone rang to say that someone from the media had arrived and wanted to see me. I told the porter that I would be down in a moment, expecting to find a journalist with a tape recorder, one of those people who wandered around Europe making interviews and selling them to radio stations at home. Instead I was greeted by John Hart who was passing through Rome on the way back from covering (presumably from the safe distance of Pakistan) the Russian invasion of Afghanistan for the American television network, NBC. In London he was due to film a programme on the possibility of World War III; during his stopover in Rome he wanted an interview with me on the Pope. Before we went on camera, his questions seemed harmless enough. But in the course of the actual interview he slipped in what Americans call a curve ball: 'Some people are saying that the Pope has two different views of human rights: one for life outside the Church and another for life inside the Church. What do you think?' Caught on the spur of the moment, I blurted out: 'Well, you can't expect a father to behave at home the same way as he does outside the family' — a response which I instantly regretted. We went on pleasantly enough for another twenty minutes or so, while my worried mind kept darting back to Hart's question and my answer.

When the interview ended, I told Hart that I was due to celebrate Mass at the Irish College, and he sent me off at once in his car. After dropping me, the Italian driver returned to the Gregorian and took Hart with his crew to the Basilica of San Lorenzo in Damaso where the parish priest had agreed to their filming for voice over scenes. The driver, instead of remaining with the car, decided to walk ten or fifteen yards to take a quick cup of coffee at a bar. When Hart and the others came out of the church and opened up the boot of the Mercedes, everything, including the film they had shot at the Gregorian, had been stolen. When I came home around ten that evening from the Irish College, there was a message from Hart asking me to redo the interview the following morning at the NBC bureau on the Piazza del Collegio Romano. He wouldn't be there as he had already left for London. But could I please give the young woman in the bureau a list of the questions he had asked me, so that she could repeat the interview? I felt grateful to the skilful Italian thieves, who had got me out of potential trouble because of my ill-judged remarks. I went off the following morning to the bureau, but omitted the tricky question in the list I handed over to the lady in the bureau before repeating the interview.

Around 1980 another phone call interrupted the post-lunch siesta. I came down to find a vague kind of person, who intended to write a life of John Paul I and wanted to talk to me about the late Pope's connections with the Gregorian: in particular, links with his relative, the saintly Father Cappello. 'I know very little about Pope Luciani's contacts with his relative,' I told my visitor. 'You should ask the secretary general of the Gregorian. He might be able to dig something out of our archives. But why write about a dead pope? Why not do a book on John Paul II?' I also expressed concern at the difficulties my visitor was likely to experience in interviewing people because of his lack of Italian. He brushed this aside and departed abruptly.

In 1984 my visitor, David Yallop, published his best selling *In God's Name*, a crudely sensationalist attempt to prove that John Paul I had been murdered, a theory already touted by one or two trashy papers, by some right-wing extremists obsessed with masonic conspiracies, and by a couple of French writers. Several of us were particularly annoyed to be included in Yallop's acknowledgements as if we had provided evidence in support of his theory. He had not in fact met some of the people listed; he misspelled the name of the Gregorian's secretary general to whom I had referred him and with whom he never brought up the murder theory. And he never raised it with me either. In 1989, John Cornwell published *A Thief in the Night* to set the record straight about the death of John Paul I,[6] who was a sick man when elected pope. He refused to seek medical help, was neglected by others, and died of an embolism. The fact that some Vatican officials tampered with a couple of details concerning his death unfortunately fed the fantasies of the David Yallops of this world. The reality was that Sister Vincenza, the papal housekeeper, had found the Pope dead when she brought him an early morning cup of coffee. It was considered more fitting that one of his two priest secretaries should have found him, and for good measure it was put about that he had died with a copy of *The Imitation of Christ* in his hands, when in fact this had been placed there after his death.

Yallop's version suggested that John Paul I had been poisoned by some villains in the Vatican — the suspects are listed — at the second attempt, the first having killed a Russian Orthodox church leader, Metropolitan Nikodim of Leningrad when he visited the Pope on 5 September 1978. Yallop reported part of the truth: Nikodim was certainly in poor health, and had already had several heart attacks before the one that killed him in the presence of the Pope. But Yallop

---

6 In *Man of the Century* (New York: Henry Holt, 1997), Jonathan Kwitny concludes that Cornwell 'ripped Yallop's book to shreds' (p. 291).

alleged that a rumor had gone around the Vatican that Nikodim had drunk a cup of poisoned coffee intended for the Pope. Unfortunately I could never persuade my interpreter friend Miguel to write up his testimony to Nikodim's death. Miguel had served as an interpreter for the meeting between the Pope and Nikodim, just as he had served in the same capacity for the meetings between Andrei Gromyko and Paul VI and then with John Paul II. 'Poisoned by someone?,' Miguel told me. 'That was impossible. After picking up Nikodim at the airport, I was at his side all the time. Over the years he had suffered several heart attacks. Suddenly he had another attack and collapsed practically into the Pope's arms. John Paul I was horrified and didn't know what to do. "Give him absolution at once, Holiness," I told him. "The man's dying."'

In June 1989 my fellow Australian Clive James descended on Rome to make a film about the city for the BBC. I had known him when we were both graduate students in England at Pembroke College, Cambridge. Before Clive came to shoot the film, two of his Girl Fridays turned up in my office, when I was serving as dean of theology. 'Clive wants to meet a decadent cardinal living in a luxury apartment and waiting to be pope,' the young women told me. I asked them to tell Clive from me that *that* kind of cardinal had died out centuries ago, and that cardinals who manage to be decadent nowadays wouldn't have a chance of being elected pope. I also asked them to suggest that Clive present Rome as an international city, one of the great crossroads of the world.

But Clive was set on decadence; he found himself a decadent Roman nobleman, and even managed to get hold of a sexologist although it was news to me that Italians needed such a person! The film included some brilliant shots of the great sights, lots of laughs, and an interview with the conductor and composer Leonard Bernstein, who happened to be in town to receive an award from the City of Rome, where he was greatly admired as the honorary president

and visiting conductor of the orchestra of the Academy of Santa
Cecilia. Songs and scenes from Bernstein's 1957 work *West Side Story*
were performed in front of a distinguished audience on the Spanish
Steps. In his continuing search for decadence, Clive inserted one or
two cracks about the performance, but couldn't manage to persuade
Bernstein to lower the moral tone when they talked together.

The roof of the Gregorian has always been ideal for television
interviews, provided one avoids those thirty minutes each afternoon
when a band accompanies the changing of the guard at the nearby
Quirinal Palace. It is also better to avoid days when marathons,
political demonstrations, or state visitors to Italy fill the sky with noisy
helicopters. I was once caught out by a low flying crow who cackled his
way into a BBC interview on the eve of Pope John Paul II's 1997 visit
to his native Poland. Hoping that viewers would pick up the reference
to John Wayne in *A Man of True Grit*, I described John Paul II as
'a pope of true grit', and reminded them of all the Pope had been
through. Operated on repeatedly after the 1981 attempt on his life, the
Pope still kept up an exhausting rhythm of trips. Before this particular
visit to Poland, he had just faced danger in freezing Sarajevo, returned
to Prague, and had endured an exhausting visit to Lebanon, which
ended with the old man shaking endless hands at the airport in Beirut
and being left to climb unaided the steps to the aircraft.

True grit was on my mind, since I had used the same image with
James Carroll when he arrived in late 1996 to prepare a piece for the
New Yorker. I knew Jim from my years in Boston (1968-72), when he
became prominent in protests against the Vietnam War. He turned
up in Rome still somewhat happily shaken by receiving a National
Book Award for *An American Requiem: God, My Father, and the War that
Came Between Us*, an autobiographical account of the divisions in his
family over the Vietnam War. Let me quote from Jim's account of our
meeting that appeared in the *New Yorker* for 7 April 1997:

I knew of Father O'Collins because, years before, he'd done a stint at the Jesuit theological school near Harvard while I, a Catholic priest at the time, was chaplain at Boston University, across the river. When I telephoned him in Rome, he agreed to meet me. 'I'll be the one wearing the red scarf,' he said proposing a rendezvous under the balcony of the Palazzo di Venezia, made famous by Mussolini ... Father O'Collins arrived, in his red scarf, an epiphany [sic] of friendly exuberance. He led me to a small neighborhood restaurant.

Jim went on to report for two pages what I said over supper to explain my admiration for John Paul II. The rest of the article did not, however, give me immense satisfaction. Those who read it might be advised to check the critical commentary by Paul Baumann in *Commonweal* for 23 May 1997.

In April 1994 the English journalist Karen Armstrong came to Rome with a television team to produce what proved to be an exceedingly one-sided attack on the Church and the papacy. I offered them the opportunity to interview two students, one an English seminarian and the other a young American laywoman. Both responded with sincere idealism, spiced with humour. When Armstrong asked Ruth, a very pretty and articulate person, 'How do you feel about ordination for women?,' Ruth threw back her head and laughingly replied: 'I don't *feel* about it. I think about it.' In the interview with me Armstrong brought up some minor decision at the Vatican of which she obviously disapproved and of which I should perhaps have disapproved if I hadn't had more important things on my mind. Two African friends of mine who had been running a centre for reconciliation had just been massacred down in Kigali, Rwanda. And I had just heard that Serbian forces were shelling a hospital in

Bosnia. It's the only time that I have ever allowed myself to show deep anger in front of the camera.

Memorable Occasions

Visitors to Rome have left so many striking memories. The saddest visit was that of Caroline, the slim and beautiful daughter of old friends. Caroline had experienced what she described as some sexual strife. I took her up to an English woman doctor who worked in a Roman hospital. Some people I knew were in the waiting room, and you could imagine their minds ticking over: 'What's O'Collins doing with that young girl?' The doctor found nothing at all wrong. Several years later Caroline discovered that she was HIV positive; she died in 1993, ten years to the day since our visit to the Roman hospital.

Right now I can hear my sister-in-law saying to me, 'Gerald, for heaven's sake finish the chapter on a cheerful note.' Let me follow Posey's advice and conclude with one of those many magic evenings Rome lays on. The great English scholar Sir Henry Chadwick was in Rome with his wife Peggy as guests of the Augustinians. Henry had just received an honorary doctorate from the Augustinianum, a centre for the study of early Christian writers. High up the hill behind the Augustinianum, we sat under ancient cedars with the president of that institute, Vittorino Grossi, enjoying the food, the wine, and one another's company on a deliciously mild spring evening. Slowly a full moon swung into majestic view above the dome of St Peter's, which seemed but a stone's throw away. For a wonderful moment nature seemed to put Michelangelo's masterpiece into the shade, so to speak. 'What an absolutely glorious sight!,' I remarked. 'Yes,' said Grossi with a smile, 'and don't forget we're looking towards Naples.' Then I remembered that he was a Neapolitan, and I wondered whether in his mind he glimpsed the Bay of Naples.

3

Students and Colleges

Year by passing year in such journals as *America* magazine (New York) and the London *Tablet*, I read advertisements praising different faculties and departments of theology and of allied religious disciplines around the world. One faculty announces: 'Ours is a place to explore intellectually in a community of adult students excited about theology.' In promoting its degrees, certificates, and continuing education, another centre may put it this way: 'We prepare women and men for service to the Church. You can study with leading theologians who write cutting edge books.' Yet another faculty advertises: 'Our students are learning ministry skills through the art of theological reflection in the context of practical ministry experience. With us financial assistance is available.' However it is put, clearly these centres feel the need to sell themselves in order to increase or at least maintain their enrollment. Such advertising is simply not needed at the Gregorian. Even after all the selection and weeding out have taken place, too many rather than too few students arrive. Very few need to be turned away by the Gregorian; the students who arrive to study with us come because their superiors or others have already chosen them as quality prospects.

Every now and then friends in other parts of the world have solemnly advised me that seminarians, young priests, religious, and lay people should study at home, in their local setting. They shouldn't come or be sent to Rome. 'There is nothing I can do about it,' I used to reply. 'I haven't asked them to turn up. Do you want me to picket new arrivals at Rome's airport with a sign, "Go back home?"'

It was the presence of those students from all over the world which motivated me to teach at the Gregorian and keep on doing so. Without that rich and varied student body, our professors would have no teaching to do and would have to content themselves with research and writing. As it is, those men and women, mainly young people, remained the focus of our lives. That was the reason behind the address I sometimes gave when writing letters to family and friends: 'On the Tiber Mission.' Many years ago in Australia I twice asked my formidable provincial (the priest who then led the four hundred or so Jesuits in my country) to give me the chance of working in India. 'Gerald,' he assured me, 'keep studying and you'll find your India elsewhere.' At the time I resented his turning down an 'heroic' offer to spend my life in a country I cherish. But, as things turned out, that old style priest spoke somewhat prophetically and I found my India in Tiber country.

The Alumni

St Ignatius Loyola founded the Society of Jesus in 1540. In 1551, when establishing what was to become the Gregorian, he had to harass other Jesuits in his fast growing religious institute to provide candidates for the student body. When St Peter Canisius wrote from across the Alps to say that hardly any prospective students could be found in Germany, St Ignatius simply wouldn't take no for an answer. Over the centuries enrollment had its ups and downs, above all during unsettled periods such as World War I and World War II. But students have always come and their subsequent lives have established a glorious tradition of Gregorian education.

By 2011 twenty-three of our alumni had been officially canonized or declared saints, and fifty-two had been declared 'blessed', a preliminary to canonization. During my years at the Gregorian it seemed that almost every year some alumnus was beatified or canonized, including twentieth-century figures such as St Maximilian Kolbe, a Polish Franciscan who was murdered in Auschwitz and Blessed Titus Brandsma, a Dutch Carmelite who was killed in Dachau, even though it was not an extermination camp in the full sense. Doubtless more will be officially recognized as saints and blesseds; I think of Archbishop Oscar Romero, who spent five years at the Gregorian from 1938 to 1943 and was martyred in 1980. Two Jesuits from Rwanda, Patrick Gahizi and Innocent Rutagambwa, whom I taught and knew well when they studied theology in Rome, were among the first victims of the genocidal massacres in Rwanda in 1994. They had committed the crime of running a centre for reconciliation between Hutus and Tutsis.

Sister Luz Marina Valencia Treviño, the daughter of a wealthy family in Venezuela, spent three years studying in our institute of spirituality and then went off to work for the poor in a Mexican slum on the outskirts of Acapulco. On the night of 20 March 1987, four men armed with revolvers broke into the cottage where Sister Luz Marina lived. After beating and raping her, they shot her in the stomach and left her in agony. She died after suffering for seven hours and forgiving her murderers. In his tribute to her, the Archbishop of Acapulco first stressed her day by day fidelity to God's grace before he named her the first martyr of Acapulco. The pastoral team with whom she had worked declared: 'In her life and death Luz Marina witnessed to the gospel values and the dignity of women.' She was only thirty-four when she died, a modern Good Samaritan who stopped to help wounded people and paid the ultimate price for her neighbourly love.

In 1997 Enrico Rebuschini, who had spent his life serving in a hospital in Cremona, a town in Lombardy known for Stradivarius and its violins, was beatified. After studies at the Gregorian in the late nineteenth century, he had entered a religious institute founded by another alumnus of the Gregorian, St Camillus de Lellis (1550-1614), and died in 1938 after years of the health care work to which the Camillans dedicate themselves. We now have seventy-five former students named as saints and blesseds, but only one professor, St Robert Bellarmine (1542-1621). It looks as if the professors teach the truth but it is the students who put it into practice. Robert Bellarmine in fact had to give up his work as professor and sometime rector when he became a cardinal and subsequently bishop of Capua.

Great numbers of alumni have risen to be bishops and cardinals over the centuries. Since the foundation of the Gregorian in 1551, sixteen out of the forty-four popes have been ex-students, including seven of the ten popes elected since 1846. Of the 115 cardinals who went into the conclave that elected Benedict XVI on 19 April 2005, 44 were former students of the Gregorian or — like Cardinal Joseph Ratzinger — had taught there as visiting professors.[7] Such statistics may confirm the worst fears of those who are already suspicious of the Gregorian as a nursery of Roman centralism and who have an antipathy to the Vatican and the papacy.

---

7 For some weeks in the first semester of 1973/74, Professor Joseph Ratzinger taught an optional course on the Eucharist at the Gregorian. When as Cardinal Ratzinger he was appointed in 1981 to head the Congregation for the Doctrine of the Faith and came to live in Rome, I suggested to the dean of the theology faculty, René Latourelle, that we might invite Ratzinger to teach again at the Gregorian: for instance, an optional course for one semester each year. 'A good idea', Latourelle commented. "But it might make other cardinals jealous." I felt like saying but didn't, 'that's their problem'. Later I realized that a little push from me might have persuaded Latourelle.

Enrolment

Why and how do the Gregorian's students — whether priests, seminarians seeking holy orders in dioceses, nuns, male religious, and laypersons — continue to come in such numbers? In 2003/2004, for example, around 3,100 were enrolled, the vast majority already possessing a degree. At least 40% belonged to the theology faculty. Well over 90% of these theological students were seeking a degree in our three-year first cycle (or M.Div. programme), the second cycle licentiate (or two-year specialized programmes), or in the third cycle (the doctorate).[8] It is a multicultural situation, with two-thirds of the students coming from Europe or North, South and Central America. The others come from Africa and Asia, and a few from Oceania. It is a multilingual situation: 26% are Italian-speaking, 18% Spanish-speaking, 10% English-speaking, with Portuguese-, French- and German-speakers then following in that order.

In 2003/2004, the average student in theology paid a little less than 2,000 euros a year; and for those clerical students attached to a diocese or belonging to a religious institute, this money was found by their bishop or religious superior. For the North Americans and some others, such fees were far lower than those they would have paid at home. But living in Rome was and is costly enough, even for those who belong to colleges, seminaries, and other institutions.

Numerous bishops, often alumni themselves, send students back to the colleges where they lived and to the Gregorian where they themselves studied. Their seminarians will thus have the opportunity to shed prejudices, meet the Catholic (that is to say, the worldwide) Church, and become more open-minded to all kinds of people. Many religious institutes maintain houses of study in Rome, and hope to

---

8 These terms and the structures that correspond to them will be explained later in this chapter.

wear down narrow nationalisms by providing their young members with a vigorous international experience through their studies in Rome. Like other university students in Germany and Austria, those who have chosen theology are expected to spend a year or at least a semester away (a 'Freisemester') at a university other than the one where they are enrolled; dozens of them regularly travel south to spend their 'Freisemester' at the Gregorian and enjoy a Roman experience. Many countries in Latin America, central and eastern Europe, and elsewhere in the world simply cannot offer a quality education to those who, having completed a first degree in theology, want to go on for higher studies in the discipline. Italian seminarians and lay persons, especially lay women, choose the Gregorian as they expect to receive there a more demanding and richer education than might be available to them elsewhere.

Over the years I was rarely involved in actively recruiting students, although I was always ready to offer the most accurate information I could lay my hands on. During the six years I served as dean of theology I had to deal with substantial correspondence from possible students, and to an extent I still get involved in this. Sometimes I encouraged prospective doctoral students to choose another centre, above all those who had already studied at the Gregorian for years. Academic incest is to be avoided, particularly in the case of Jesuits earmarked for appointment as Gregorian professors. Those who had done part of their studies, including their doctorate, in Canada, England, France, Germany, Spain, or the United States constantly brought fresh ideas and perspectives to our common work. On one of my two visits to Colombia in the 1980s I was able to put a similar point of view at the major seminary in Bogotá. Almost all the teaching staff of a dozen or so priests had done their higher degrees at the Gregorian. 'It's very flattering,' I observed. 'But please think of possibly taking further studies in France, Belgium or the United States. A variety of contacts and experiences for the future teachers will enrich your faculty.' The Colombians normally arrived as young priests, with their first degree in theology already behind them — as is the usual practice for those who came to us from other parts of Latin America, as well as from Asia, Africa, and Spain.

The international, transcultural variety of the student body taught me many things, including the fact that studying theology in Rome at the age of twenty-five or thirty can unmask the poor quality of high school education received a decade or so previously. Some students have to be remarkably tenacious, if they are to acquire the skills necessary for analyzing texts and composing papers which they should have been taught in their high school days. Those who were so fortunate as to have received their schooling in France, Germany, most provinces of Italy, and some other countries regularly seem to have a head start over many of their companions when they come to the Gregorian.

Through reading their papers and listening to the oral examinations in their languages, the students were responsible for teaching me Spanish, reviving my dormant French, and keeping my German alive. Through the diversity of their background, they enabled me to see that there are three distinct styles of theology: the classical European style of articulating the truth in an academic setting; the practical, Latin American style of liberation theology that is concerned with living the truth in seeking justice for the oppressed; and the worshiping style of eastern Christians who praise the infinitely beautiful God who will be our future happiness for ever. John O'Brien, an Irish missionary priest of whom more later, helped me to feel fully at home with these three styles, which became a major theme for my *Retrieving Fundamental Theology* (1993). Upbringing and education in Australia and England made me primarily an exponent of the first style: the articulation of truth in an academic setting. I have tried to respect and love the liberational and liturgical styles; and for years I drew encouragement and consolation from what the Cardinal Archbishop of Bogotá said to me in 1986: 'Please teach the students the scriptures and the major themes of the great tradition. They can translate all that into their own cultures when they return home.' For good measure, he added: 'In Rome you can't pretend to know all the cultures and experiences they bring with them. Just respect them; that's sufficient.' This was easily done with the Latin Americans. Like students from other suffering parts of the world, they were persistently grateful and seldom complained.

Colleges and Courses

Many of our Latin Americans live in the Mexican College, the Brazilian College, or the Latin American College (the Pio Latino). The Brazilian College and the Pio Latino were comparatively recent foundations (in Roman terms!) and staffed by Jesuits.

As well as founding the Gregorian, Ignatius Loyola also established the German-Hungarian College, which is still staffed by Jesuits. The origins of the Germanicum give it a special link with the Gregorian, expressed by the way in which at the start of the academic year its graduates from the first cycle are ordained together in the Gregorian University's church, Sant'Ignazio. In the litanies of the saints recited or sung during the ordination ceremony, they invoke their founder and ours: 'Holy Father Ignatius'.

During my early years in Rome I would never miss that October ordination for the students of the Germanicum. It sometimes involved assisting at Mass the following morning with one of the new priests and joining him for the celebration meal which he and his family offered in a restaurant in Rome or out in the nearby hills. On one memorable October day the new priest had me seated right opposite a stunningly beautiful relative who wore an low-cut dress. I remembered the advice a prince had given his son about coping with similar eventualities: 'Look them in the eyes!' The problem there was the dazzling quality of her blue eyes, which naturally seemed even more striking in a country where dark eyes are the norm. I spent the two- or three-hour meal speaking German but gazing across her shoulders and golden hair and out at Lake Nemi.

The North American College, a pentagon-like structure up on the Janiculum Hill, regularly supplies twenty or more students for the first year of first cycle theology. Other substantial groups come from the French Seminary and the Major Seminary for the diocese of Rome. From the late 1980s another source of students has been 'Redemptoris Mater', the seminary for priestly candidates of a modern movement aimed at helping all Christians discover or rediscover what faith and baptism really entail, the Neocatechumenal Way.

A number of those following the first cycle and aspiring for ordination are Byzantine rite Catholics, who marry before they are ordained deacons. Others again are Latin rite Catholics and members of religious institutes with whom I came into contact for the first time. The Resurrectionists are an institute that takes its name not, like so many other institutes, from the passion and redemptive death of Jesus but from his triumph over death. As their house was next to the Spanish Steps, they were close neighbours and became good friends. The tragic end of one Resurrectionist is a painful memory that still haunts me. He would fall asleep in class and at least on one occasion I reprimanded him for that. I didn't know that he suffered from chronic insomnia. When he returned to Poland for military service, his tortured condition sent him out of his mind and he shot himself.

First-year students have normally been a happy bunch, who cheerfully put up with my Australian accent coming through the language of Dante! Forty-five minutes in Italian seemed an eternity on my first-day lecturing in October 1974. René Latourelle, then dean of theology, had loosened me and the students up by his final words of welcome and introduction: 'Father O'Collins will teach the course on revelation, and, I guarantee, his accent will be a revelation to you!' I will never forget the kind applause led by the American students at the end. I was certainly not the only person in the hall for whom this had been the first experience of a lecture in Italian! We were united by our common struggle in learning a foreign language.

The second cycle audience seemed to offer a higher percentage of unforgettable personalities than the first. During a course I taught on the use of the scriptures in theology, a mature Italian lady confessed to be a great-grandmother. 'You and your daughter must have married very young,' I responded without too much flattery. Her husband had died, and the mature Italian lady was caring for an old friend suffering from Alzheimer's; the graduate courses at the Gregorian acted as a happy distraction. One of the other students was a Russian, a Lutheran bishop, presumably the only Russian-born Lutheran bishop. In our conversations we had to muddle along in a mixture of English, German, and Italian. Yet another student, a German deacon from Cologne, could not always attend the lectures, but passed the examination well, and eventually defended his doctorate. He had to be cautious about picking up any infections going the rounds, since he was still gathering strength after a heart transplant.

At the licence level I enjoyed the contributions which the English writer, Margaret Hebblethwaite, made to at least one course and a seminar. In the late seventies she came to Rome with her husband Peter and their children while he was working as the Roman correspondent for the American newspaper, *The National Catholic Reporter*. Margaret, who had previously studied theology in Oxford, used to cross the city on a motor scooter. With a white helmet on top of her beautiful red hair and wearing a fur coat in cold weather, she certainly succeeded in distracting Italian drivers. Unfortunately Margaret couldn't finish the two-year licentiate program, since she and Peter returned to Oxford after she had completed only three semesters with us.

For their examinations first-cycle students can normally choose either to take a ten or fifteen minute oral or to sit for a two or three hour written examination. For second cycle courses they often have three choices: oral examinations, written examinations, or a paper to be submitted before the end of the course. Each semester they attend an afternoon seminar once a week and at times follow language courses in the afternoons: Latin, Greek, Hebrew, or some modern language. Although required courses are taught in Italian, for their written papers and written examinations students may use English, French, German, Italian, Latin, or Spanish. Some professors also accept written work or orals in other languages: for instance, in Portuguese.

Licence Students

Licence students and doctoral students have the right to use one of the official six languages for their dissertations. Tradition also allows for the use of Portuguese, which suits the numerous Brazilians who greatly outnumber those from Portugal itself. By June 2006 ninety-two doctoral students had successfully completed and defended theses written under my supervision in English, French, German Italian, or Spanish, and over three hundred students had completed their licence dissertations with me (in those languages and Portuguese), usually writing around eighty or ninety pages.

Each year brought evening meetings with the licence and the doctoral students. Generally that involved a concelebrated Mass, followed by a discussion of topics of common interest, and ending with beer and a pizza. On one memorable evening in the late 1970s my licence students were to gather across the Tiber and up the Janiculum Hill at the North American College. Riot police had been spending the late afternoon teargassing and making baton charges against thousands of young people who, angered by the corruption of the government, had flooded the historic heart of the city for an illegal demonstration. I decided to make my run down side streets and set off at an energetic pace through the centre. By now Rome was eerily deserted and reeked of tear gas. When I slipped across a long street near the Piazza Navona, a helmeted policeman hundreds of yards away to my left spotted me and fired a tear gas grenade. As it spun around on the ground, I gazed at it in fascination, until I suddenly saw again the face of Prince Andrei at the Battle of Borodino in a film version of *War and Peace*. He stared helplessly at a shell until it exploded and fatally wounded him. That snap memory set me moving at speed along the narrow streets and up the Janiculum.

John O'Brien, one of my group of licence students, was waiting up at the North American College with the others and led us in Mass. This slim and bearded Irish missionary constantly reminded me of the face that popular art often gives to Jesus, especially as John used to close his eyes when reciting the eucharistic prayer at the heart of Mass. Highly intelligent, he had a remarkable command of languages and a radical life style that enthralled me. Drama and tragedy were never far away, whether he was working at home in Ireland or abroad in Africa and Pakistan. My favorite O'Brien story concerns the dissertation he wrote for his licence. He wanted to trace the evolution of Karl Rahner's thinking about the incarnation or the Son of God assuming a human existence in our midst. Brushing aside my proposal that he limit himself to Rahner's early essays on this theme, John examined years of writing from that superlative but difficult twentieth-century theologian. He ended up with hundreds of pages of manuscript, three or four times the length of a normal licence dissertation. With the deadline for submission imminent, he asked the then dean of theology for two further weeks, which coincided with our Easter break. The dean agreed, but added that John *must* hand the work in on the day classes resumed.

John went away over the break to help in a parish, leaving the manuscript with an Italian lady who had promised to have it all typed and ready for his return on the Friday after Easter. When he came back, he found to his horror that she hadn't typed a single page. In fact the poor woman couldn't type at all and had accepted the work (along with the terms of payment) because of some kind of psychological incapacity to say 'Sorry, I can't type.' Totally dismayed, John turned up in my room around midday on the Friday. Neither of us could think of any way of finding the necessary help to do all the typing, make the photocopies, and have the work ready for the dean in three days time. But late on the Monday morning John returned and presented me with my copy of his dissertation. 'A miracle,' he declared grinning from ear to ear. On the Friday afternoon he had gone off despairingly to smoke and drink Coca Cola in one of the first Irish pubs in Rome, 'the Fiddler's Elbow'. A girl sitting with two friends at a nearby table took pity on the lonely young man, invited him to join them, and asked: 'What's your problem?' John explained; the three Irish girls looked at each other and said: 'We'll do it for you.' They were secretaries who worked for an international organization in Rome. Off they went with John to the French Seminary where he lived. He put them in different rooms and in front of different electric typewriters — this being before the days of computers. Through Saturday and Sunday John hurried from room to room, correcting the chapters as they rolled off the production line. First thing on Monday morning he went to a local agency to get the text copied and bound — a couple of hours work — before coming to my room. The 'Luck of the Irish' had for once prevailed over Murphy's Law ('if anything can go wrong it will').

John returned to the Gregorian several years later to undertake a doctoral thesis. He left Rahner behind him this time. His study of theological method from the perspective of the poor helped me to clarify my own thinking about the three styles of theology which characterize the life of my discipline around the world: theory, practice, and worship.

Doctoral Students

Here I want to pay tribute as well to other doctoral students. I enjoyed collaboration with them and learned from all of them. It seemed more like 'super-vising' or looking over their shoulders to see what they were writing, rather than 'directing' or pushing them along a road I had chosen for them.

My first doctoral student, Dan Kendall, showed me the value of exploring the reception of New Testament texts in the subsequent development of Christian thinking. He examined the way a passage from St Paul (1 Corinthians 3:10-15), which reflects on the work of some Christians (namely, missionary preachers), was subsequently pressed into service to illuminate belief in the purgatorial cleansing that takes place after death of human beings. Years later Nunzio Capizzi, fresh from an excellent course at the Biblical Institute on St Paul's Letter to the Philippians, scrutinized a typical group of late twentieth-century theologians on their use (or sometimes misuse) of a wonderful hymn written or, more probably, quoted by the apostle: Philippians 2:6-11.

An Australian student, Paul Gwynne, turned to good use earlier studies in natural sciences and critically evaluated the particular issues that have emerged in a contemporary debate on special divine activity. Michael Heher, an expert on the work of the American novelist Flannery O'Connor, showed how her bizarre stories illuminate the human condition in its need for and openness to God's saving self-revelation. An English Holy Child Sister, Anne Murphy, took advantage of critical editions of the writings of the man for all seasons, St Thomas More, to tackle his reflections on Christ's cross and our share in it. More developed these reflections during his stay in the Tower of London before he was beheaded for his alleged high treason in refusing to acknowledge Henry VIII as head of the Church in England.

An American Capuchin priest, William Henn, turned to another 'man for all seasons', Yves Congar, the learned French Dominican who played a leading role as an advisor during the Second Vatican Council and encouraged the bishops to think of the revealed truths of Christianity in a certain order of importance. Bill's thesis spelled out the elements that led Congar to develop this principle of 'the hierarchy of truths'. When published in our dissertation series, the *Analecta Gregoriana*, the volume included a friendly letter to Bill by Congar himself. When neither of our professors of ecclesiology or doctrine of the Church could propose a suitable candidate for a chair in that field — one of the professors simply had no one to suggest, and the other proposed a candidate who was rejected by the dean of theology's four counsellors — I encouraged the counsellors to think of Bill, who was in due course appointed to the vacant chair.

Several of my doctoral students have already gone to the grave, a number have sunk out of sight, but all remain in my memory, even those who never finished and defended their dissertations. That is the fate of around 25% of our doctoral students, a percentage which is slightly better than that in the larger universities of the Western world. Sickness, a major change of direction, or too much other work left these friends marked up as ABD (all but the dissertation).

The most painful case of ABD was that of a priest who generously helps everyone who needs him — and they are many — and is at the same time a perfectionist rather than a realist. Alfred wrote more than a thousand pages, and still remained dissatisfied. At one point I tried to lay my hands on his work, so that I could have it photocopied, bound, and presented to the faculty. 'That'll force him to defend it,' I thought. But Alfred must have got wind of my intention and allowed me to have only part of what he had written. Yet I learned much from Alfred; he helped to shape my thinking about human experience, which was part of his problem. Unless you keep a firm hand on 'experience', you can be overwhelmed by the vague and loose feel to that notion, as Alfred was.

With so many licence and doctoral students there has inevitably been much socializing. Doctoral students celebrate the defence of their thesis with a post-defence meal. On such occasions no one has a public image to defend; there is plenty of entertainment — sometimes at the expense of members of the faculty. The boldest crack I ever heard came from Father Milton Walsh of San Francisco; he had successfully defended his fascinating study of Monsignor Ronald Knox as apologist. In the presence of his archbishop and other dignitaries, he turned to his two principal examiners, Father Jared Wicks and myself as his director, saying: 'Thanks very much for what you said at the defence. I want you to know, boys, that the checks are in the mail.'

Doctoral students never fail at their public defence. If inadequate theses have been submitted, these are turned down beforehand, with detailed reasons provided. The defence can, however, affect the final grade, which might be anything between a bare pass and *summa cum laude*. Students are free to invite anyone to attend the defence, and the chosen audience might include bishops, representatives of the media, and ambassadors. Milton Walsh brought along not only his archbishop, John Quinn, but also the first US ambassador to the Vatican, William Wilson. One Columbian priest invited at least three cardinals to sit in the front row. He needed all the help he could get, since his thesis was barely up to scratch. In 1991 Croatian television filmed the defence of an excellent thesis by a Croatian priest, and succeeded in making the hall almost unbearably hot with their lighting. As director of the thesis and dean of theology I could have refused the presence of TV cameras. But I hoped that a programme on the civilized defence of a doctorate in Rome might do a bit of good in the priest's homeland, where savage fighting was about to erupt in former Yugoslavia.

Like most of my American doctoral students, Milton stayed in the Casa Santa Maria. Living right in the heart of old Rome not only carries advantages for those students but also leads to distractions coming from a flow of visitors. In their local jargon, 'Pits' stands for 'persons in town' and 'Fits' for 'friends in town'. The student priests at the Casa also speak of 'consigning' their theses, rather than submitting them or handing them in. Nothing can eradicate that term — not even pointing out how in ordinary English usage it takes trucks to bring 'a consignment of goods' and when exasperated we might feel like 'consigning' someone 'to the devil'. Italians, who use 'consegnare' when they speak of submitting theses, might be flattered to learn that linguistically the road between English and Italian is not simply one way.

Two Old Colleges

'The Casa' and even more the older colleges such as the Venerable English College made me feel connected with an unbroken tradition. The Venerable has extended a welcome to English students and pilgrims since its foundation in 1579. When walking to the English College, I frequently went by way of the Campo dei Fiori, passed the statue of Giordano Bruno (burned there in 1600 by the Roman Inquisition), and took a tiny alley which enabled me to look up at the Borgia arms that mark the home of one of Pope Alexander VI's mistresses! For many years the English College excelled itself at the Christmas pantomime which had several performances. An adapted version of 'Pinocchio', 'the Wizard of Oz', 'Jack and the Beanstalk', or some other favourite turned into a vehicle for hilarious jokes at the expense of the College staff, other colleges, Roman institutions of all kinds, and, naturally, the professors. Variations entered the text from evening to evening, to include particular individuals and groups attending a given performance. No one could be left out, and the professors and bishops present were well aware that they might be called onto the stage and turned into a snowman (myself on one occasion) or something worse. A prayer service and variety concert now take the place of those elaborate pantomimes.

Another community that reaches back centuries is the International College of the Gesù, which houses forty or fifty young Jesuits in the building where Ignatius Loyola spent the final years of his life and died in 1556. Although I never lived at the Gesù, on two occasions I served as dean of studies for the Jesuit scholastics or seminarians. Successive rectors always gave me the green light to turn up at the Gesù whenever I wanted to share the buffet evening meal, between 6.30 and 8. The scholastics came from Africa, the Americas, Asia, and Europe, making the College about as international a mix as my heart could desire. The vivacity of those young men, especially the Africans, Asians, and Latin Americans, gave me a regular break and provided a necessary psychological balance to life with my older, mainly European colleagues in the Gregorian community. The words of my one-time, German spiritual director frequently popped into my mind when I visited the Gesù: 'O'Collins, your only hope, humanly and spiritually, is to hang around with the young.'

In the *The Pope's Divisions* by Peter Nichols, the London *Times* Roman correspondent for many years, the first chapter set the scene with the eleven o'clock Mass in the Church of the Gesù.[9] The Italian congregations remained relatively passive, but they always appreciated the lively singing and sermons that were sincere, short, and to the point. Along with Nichols I found the eleven o'clock Mass in the Gesù one of the striking indications that Rome remains the city of all nations. In a later chapter I must tell two stories about Masses in that church: the Sunday morning when Father (later Cardinal) Paolo Dezza packed the church, and the evening funeral Mass in November 1989 celebrated by Father Peter-Hans Kolvenbach for the six Jesuits, their cook, and her daughter murdered by security forces in El Salvador.

Extra Activities and Real Needs

Before ending this chapter, let me walk in imagination across the Piazza Venezia and the Via del Corso back to the Gregorian and answer three questions in that setting. First, apart from their regular

---

9 Since they had similar names, Peter Nichols and Peter Nicholson, a cartoonist who spent the better part of a year living outside Rome before becoming famous for his cartoons in the (Melbourne) *Age* and *The Australian*, suffered from Italian postal workers confusing their mail. Even worse for the cartoonist was the outburst he provoked when making a routine phone call to a Roman bank about a cheque that had not arrived. When he gave his full name, the bank official instantly took it as pure mockery from an Australian confidence man who had not yet been arrested. He was defrauding the banks, and by pure chance used the same name, 'Peter Nicholson'.

programme of studies, what extra lectures and speakers could students enjoy at the University? Over the years they had the opportunity to hear talks from Mother Teresa of Calcutta, from Jean Vanier, founder of the L'Arche communities for mentally handicapped people, or from that defender of human rights in South Africa, Denis Hurley (1915-2004), an alumnus of the Gregorian who became Archbishop of Durban. Stanley Jaki, a winner of the Templeton Prize for his work on the interface between science and religion, lectured for us, as well as Jewish scholars, Buddhist leaders from Asia, and our former rector, Cardinal Carlo Maria Martini of Milan, to name but a few.

From time to time the Gregorian hosts international meetings such as the 1996 symposium on fundamental theology, which drew American speakers like Avery Dulles and David Tracy and German stars in the discipline. In 1997 we had an international meeting on the Holocaust, and in 1998 a dialogue lasting several days between members of the Japanese Tenriko religion (centered on God the Parent and the practice of a joyful life) and Christian thinkers including Ninian Smart from Santa Barbara. In March 1992 a fascinating conference marked the production of CD-ROMs which would greatly facilitate research into the works of Ignatius Loyola. This meeting was promoted by Father Roberto Busa, who proudly told English speakers that his surname is pronounced 'boozer'. A pioneer from the 1950s in electronic means for research, Busa had strong Venetian connections, knew very well Patriarch Luciani, the short-lived John Paul I, and remained a good friend of the veteran and much maligned Italian politician, Giulio Andreotti. Andreotti was to go on trial for murder and for association with the Mafia. The trials went on for years until he was definitively acquitted of both charges. At the conference on the Ignatian CD-ROMs, I was astonished to catch Andreotti quietly attending one of the sessions. He had taken time out from the frenzy of a national election to come along. All in all, students have enjoyed many extra and stimulating offerings at the Gregorian, and not least some astonishing art exhibitions.

Our atrium was well suited for small exhibitions. In May 1997 it displayed seventeen works by the Georgian artist Irakli Parjiani on such sacred themes as the Annunciation, the Adoration of the Magi, the Last Supper, the Crucifixion, and Mary Magdalene at the tomb of Jesus. This painter had died prematurely, some years before the fall of Communism. The exhibition was opened by Eduard Shevardnadze, former minister of foreign affairs for the Soviet Union and subsequently President of Georgia.

A year after the Parjiani exhibition, our atrium was filled with the works of an Egyptian Muslim, Ahmed Moustafa. The Israeli Ambassador to the Holy See, the President of Italian Jewish communities, many ambassadors of Muslim countries represented at the Holy See, and a large number of other visitors attended the opening ceremony and were moved by the painter's translation of mystical experiences into visual images. A year earlier, in 1997, when Pakistan celebrated fifty years of independence, the British government had commissioned and presented to the people of Pakistan a work by Moustafa entitled 'Where the Two Oceans Meet'. To thank the Gregorian for providing him with a venue, the artist gave the university one of his works. It filled a wall facing the office of our Institute for the Study of Religions and Cultures.

The second question concerns the teaching faculty. When did Gregorian students and, in particular, those studying theology first find women professors teaching them? Although women had started teaching in our faculty of social sciences and institute of psychology shortly after the Second Vatican Council ended in 1965, progress was slow. From the early 1980s the faculty of theology began to hire women biblical scholars to direct seminars, the first being Maria Luisa Rigato who was to contribute a chapter to a book I co-edited in 1991,

Luke and Acts

Letters from my first years in Rome reflect my discomfort at the limited roles assigned to women — in classrooms and beyond. On 8 December 1975 faculty and students from the ecclesiastical universities and other institutions went in large numbers to a special Mass celebrated by Pope Paul VI to recall the tenth anniversary of the closing of the Second Vatican Council. Ten days later I wrote to a friend in Australia and described the scene in St Peter's:

It was sad to see that women are still not allowed to read lessons or participate in the prayer of the faithful. Two women carried vases of white flowers to the altar at the offertory, and that was all. The refusal to let women play a more significant role in the celebration looked even stranger, as it was a feast of Our Lady and the Pope's sermon (and long prayer after the sermon) stressed the sublime dignity of one woman.

The following year I began a correspondence with several leaders of American women religious groups about the possibility of their sponsoring women theologians as visiting professors at the Gregorian.

Although nothing resulted from these initiatives, women scholars from Canada, England, France, Italy, Norway, Spain, and the United States came to find a place on our theological roster. In the first semesters of 1978/79 and 1979/80 the Norwegian scholar Kari Børresen encouraged feminist thinking in her seminars on ancient and medieval Christian authors. She was subsequently to teach at Harvard Divinity School, and eventually secured a well-deserved chair at the University of Oslo. From 1983 Mariette Canévet, a professor in ancient Christian literature at the University of Strasburg, began to conduct six-week, optional courses on such Greek authors as St Athanasius of Alexandria and St Gregory of Nyssa. From 1986 to 1989, Francesca Cantù, a professor at the University of Rome and the daughter of a retired Italian admiral, offered optional courses on Latin American history for our theological students.

In 1989 a big breakthrough occurred when I recommended the Italian Sister Elena Bosetti and secured her appointment as the first woman to teach a required course — on the Gospels of Matthew, Mark, and Luke in our basic or first cycle of theology. In the spring of 1997 Janet Martin Soskice, a Canadian who teaches at Cambridge University, became the first woman to hold the McCarthy Visiting Professorship (of which more below).

The third question concerns the funding of the Gregorian and the recruiting of professors. Although students of superlative quality arrive without the Gregorian needing to advertise, money remains a problem. Despite the vigorous efforts of such rectors as Giuseppe Pittau (who became Archbishop Pittau and until his retirement worked for the Vatican's Congregation for Catholic Education), it proved difficult to put the Gregorian on a stable financial footing. Expenses rose enormously, not least through the need to hire more non-Jesuit teachers and pay them adequately. Fees had, of course, also risen, but they remained well below those of comparable institutions in North America. The Gregorian had no wish to make the cost prohibitive to those from poorer countries.

The crucial challenge, however, was and is that of recruiting professors, in particular, Jesuits who are academically well prepared, able to speak several languages, open to a very international student body and willing to live permanently away from home. During my six years as dean of theology, I found that suitable professors from around the world would gladly agree to come and offer courses for six weeks or an entire semester. Stars of the theological world would in fact give a broad hint that they expected to be invited! The difficulty, however, was that of renewing our full time faculty. Our life in Rome was a missionary one, not the most gruelling of foreign missions, but still a missionary existence. My colleagues and I spent years searching, not always successfully, for those ready to accept the invitation: 'Come and join us on the Tiber mission.'

Lunch at the Vatican with Cardinal Castillo Lara, c. 1996

4

Italy and the Italians

This chapter threatens to be one of the longest in this book, because it aims to share the good news about Italy and the Italians rather than any bad news. You can be reminded of the latter right in the heart of Rome on the Piazza Venezia, where *the* Italian problem is carved on the Victor Emmanuel monument: 'unitati patriae, libertati civium (to the unity of the fatherland and the freedom of the citizens).' As any observant visitor will notice, Italian society blatantly favours individual freedom over national unity. The level of diversity is such that it leads to fragmentation. But let me sum up the good news by assuring my readers that Italians rank among the world's leading role-models in human living. There is a universal need to belong somewhere and to someone. The Italians belong to their families and friends, and their families and friends are windows through which religion comes into view.

Families and Faith

In 1986 I was back in Naples, on one of my many visits to a city that never failed to revive and astonish me with its warm humanity. Little Chiara, fresh from her first communion, was there to welcome me. Bright and ready to go at the age of nine, she told me about her lessons in geography and English. Twenty-year-old Giuseppe took time off from his work in the Royal Palace of the Bourbons and guided me through the city's opera house, the Teatro San Carlo. I went up front and tested the legendary acoustics with my rendering of 'La donna è mobile.' We then crossed the road to drink excellent coffee in the huge arcade of King Umberto I. Two young friends, Gino and Fausta, captivatingly in love with each other, took me out to Pozzuoli, a village on the Bay of Naples. After hours of wonderful talk, delicious fish, and gleaming wine, we walked along the waterfront to lift our eyes above the boats and see the stars. The following day I lunched with two old men who recalled highlights from their past: for one his years as a tailor in Rome, and for the other a long stay in Australia that had initiated him into the dangers of surf beaches in Queensland. Yet the best of the day was yet to come; I went on to the Gesù Nuovo and met an ancient Poor Clare sister. Angelina greeted me with a widest of smiles when we met at the entrance to that most ornate of the baroque churches in Naples. In the crowded streets of Naples, kindness and love abound, as well as crime and violence. No one has caught Naples better than the late Francis Steegmuller in his *New Yorker* story (21 April 1986) about being attacked by two young men and then rescued by others with efficient kindness. The husband of Shirley Hazzard, Steegmuller was a world expert on Gustave Flaubert.

On the train back to Rome from Naples, I thought about Chiara, Giuseppe, Gino, Fausta, the two old men, and Sister Angelina. For two days they had let me into their lives. On those warm days and magic evenings I had once again enjoyed the rich humanity of Neapolitans of all ages. Yet Romans too know how to blend faith with the way they live their family values.

Just before Christmas 1976 my family sent me a ticket to fly home to Melbourne, as my mother was fading fast. Classes had ended and I was to catch a flight the following day, when a couple of Irish students decided to take me off to a 'trattoria' where I had never been before. At the end of the meal our waiter cheerfully asked us what we were going to do at Christmas. When I informed him that I would be going home to Australia since 'la Mamma sta molto male (my mother is very ill),' his face turned serious and he kissed me on both cheeks. This stranger instantly became a brother when he found me facing a painful loss at the heart of my family life. Where else in the world would a waiter whom I was meeting for the first time express his concern with such spontaneous affection? In March 1977 my mother died. One of the memories which softened the pain was the impromptu kindness of that Italian waiter on a December evening a few months earlier.

Years later some friends invited me to join them for a funeral Mass celebrated in the monastery of Santa Sabina up on the Aventine. We stood and knelt in history, when they conducted the service in the cell where St Dominic had stayed and where, on one remarkable occasion, he spent hours in prayer and spiritual conversation with St Francis of Assisi. When we came down from that holy place, they took me to a 'trattoria' right next to the Pyramid, the Porta Ostiensis, and the old Roman wall. A young mother with a tiny child in her arms stood at the entrance of the Taverna Cestia. They both deserved to have modelled for Raphael. I smiled, blessed the little boy, and asked: 'What's his name?' 'Riccardo,' she told me. When we left a couple of hours later, I paused to chat with a young man who was as handsome as any legendary Greek god. 'Gone to bed,' he told me when I asked what Riccardo was doing. Then, looking almost mystically into the distance, he said quietly: 'Children are the salt of life.'

Mothers and children structure the Italian philosophy of life, shape the experiential and emotional depth of religion, and make it a vital ingredient in the culture. Young Italian men furtively bless themselves when they pass a 'madonnina', or little image of the Madonna and baby Jesus tucked away in a niche on a street corner. I was once driving around Naples with a highly successful woman who had risen to become a judge in her late thirties. I noticed that she crossed herself whenever we passed a cemetery. She had leapt ahead professionally but an instinctive gesture of prayer for the dead seemed utterly natural to her. Visit Italy on 2 November, All Souls' Day, and you will see people crowding the cemeteries. They return to pray at the graves of their dear ones, and leave pots of chrysanthemums, the flowers which Italians reserve for their dead. It is easy to write off such material expressions of religion as a cultural hangover from the time when Italy was the heartland of Catholicism or even to dismiss them as semi-pagan superstition. I believe that the furtive signs of the cross in front of the 'madonnine', the flowers at cemeteries, and so many more customs are windows into the other world that gives Italians that vision and hope we all need.

Back in August 1974, when learning Italian in Florence before taking up my lecturing at the Gregorian, I went to an outdoor Sunday Mass celebrated by the archbishop in thanksgiving for the liberation of Florence from German occupation thirty years previously during the Second World War. The crowd filled the Piazza Signoria, military representatives stood up near the altar, and I found myself surrounded by men from a Communist trade union. They talked and even smoked throughout the Mass, but at the moment of the consecration they took their cigarettes from their mouths and held them down towards the ground in a kind of salute to Jesus now present among us through the Eucharist. There are plenty of jokes about Italian men, who if asked whether they attend Mass every Sunday reply: 'I'm a Catholic but not a fanatic (sono cattolico ma non sono fanatico).' One legendary character apparently went to confession and told the priest that he had committed the sin of fornication. 'How many times?,' asked the priest. The reply was: 'Look, Father. I came here to confess my sins, not to boast.'

In April 1997 the world's media carried the story of the 44-year-old Italian fireman, Mario Trematore. He dashed into the burning Savoy Chapel in Turin Cathedral and, as chunks of masonry fell around him, rescued the Shroud, that most moving image of the crucified Christ. The press quoted Trematore: 'I was afraid for the Shroud, because when I smashed through the bullet proof glass, I could easily have smashed the casket and the Shroud, and then I would have been known as the biggest cretin in the world.' But not every foreign paper included his additional comment: 'At a certain point I felt something within me, a higher force that guided me. I grabbed a sledge-hammer and began to hit the anti-projectile glass. I struck and struck and struck, but the glass did not give way. Then finally it broke. I believe that in that moment God gave me the power to save the sacred Shroud.' The Italian daily papers carried the front page story: 'Shroud safe.' Trematore became an instant national hero. No matter what their politics or the degree of their anti-Church feelings, it mattered deeply to the Italian public that they did not lose the Shroud in that fire.

Terrorists

The topic of Italian men and religion brings back my surprise when a friend asked me: 'Do you know another country where the prime minister attends daily Mass?' The prime minister at the time was Giulio Andreotti, who went to Mass in different churches during the course of any given week. That practice probably saved him from the fate of Aldo Moro, who had been prime minister five times, was encouraging national solidarity by his shift to the centre-left, and was widely expected to become the next Italian president, only to be kidnapped and assassinated by the Red Brigade in 1978. The terrorists could plan meticulously their way of killing the five bodyguards and kidnapping Moro, since he always attended the same church at the same time every morning. Andreotti was too street-wise for such a thing, although he frequently attended the Jesuit Church of the Gesù for his morning Mass and would take his turn reading the first lesson. In the late nineties Andreotti, now a senator for life, faced charges of Mafia connections; the only seemingly solid piece of evidence was testimony that a Mafia chief had been seen embracing Andreotti. He brought a smile to the faces of the early morning congregation as he read Paul's advice to the Roman Christians: 'greet each other with a holy kiss' (Romans 16:16). The question before the court was whether Andreotti had in fact kissed one of Sicily's bosses. Presumably kissing a Mafia chief could never be a holy kiss. Andreotti himself said: 'If I kissed that guy, I should be taken away to a psychiatric clinic.' The 'repentant' ex-Mafia member who testified to having seen the kiss ruined his credibility by committing yet another murder.

On the sad day in March 1978 when members of the Red Brigade succeeded in kidnapping Aldo Moro on the outskirts of Rome, shops around the city closed in protest. It was the Red Brigade's biggest success in their attempt to strike at the heart of Italy's political life in the hope of destabilizing Italian democracy and preparing the way for an extreme left-wing government. I went up to the Gregorian's roof garden far above the streets, looked across the rooftops, and wondered where on earth the terrorists could be hiding Moro. Then a message arrived from the radio section of RAI, the national media organization to say that my interview would still take place later that morning, and could I please come to their studio on the far side of the Tiber. By a cruel coincidence the topic they had given me was Jesus' death and its significance for us.

Living in Rome in those 'anni di piombo (years of lead)', as the late seventies and early eighties came to be called, one was all too aware of the merciless and senseless killings carried out by terrorist organizations. But at the same time, the funeral services for their victims repeatedly revealed the faith of grief-stricken men and women and their willingness to hope and to forgive. At the funeral of Walter Tobagi, a young journalist assassinated in May 1980 in revenge for what he had written about terrorists, Archbishop (later Cardinal) Carlo Martini of Milan spoke of a 'mystery of meaninglessness and madness'. But he also reminded the congregation of that great certainty to be found in the Bible: 'What is meaningless can gain a meaning.' The prayers of the faithful which followed the Archbishop's homily showed most movingly how Jesus can bring those in terrible sorrow to see and affirm meaning in their experience. Stella Tobagi, now widowed with two small children, had written a prayer. She sat with her arms around her son and daughter while her sister read it for her: 'Lord, we pray for those who killed Walter, and for all people who wrongly hold that violence is the only right way for resolving problems. May the power of your Spirit change the hearts of men, and out of Walter's death may there be born a hope which the force of arms will never be able to defeat.'

At a wedding reception outside Vicenza some years later I noticed two people standing slightly apart from the elegant and vivacious crowd. They turned out to be the parents of a young terrorist woman, who had been rounded up and jailed in the rapid collapse of the Red Brigade. When I met her grieving parents, they told me that they had just published a book about their daughter. It was part of their effort to understand how life had failed those idealistic young people, who desperately wanted to improve Italian society but had then turned to violence. Was it the Church which had failed them? Was it the state? Were the parents themselves primarily responsible? I shared with them my conviction that the Red Brigade showed, in a terrifying way, how ideas matter and how, for good or evil, beliefs shape actions.

It does matter enormously that what we hold to be true is in fact true to reality, both in terms of the here and now and of the hereafter. The Red Brigade illustrated tragically the importance of sharing our ideas with those who are not our close friends and of listening to those who do not think like ourselves. The young terrorists listened only to one another, and that self-reinforcement drove them to horrible extremes.

Six Weddings

Italian weddings have a magic all their own. A wedding in the mid-seventies, between Mario and Tina, took me up to Marta, a charming village on Lake Bolsena about sixty miles north of Rome. After endless courses had been consumed or put into doggy bags, Mario and Tina made a cascade of champagne down a mountain of glasses without any loss or breakage, and the final toasts were drunk. We then moved to the home of Mario's parents down by the water for further festivities. I knew that the last bus back to Rome had already departed. When I asked the bridegroom about transport possibilities and mentioned that I had a class to teach the following morning at 8.30, Mario gave the classic answer: 'Ci penso io (I'll take care of it).' Around ten o'clock Mario bundled Tina, still in her wedding dress, into the back seat of his Fiat 500, put me in beside him, and with much song and merriment we hit the road for Rome. Never had I seen or heard of a priest sharing a ride with the newly married couple heading off for their honeymoon. It was around midnight when we swung into the Via della Pilotta and arrived at the Gregorian. One solitary tourist stared in amazement as a bride and bridegroom piled out of the tiny car to hug a priest who had obviously blessed their wedding. Was this a latter day version of Romeo, Juliet, and Brother Lawrence?

In Rome itself I did three weddings in the Doria church, St Agnes on the Piazza Navona: for Gesine Doria and for two sisters, Mary and Diana, who had grown up with the Doria children. When we were rehearsing Gesine's wedding, the short aisle meant that her father walked her from the door to the altar in a minute or so. 'Frank, let's do that again,' I told him. 'You'll have to take it more slowly.' With a laugh the Prince Doria excused himself: 'I'm trying to get rid of her more quickly. Can't you see?'

When I officiated at the wedding of Emanuela and Mammo (short for Massimo) just outside Rome, she arrived a good ten minutes early and managed to reach the altar before I did. Emanuela worked for the elegant firm of Gucci in the Via Condotti. I became a good friend of several girls there after a Maltese nun asked me to take over as chaplain to them.

Donatella and Leonardo provided me with my second visit to Venice for their wedding in the Church of John and Paul, where I was delighted to meet a very friendly pastor with the charming name of Padre Camelotto. It conjured up legends of King Arthur, Tintagel, and old Camelot. Unfortunately, the overcast weather cancelled the original plan, which had been for Donatella, Leonardo and myself as celebrant to leave the church in a gondola for a restaurant on the island of Murano. A less direct route, down the Grand Canal in a motorboat, however, allowed the public to admire us and see what we had been doing.

Unlike the Romans, Venetians don't force you to eat a vast amount on festive occasions, but the food is wonderful. The restaurant on Murano belonged to Donatella's brother. His eleven year old daughter, Veronica, and I enjoyed one another's company on the motorboat journey to Murano, and she told me of her hopes of becoming an outstanding violin player with the Venetian orchestra. Some years later I returned to Venice to baptize the second son of Donatella and Leonardo, and again we took a boat trip across to Murano for another lunch at the family restaurant. We were one course into the meal, when Veronica arrived home from her violin lessons. She saw me and ran across the restaurant to give me a big hug. For several weeks life seemed even more worth living, because a young girl who hadn't seen me for several years had remembered me and could show me such spontaneous affection.

The Dorias

In the heart of old Rome, Frank and Orietta Doria gathered their friends and made us all feel that we lived in village community. Daughter of a Doria prince and a Scottish mother, Princess Orietta Pogson Doria Pamphilj inherited the patrimony of one of Italy's greatest families. It was after the liberation of the city in June 1944 that she first met the English naval officer Frank Pogson, whom she was to marry. He had docked his minesweeper in Ancona where she came to work in a canteen as a volunteer for the Catholic Women's League. She had just emerged after hiding out in Rome with her parents during the Nazi occupation of the eternal city.

Months earlier, when German soldiers raided the Doria Palace, Prince Filippo Andrea, Princess Gesine, and their daughter Orietta hid in a lavatory behind a sliding bookcase and heard the soldiers clumping around the gigantic building. The parish priest of Santa Maria in Trastevere then hid the three Dorias for months and shared his food (mainly vegetables) with them. Everyone went very hungry and lived in constant fear. Prince Doria, continued working secretly with Msgr Hugh O'Flaherty, a Scarlet Pimpernel figure who organized hiding places for Allied soldiers, Jews, and others on the run from the enemy forces.[10] In 1943-44 there was a high price on the Prince's head.

Born in 1922, Orietta's education was divided between Rome, England, and Switzerland. Her father's chronically poor health involved a long stay in the Swiss mountains in 1938-39 with his wife and daughter. In Switzerland Orietta developed her love for mountaineering and skiing. Her education may have been fragmented, but she grew up speaking excellent French, as well as English and Italian.

She had a great affinity with her father. When Prince Filippo came out of hiding in June 1944, the Allied authorities appointed him mayor of Rome and he led the city until democratic elections could once again be held. Orietta shared deeply his sense of service. She handled motor vehicles with skill, and from the 1940s to the end of her life had a truck driver's licence. That licence also let her drive vehicles for the girl guides, an organization which she supported with energy and generosity.

When she married Frank in 1958, her father had given his full blessing to their union but, sadly, died a few months before the wedding took place. Mean-minded gossips among the Roman nobility falsely suggested that Prince Filippo opposed the marriage — something that in any case he was unlikely to do since he had himself married a Scottish nurse and was related to the Dukes of Newcastle and the Earls of Shrewsbury. Orietta felt deeply let down by that gossip coming from Roman families, some of whom had already compromised themselves by earlier accepting Mussolini's fascist regime. In any case she had the strength and the wisdom to adapt to the post-war world, which was very different from the one in

---

10 In a film about the German occupation of Rome, *The Scarlet and the Red*, Gregory Peck played the role of O'Flaherty.

which she had been raised as the only child in an immensely wealthy, aristocratic family that spent its summers in the Villa Doria Pamphilj on top of the Janiculum and its winters in their 1000-room palace in the heart of Old Rome. She could never identify with the nobility who pretended that everything had remained just the same. One only needed to see tall Orietta riding her bicycle around the city or hear her talking with shopkeepers to realize how she identified with ordinary people.

She never agreed with the post-war critics who attacked Pope Pius XII for deciding that it would be counter-productive to denounce the Nazi genocidal persecution of the Jews. The Dutch bishops spoke out strongly, and the Nazis reacted by deporting from Holland more Jews and killing them in Auschwitz.[11] Yet Orietta had little time for some who worked later in the Vatican. 'They're a dreadful lot', she remarked to me more than once.

She and Frank, both devout Catholics with a life of daily prayer, gave strong support to inter-church relations when Pope John called the Second Vatican Council. In their palace overlooking the Piazza Navona they made available a meeting-place for non-Catholic observers who attended the Council. Part of that palace became Foyer Unitas, a residence for non-Catholic visitors administered with skill and devotion by the Ladies of Bethany. The Franciscan Friars of the Atonement were welcomed and continue to run there the Centro Pro Unione, one of the world's most important ecumenical study-centres. On the Via del Corso the Palazzo Doria itself came to

---

11 See David Dalin, *The Myth of Hitler's Pope* (Washington, DC: Regnery, 2005). In making a strong case for Pius XII, Palin drew on many sources, but, surprisingly, did not use Owen Chadwick, *Britain and the Vatican during the Second World War* (Cambridge: Cambridge University Press, 1986). Among other things, that work documents how in the winter of 1939/40 Pius XII became involved with two leading German generals in a plot against Hitler.

house the Anglican Centre, the fruit of a 1966 meeting between Pope Paul VI and the then Archbishop of Canterbury, Michael Ramsey. When Archbishop Robert Runcie came to Rome, Orietta and Frank offered him a wonderful reception in their home. It was also in the Palazzo Doria that I renewed my friendship with George Carey when he returned to Rome as Archbishop of Canterbury.

Orietta was also a Roman to the core. One memorable Sunday she and Frank joined me for a day of prayer out at Villa Cavalletti in the Alban Hills. When we turned a corner on the Via Quattro Novembre and drove down the hill towards the Piazza Venezia, I felt a little bump. 'That hole has been there since the war,' Orietta explained. She cherished her city right down to minor potholes and the sheep that used to be driven late at night down the Via del Corso.

Frank and Orietta were a great twosome; his sense of fun checked her tendency to over-seriousness. After she underwent a serious operation in the Roman hospital of Salvator Mundi. I came one afternoon, found her alone, and blurted out something I had been waiting to say for years: 'I find it very touching to see how much Frank loves you and misses you right now.' In her usual matter-of-fact style, she brushed my remark aside but could not help letting me see how I had caught the heart of her existence, the trim ex-naval officer who had married her.

It was no accident that I first met Frank and Orietta through a young American who was writing his thesis with me. The priest belonged to those generations of students who came from all round the world to study in Rome and enjoyed a delicious surprise: the unassuming friendship of the Dorias. Year by passing year, the Christmas carols in the Palazzo Doria were vividly memorable occasions when Frank and Orietta brought together family and friends around the piano in their home. Led by a student from the

English College, we had to sing our way through a booklet before being allowed to move to supper.

At buffet meals I frequently gravitated towards Frank, unless first summoned there by his incomparable butler, Mario. Frank was always happy to talk about his years at sea during the Second World War, when he served on North Atlantic convoys and then mine-sweeping in the Adriatic. Courageous man that he was, he never spoke of the dangers, but recalled the friends he made in the armed forces. He was always a great teaser, and he joked about my persistent failure to distinguish being 'in' a ship or 'on' a ship. I never knew him to tell set piece jokes, but he inserted brilliantly funny remarks into the conversations going on around him.

When a heart condition meant that Frank could only move around in a wheelchair, I started coming each week to say the Sunday Mass for him and Orietta in their sitting room. 'You are the specialist in St Paul', I told him, and always asked him to take the second reading. From his armchair he proclaimed the apostle's words with care and concentration. His quiet devotion touched me over and over again. Then the minutes after Communion when the three of us, sometimes joined by house guests, sat in silence gave me a fresh sense of how we can experience the communion of saints in the presence of Christ. For me and so many others, Frank was love, loyalty, friendship, and fun personified. He was all that for his wife, their children Jonathan and Gesine, and the rest of the family. Sadly for me, Frank died when I was spending a semester at Marquette University, Milwaukee. But I know that one day we will be merry together at home with our God.

Orietta struggled for years against cancer, with cheerful courage and never a hint of self-pity. Only a month before she died, she went to the Quirinal Palace, was invested by Queen Elizabeth II with an OBE, and a few hours later attended the pre-lunch drinks party for the Queen in the Anglican Centre, now housed in splendid new quarters above the Doria Gallery. It was Orietta's final and most fitting public appearance. In October 2000 twelve priests concelebrated her funeral Mass, including the rector of the Beda College, the rector of the Scots College, and the acting rector of the English College — fittingly, for those colleges were very dear to Orietta. The chief celebrant was her very old friend, Bishop Luigi del Gallo di Roccagiovine. He preached in Italian and I preached in English. The basilica was packed. Afterwards I buried Orietta in the family chapel, up in the grounds of the Villa Doria Pamphilj, in a tomb right next to Frank's. In the Doria village at the heart of Rome, along with many others I felt that we had lost our 'mum'.[12]

'The Kids'

Leonardo, Donatella, Laura, and many other young Italians entered my life thanks to Mimi Sbisà, a high school teacher who lived opposite the papal villa outside Rome at Castel Gandolfo. I first met Mimi in 1978 over lunch with our Jesuit scholastics at the College of the Gesù, when this elegant Milanese lady was discussing with one of the priests a plan to emigrate to Australia. I was called in and asked to tell her about my native country. Mimi eventually decided to stay in Italy, and introduced me to her circle of younger and older friends. She was rather similar to Christina Kay, the Edinburgh teacher transformed and immortalized in Muriel Spark's *The Prime of Miss Jean Brodie*. Like Kay, Mimi left her mark on all her pupils. She was charm and dignity personified, full of culture and high principles, and spoke English, French, and German as well as her native Italian.

For a couple of years one afternoon a week I would catch the

---

12 In the London *Tablet* I published an obituary for Frank (10 October 1998) and for Orietta (25 November 2000).

Gerald O'Collins with those who contributed to Friends in Faith (1988)
Top: At Lake Albano. Below: Outside the Papal Villa, Castel Gandolfo

little train that runs beyond the walls of Rome, along miles of an old aqueduct, around vineyards, through a tunnel, and finally to the tiny railway station of Castel Gandolfo above Lake Albano. Mimi had asked me to help her young friends with their English conversation. I used to bring photocopies from the London weekly *The Economist*, preferably an article on Italy. Mimi's students would read and comment on the text. Mimi would provide them with an English accent superior to mine, and I was available as the ultimate arbiter on matters of grammar and idiom. Those 'kids,' as Mimi called them, filled a hole in my life. They cared for me deeply, because — as Mimi said years later — 'they saw that I had time for each of them, was deeply interested in their studies and plans, and was obviously relaxed and happy in their company. The age gap did not matter.' My old German spiritual director was right in his advice 'to hang around with the young'.

Eventually I wrote a book with them, *Friends in Faith*, which also appeared in Italian, Portuguese, and Slovakian. You will find the photographs of some of the kids on the cover. They had each taken a section from the Apostles' Creed and talked to me about what it meant to them or how it puzzled them. We moved from the opening words of the Creed, 'I believe', right through to 'Amen'. In retrospect I think a little more distancing of myself from the kids might have improved the final product; in the book my affection for them is too much in evidence. Yet I very much wanted to pay a tribute to them all and to record them in their own words at a time when none had yet married and most were still finishing their post-high school studies.

Maria Franca, Enrico, and Giorgio

Mimi also introduced me to some of her closest adult friends: Maria Franca Lamaro, Enrico Massa, and Giorgio Barzilai. I sometimes spent Christmas Eve with Maria Franca and her family near Castel

San Angelo. After the meal we would walk to St Peter's Square to admire the huge Christmas crib, and then along the Via Giulia to the English College for Midnight Mass. With black hair, brown eyes, and an olive complexion, Maria Franca was all heart, a luminously beautiful woman who lived her separation from her husband with great dignity and was the quintessentially loving Italian mother and grandmother.

My Italian friends seemed to love all things English, especially a lawyer friend Enrico Massa who dressed like a London professional man. His office, just off the Via Veneto and right behind the Hotel Excelsior, resembled an English solicitor's office or barrister's chambers — in its choice of desks, pictures, and the mild disorder of documents piled in corners. This bald, courteous gentleman in his pin-stripe suit seemed to have been parachuted into Rome from London. He was English too in his desire to maintain his privacy. I often came to his office at six thirty when he finished work, and we would walk a short block to buy a cake in a pastry shop in the Via Veneto. The lady behind the counter never knew Enrico's name; she simply called him 'professore'.

Enrico was a great friend to the kids out in Castel Gandolfo and Albano, and would entertain them with his fund of knowledge and his slightly off-colour jokes. They enjoyed his company over a pizza in Albano, for our annual picnics at the English College summer residence, Palazzola (of which more later), and at his home in the Via Giulia. Enrico was a 'freddoloso', an Italian who disliked the cold and could never be warm enough. One evening the kids and I were dining at his home with the central heating roaring away. The kids started taking clothing off: first jackets and sweaters, then shirts and blouses. But Enrico sat unperturbed in his jacket and tie at the head of the table.

He sometimes joined me for supper at the Gregorian, and became very friendly with a young Indian Jesuit who was writing a doctoral thesis on St John's Gospel. Enrico wanted to know everything about the University and the students who came to us. 'Are there any women students from abroad?,' he once asked me. 'Yes,' I told him. 'We have two laywomen from Colombia, for example. Each is preparing a doctoral dissertation in theology.' Two years later, seemingly out of the blue, Enrico wanted to know whether Dora and Marta were still with us. He asked me to invite them on his behalf for a meal. When the four of us sat down in a restaurant, the three of them went chatting away. Those radiantly lovely South Americans spoke Italian as their second language, but they could match the flow of talk from Enrico. In his beliefs, he seemed to me a Christian pantheist, and the two girls soon realized that. While he basked in their company, they insisted with him that following Jesus was a very good thing to do. When we had finished our meal, Enrico asked: 'Do you have time for a quick drink at my home?' So off we went to the Via Giulia for a 'digestivo'. I could see how he continued to be amazed that the blatant faith of Dora and Marta did nothing to dampen and everything to increase their zest for life. I just got them home as the curfew came down in the 'pensione' run by nuns where they stayed and where the fare was normally frugal.

Although Enrico would walk across the city to his office every day and also return home on foot in the evening, his heart was giving out on him. Tragedy struck when the son of Enrico's associate took his own life. I sat with Enrico and Maria Franca in a church on the Via Nomentana which was packed with the young friends of the boy who had died. 'Please God,' I prayed, 'make the junior curate say it right,' and he did. The priest, who could have been no more than ten years older than all the young people mourning the death of their friend, spoke with compassion, insight, and real hope. When we left the church, Enrico insisted on keeping our appointment for an evening meal with Mimi at Castel Gandolfo. 'This is his Last Supper,' I felt, as Enrico fought his mortal weariness and chatted away at table. A few days later he collapsed and phoned Maria Franca. In the ambulance he repeated our names and the name of Jesus. In the hospital there was nothing they could do for him, and we all lost a devoted friend.

By then Giorgio Barzilai had already died. In his youth he had been one of the young men gathered around the atomic physicist Enrico Fermi (1901-54), who settled in the United States before the Second World War. Fermi had gone to Sweden in 1938 to collect his Nobel Prize, and did not return to Italy because the anti-semitic laws affected his Jewish wife. Giorgio himself rose to be a professor of electrical engineering at the University of Rome. His Jewish father Salvatore Barzilai was a notable politician and trial lawyer, and one of the delegates who had created the Treaty of Versailles at the end of World War I. Giorgio had a photograph of the delegates which included himself, a small boy standing in front of all the adults.

Giorgio enthralled me with his stories about his father's skill in court. In one case Salvatore was prosecuting a man who had propositioned a nun working in the same hospital, and then killed her in a fit of rage when she refused his advances. The defence lawyer instructed his client to admit that he had killed the nun but then to allege doing so because *he* was outraged *at her propositioning him*. When he rose to address the jury, a normal enough selection of practicing and non-practicing Catholics, Salvatore said with righteous anger: 'You know that I don't share your religion. But I find this plea an outrageous insult to a woman who dedicated her life to serving the sick and the dying.' The killer was convicted. In another murder case Salvatore appeared for the accused, a brother in a religious order who had shot his superior. 'My father got him off with only seven years,' Giorgio proudly added. 'That doesn't sound like a win,' I replied. 'Why didn't he get him acquitted on the plea of being seized by a moment of insanity?' 'That was a bit difficult,' Giorgio explained. 'The brother had previously gone out and bought the weapon.'

Italy has blessed me with extraordinary friends. Many of them made me their unofficial chaplain. After officiating at the weddings, I was also expected to baptize their babies and to bury their dead. We celebrated our friendship with an annual Mass and picnic in the garden of Palazzola, a medieval monastery that became a villa for the English College from the start of the twentieth century. High up on the wall of an old volcanic crater and surrounded by woods, Palazzola looks across Lake Albano to the papal villa at Castel Gandolfo and beyond it, towards Rome and the sea. At the far end of the garden a staircase hollowed out of the rock gives access to some woods and beyond them to a field, which boasted a large oak tree at one side and was the perfect setting for village cricket. For years Australian and English seminarians used to play a summer match there, imagining themselves to be Australia battling England for supremacy in world cricket.

I never felt more at home with a congregation than on those late spring days of our annual Mass in the Palazzola garden. In later years my now not-so-young friends brought their exquisite children for the day. Woe betide me if I mixed up their names: Francesco, Piergiorgio, Alessandro, Margaux, Pietro, Andrea, and the rest. For the little ones the Mass was a break in their efforts to catch the goldfish in the fountain. They sat on stone benches near our makeshift altar, and helped me by lighting the candles and bringing up the water and the wine at the right moment. It delighted me to see Italian children running free and chasing each other around a huge garden. So often in Rome I passed children smothered in clothing and strapped into push chairs almost as if they were tied into a straight jacket. But their eyes were free, and swivelled to follow me when we caught each other's gaze and engaged in some non-verbal communication about the freedom to come.

Politics

Let me leave Palazzola and my friends to say something about the bigger scene: Italian politics, medicine, and the press. One ambassador who lived for years in Rome used to give vent to his frustration by declaring: 'Italy isn't a corrupt country; it's a very corrupt country.' I have seen surveys on corruption in the western world, which name New Zealand and the Scandinavian countries as the least corrupt, and Italy comes a close second to Greece as the most corrupt country.

In the 1980s modern Italian history was sometimes summed up as 'Rex, Dux, Crux, and Crax.' The 'Rex' or king referred to the monarchy which presided over Italy from 1870 until voted out by a referendum after the Second World War. The 'Dux' was Latin for 'il Duce', 'the Leader' or Benito Mussolini whose fascist dictatorship ruled the country from 1922 to 1943. When democracy was restored after 1945, the Christian Democrats led the government or acted as the power brokers down to the early nineties. They used the cross ('crux' in Latin) on their coat of arms. Then came 'Crax' or Bettino (allegedly baptized 'Benito' in the days of Mussolini) Craxi: hence 'Crax'. During Craxi's four years as prime minister (1983–87) corruption reached a level that amazed even the Italians, who were tolerantly ready to accept a certain level of crooked practices on the part of their leaders. The crusading magistrates led by Antonio Di Pietro spelled the end of Craxi and the old guard. Craxi hastily retired to Tunisia rather than spend his declining years serving a jail sentence. For a few years I enjoyed the experience of living in a country which seemed controlled by judges who had no hesitation in prosecuting government ministers. Many members of the Italian parliament were voted out by the enraged electors, and a few of them finished up in jail as well. But only an optimist would say that corrupt patronage is dead.

Few countries bear close political scrutiny. Public heroes and heroines are another matter, and Italians can be proud of their great men and women. The world has heard about the saintly Padre Pio, who worked miracles and played his part in attracting heroic recruits to his order, the Capuchin Franciscans. Many of Padre Pio's confreres spent years in Africa, often on most dangerous assignments in Angola, Mozambique, Uganda, and other war-torn countries. Since World War II many Italian priests, religious, and lay people have been killed in what are euphemistically described as the trouble spots of the world. The Capuchins have been prominent amongst those martyrs for faith and justice.

Italian laymen and laywomen have also been prominent in courageous activities abroad. I think, for example, of Francesco Stripoli, who from 1979 worked in the field of humanitarian aid, chiefly in Africa. After 1998 Stripoli coordinated aid to Angola on behalf of the United Nations. The country was lacerated by civil war for more than twenty-five years; by early 1999 a million Angolans had fled the countryside to endure a wretched existence as internal refugees in their three cities. On the other side of Africa, Annalena Tonelli worked for thirty-five years in health care for the poorest of the poor in Somalia. In 2003 two shots in the back of her neck ended the life of someone who was known as the Mother Teresa of Somalia. Moved by Tonelli's heroic dedication, one old local leader said, 'we Muslims have the faith, you Christians have the love.'

Heroes and heroines have not been lacking at home in Italy. General Alberto Dalla Chiesa and his pregnant wife Emmanuela, were both shot dead in 1982 in Sicily when the General was leading the fight against the Mafia. Ten years later in May 1992 a gigantic bomb under an expressway outside Palermo 'removed' the leading anti-Mafia judge, Giovanni Falcone, his wife and three of their bodyguards. Two months afterwards Paolo Borsellino, another anti-Mafia judge and one of Falcone's closest colleagues, was also killed together with four of his bodyguards, this time by a car bomb.

The only political episode that has made me question and even feel ashamed of my living peacefully and comfortably in Europe concerned the genocidal breakup of former Yugoslavia between 1991 to 1995. At some western embassies in Rome it almost seemed bad taste to pass on the news that we regularly received from across the Adriatic. Outrage was definitively out, and soft talk about diplomacy was in. Those years taught me much about international selfishness and the evils of self-pitying nationalism, including Croatian nationalism.

It was not that I expected Italy to take the lead in ending the rape, torture, and murder that left around 200,000 dead, a million or more people driven from their homes, hundreds of churches and mosques blown up, and towns devastated by thugs masquerading as freedom fighters. But dishonest catchphrases served as an excuse for not getting involved: political leaders, particularly in Britain, tried as long as they could to avoid action by talking of 'tribal tensions', 'ancient ethnic hatreds', the risk of a 'dangerous precedent for secessionists around the world'. In his *Unfinest Hour: Britain and the Destruction of Bosnia* (London: Penguin, 2002), Brendan Simms tells the sordid story of high officials who connived at criminality.

Television commentators on the spot in Sarajevo, Mostar, and other ravaged places made it quite clear who were the victims and who were the aggressors. And so too did cartoonists in many daily papers of the western world, as well as journalists like Melanie McDonagh. In the columns of the London *Tablet* she regularly denounced the politicians who first looked the other way and then went off to do business deals with the evil genius of the war, Slobodan Milosevic. Over dinner in 1993 two tense priests from Bosnia told me of a colleague fastened onto a cross by Serbian militia. 'He didn't have to hang there too long,' they added. 'They used him as a target for their weapons.'

Medicine and the Press

Italy, though spared some of the worst features of nationalism, hardly commands universal respect for its health care. But how few countries do? As one dear friend in England said to me, 'hospitals are good if patients stagger out alive.' Italian medicine and hospital care are a mixed bag — with features both good and bad. The bad features lend credence to one remark still often repeated in Rome: 'The best doctor's waiting room here is the departure lounge at Fiumicino airport.' My surgeon brother when visiting me rarely failed to advise, 'If you have a prostate problem, get a catheter put in and fly home to Australia.' Since he, a brother-in-law, and a nephew proved outstanding urologists, I would have fallen into the best of hands in Australia. Nevertheless, I must put in a good word for some Italian doctors and health care. When an elderly visitor with a bad heart slipped and broke a hip on what was to be her last night in Rome, the post-operative care left much to be desired but the operation had been performed well enough to enable her to return to Australia. Given her uncertain heart condition, I feared that she might die on the table. Another who managed to get home safely was a young woman from the United States who in a fit of depression flew to Rome and took an overdose. Her close relatives appeared perfectly satisfied with the hospital care that pulled her through and put her back on her feet. On balance, I share the grateful respect Francis Steegmuller showed in his *New Yorker* story (see above). What was done for his broken collarbone in an ancient hospital in Naples turned out both better and, as they wouldn't charge him, much cheaper than the treatment he subsequently received in New York.

Sadly I cannot write well of the Italian papers, including those under the auspices of the Church: *Avvenire* (run by the Italian bishops) and the Vatican's daily, *L'Osservatore Romano*, in which the failure to publish any letters to the editor causes me to question whether it qualifies as a newspaper. During the dictatorship of Mussolini *L'Osservatore Romano* courageously published news that the other papers were afraid to carry. Fascist thugs sometimes attacked those selling *L'Osservatore* and even individuals found in possession of copies. In those days *L'Osservatore* had a big circulation and was widely considered to be the only paper that told the truth.

In 1976 one of our former professors was held by the police over a weekend after they arrested him for writing 'frocio' (sodomite) on public notices expressing sorrow for the murder of the film director, Pier Paolo Pasolini. Naturally the papers all mentioned that Arturo had taught at the Gregorian. When Jesuit authorities let them know that he had stopped teaching and had spent time in a clinic because of his condition as a manic depressive, all but one of the papers reported that more or less as I have stated it. The *Messaggero*, however, insisted on underlining the fact that Arturo's mental condition first began to manifest itself seriously when he was a professor at the Gregorian.

In 1981, when John Paul II appointed Father Paolo Dezza his delegate to lead the Jesuit order for an interim period, newspapers clamoured for an interview with Dezza. When no interviews were forthcoming, one enterprising journalist cut up a recently published lecture by Dezza, inserted into the text his own questions, and published an 'interview'. It was pointless for Father Dezza or anyone else to protest.

When I returned to Rome from the Resurrection Summit held in New York at Easter 1996, I felt happy that the three main-line American weeklies, *Time*, *Newsweek* and *US News and World Report*, had all carried cover stories on Jesus for their Easter numbers. *Time* and *US News and World Report* had, admittedly, focused too strongly on the odd 'results' from the California based Jesus Seminar, which for a decade had been publishing their supposedly scientific assessments. In what was easily the best of the three reports, the religion editor of *Newsweek*, Kenneth Woodward, centred squarely on the resurrection of Jesus, citing some contemporary rejection of the belief but giving considerable space to those who do accept Jesus as personally risen from the dead. In a secular journal such as *Newsweek* space had to be given to both points of view. Woodward was not writing for a parish magazine! And it was quite clear that he stood with the believers. To my astonishment the Italian church paper *Avvenire*, nevertheless, attacked Woodward for rejecting the resurrection.

On 8 November 1997, *La Repubblica* carried a startling report from Australia: Bishop Geoffrey Robinson of Sydney had published a statement on the evil of paedophilia the previous August, and this statement had apparently caused a hundred priests to resign from their ministry. When I contacted reliable Australian sources, I found that Bishop Robinson had indeed published such a statement. When asked by an Australian newspaper for an indication of the number of priests who had resigned from the ministry for all kinds of reasons in recent years, he replied that it was between ten and one hundred. An Australian newspaper had initially misreported Robinson but then published a correction. The Italian journalist ran his story without checking his sources.

I had a personal experience of misrepresentation while I was serving as dean of our Theology Faculty. An outstanding professor of moral theology — let me call him Richard — went into one of his periodic downs and phoned me in distress. I went at once to visit Richard and discovered that part of the problem came from taking on too many extra courses and lectures outside the Gregorian. Since I knew how hard it would be for him to withdraw, I asked him for the list of those extras and, with his permission and as his dean, set to work telephoning his hosts and cancelling his appearances. The only person who seemed disgruntled and unsympathetic to his condition was a representative of a foundation, who had organized an international meeting with fifteen moral theologians and ethicists. '*He* is worn out, and *you* already have his paper,' I insisted. 'Haven't you ever been to meetings where some speaker was sick and couldn't come, and the paper was read by someone else?' I didn't want to go into details about the condition of my professor who seemed to me on the edge of a serious nervous breakdown.

A few days later a two-page spread in the *Repubblica* informed me that in telephoning the foundation I had been acting on behalf of the Vatican who wanted to silence the professor in question! In Rome friends laughed it all off and teased me for being a Vatican agent. But the journalist had never bothered to phone me and check the story before it went to press. In Germany the following summer I learned how lies can travel. On a visit to Tübingen I called on Walter Kasper, still a professor on the Catholic faculty there, not yet ordained bishop for Rottenburg-Stuttgart, and years away from becoming a cardinal in Rome. We chatted away and then Kasper, slightly nervously, cleared his throat and asked: 'What's this about the Vatican and the *Lehrverbot* [official order to stop teaching] for Richard?' I laughed, pointed to myself, and told him: 'Ich bin das Lehrverbot (I'm the Lehrverbot).' It was a salutary lesson also for Kasper.

With the possible exceptions of *Corriere della Sera* and *La Stampa*, no one should believe what they read in the Italian newspapers until

they have the news independently confirmed elsewhere.[13] In fairness
to Italy I should add that there are very few newspapers in the world
that I instinctively respect and trust beyond the sporting pages. In
reporting sport no newspaper can afford to make mistakes. But why
can't they keep up that standard in other areas? Why don't they all
imitate the healthy example of the *New York Times*, which regularly
publishes corrections of errors that it has allowed to slip in? So
many newspapers in Italy and elsewhere often seem to offer slabs of
entertaining fiction or semi-fiction.

The Italian Language

I round off this chapter with some light-hearted comment about the
Italian language. The most economic exchange I have enjoyed with
an Italian official came one Sunday when I caught an afternoon train
back to Rome from Castel Gandolfo. I was perfectly truthful in saying
to the ticket collector: 'I did buy a return ticket this morning, but over
lunch with some friends I left my ticket inside their copy of today's
paper.' 'Beh!,' said the ticket collector as he shrugged his shoulders and

---

13 One should also be cautious about accepting what papers have to say about history. On
13 March 2000 *La Repubblica* reported satisfactorily the Mass celebrated by John Paul II in
St Peter's Basilica on a day of repentance when the official Catholic Church asked pardon
for past and present sins. But on the very same page an article reported astonishing
figures for one of the past sins: the execution of 'millions' of witches. "That would have
depopulated Europe,' I thought, and went off to check some standard historical sources.
Around fifty thousand witches were executed by Catholics and Protestants over four
centuries—a horrible crime but still nothing like killing 'millions'. Three months later, on
12 June 2000, the Colonna family staged a huge and noisy party to celebrate nine hundred
years of their recorded existence. When reporting the party, which was held right next
door to the Gregorian in the Villa Colonna and kept many of our community awake,
Corriere della Sera ran a headline announcing that the Colonnas had 'given five popes to
the Catholic Church'. In fact they had supplied only one, Martin V. Maybe 'the fifth'
suggested to some journalist that the other four popes, from Martin I, who died a martyr
in 655, to the French-born Martin IV, who died in 1285, must have all been Colonnnas.

moved on. The tone of his voice suggested interpreting the 'beh!' as: 'Well, it doesn't matter. That could happen to anyone.' 'Abusivamente' is another wonderfully short word that packs in a lot of meaning: it has nothing to do with physical or verbal abuse but often means building a house or making substantial alterations without the proper permit. 'Obliteratrice', far from being a new super-gun, is simply the machine for putting a date and time on your ticket when you board buses and trams. 'Rumori' are noises, not rumours, which are 'voci correnti' (voices in circulation). A 'preservativo' is neither an ingredient used when bottling fruit nor a life-jacket but a condom. A 'fatalità' does not refer to a death but to some act of fate, a piece of hard luck. 'Matrimoni bianchi' (white marriages) are not unions

Meeting Italian President, Francesco Cossiga, 1990

between whites (even less wedding ceremonies for which the bride wore white) but unconsummated marriages.

At one stage of work with Mimi and the kids, I thought of writing a small book on 'false friends' or Italian words that look familiar to English speakers but carry different meanings or at least different nuances. 'Domandare' is not to demand something but merely to ask a question. A 'discussione' goes beyond a relaxed discussion with someone and means a more or less heated argument. 'Irreducibili' are not people who find it hard to lose weight but those who obstinately support lost causes. At a railway station a 'deposito' is the hall where you can leave or deposit your baggage. But when a railway carriage goes 'in deposito', it is being left in the yards. Those in academic life should remember that a 'conferenza' is one lecture and not a meeting or a 'simposio', which may run over a weekend and involve many speakers and lectures. If a student tells you that he has been 'interrogato', don't worry that he has been arrested and interrogated by the police. He has probably just done an oral examination, at the end of which he was hopefully told by the examiner(s) that he was 'promosso' or had passed. Hence you should also keep in mind that his 'promozione' could signify merely passing another exam and is not necessarily a rise in military rank or in the hierarchy of a business firm. When a speaker uses the word 'ultimamente', don't imagine that he means 'finally' and is about to conclude. He is merely saying 'in recent years', and could well intend to take you through them in detail. If he then announces that he wants to 'delineare le peculiarità' of some organization, he intends to summarize its special features rather than its peculiarities.

As with many other western languages, Italian now includes euphemisms to upgrade certain 'lowly' occupations. Garbage collectors used to be known as 'netturbani' (city cleaners), but they have turned into 'operativi ecologici' (ecological workers). Italian, like many European languages, has taken over various English expressions, introducing at times some local nuances. Jogging is called 'footing'. Traffic jams or delays are often reported as the traffic being 'in tilt', as if the cars and trucks caught on a jammed freeway were up on one side. My favorite example comes from a firm that is legally authorized to provide valid information on 'infedeltà coniugali' (acts of infidelity on the part of married people). The cheapest rate, when I last picked up one of the agency's flyers, was over one hundred U.S. dollars. Naturally their services are available twenty four hours a day. The agency uses an English and an Italian word to call itself 'Terminal Investigazioni' (Terminal Investigations). 'Terminal' strikes me as an inspired borrowing for that line of business.

Like many foreigners and Italians themselves, I have delighted in local surnames. They include 'Indelicato' (Indelicate), 'Innamorato' (In Love), 'Santopadre' (Holy Father), 'Mangiaprete' (Priest Eater), 'Castracani' (Dog Castrator), 'Saltamerenda' (Meal Skipper), 'Vacchina' (Little Cow), 'Gatto' (Cat), 'Saraceno' (Saracen), 'Maglione' (Heavy Sweater or Pullover), 'Uccellatore' (Bird Hunter), and 'Casalone' (Big House). When I received the class list for a course I was to teach at the Gregorian in 1996, 'Buontempo' (Good Weather) preceded 'Cantagallo' (Cock Crow). One tall Sicilian priest I know is 'Alessandro Magno' (Alexander the Great), and a former bishop of Frascati, a town near Rome, was grandly called 'Dante Bernini.' A little investigation has uncovered interesting surnames among Sicilian bishops: the late bishop of Trapani was 'Amoroso' (Amorous), whereas an archbishop of Catania was 'Bommarito' (Good Husband).

I can't help wondering about the stories behind 'Dell'amore' (Of Love), 'D'Amico' (Of a Friend), 'D'Antico' (Of the Old One), and 'Della Vedova' (Of the Widow). 'Esposito' (The Exposed One) derives from those babies (presumably mainly illegitimate) who were 'exposed' in the sense of being handed over, often anonymously, to the care of others. Ancient scandals lie behind such surnames as 'Del Prete' (Of the Priest), 'Del Monaco' (Of the Monk), and the more precise 'Dell'Arciprete' (Of the Archpriest). One Church-sounding surname that leaves me puzzling over its derivation is 'Quaresima' (Lent). Was someone excessively devoted to the Lenten fast? And why do the Sardinians continue to tolerate the surname 'Porcu' (Swine)?

At Palazzola, Lake Albano, with the Dorias' dog Roldano, 2002

But long live the Italians *and* their names. They roll off my tongue like honey and music, especially when I ask at a marriage ceremony: Do you Daniela Bellardinelli take Stefano Ponzini as your husband for better or worse, in sickness and in health, for richer or for poorer, until death do you part? Italy and the Italians have taken me for better or worse, and all I can say is 'Grazie, grazie, grazie' (thank you, thank you, thank you).

5

Three Popes

The world arrives in Rome to see the Pope. The papacy, as much as anything, makes the eternal city an exotic locale and invests life there with a dreamlike quality. In other parts of the world people sooner or later start asking a visitor from Rome: 'How's the Pope's health? When did you last see the Pope?' Or else they question the visitor about papal contacts: 'Do you meet the Pope often? Ever had a meal with him?' A chapter of this book must report on three popes who were part of my life in Rome: Paul VI who died in 1978; John Paul I, with his cruelly short pontificate of thirty three days in 1978; John Paul II who for over twenty-six years 'bestrode the narrow world like a colossus'. On a scale previously unknown, John Paul II made the Pope a world presence for a world church. Before his death on 2 April 2005, he completed 104 journeys outside Italy, which had taken him to at least 130 countries, including eight times home to Poland.

Pope Paul VI

When I arrived in August 1974 to teach full time at the Gregorian, Paul VI, who had been born in September 1897 and elected Pope in June 1963, was almost seventy seven years of age and had slowed down. During the last years of the Second Vatican Council (1962-65) and its immediate aftermath, he had worked energetically, internationalized the Vatican offices by bringing in a number of non-Italians, and initiated a pattern of travel that John Paul II was to continue with great energy. Paul VI's papal pilgrimages had taken him to Colombia, India, Uganda, the Philippines, Jerusalem, Sydney in Australia, and to the United Nations in New York. But he had not gone out of Italy since 1970. He was still to publish one of his most fruitful and enduring documents, *Evangelii nuntiandi* ('announcing the good news') (1975). The Pope described Jesus as the first and greatest 'herald' or 'preacher'. But when the original Latin text was translated into modern languages, somehow Jesus became 'the first evangelizer', and a new title was launched into popularity. Paul VI gave that document the status of an apostolic exhortation, rather than the higher grade of a papal encyclical. After the worldwide debate stirred up inside and outside the Catholic Church by his 1968 encyclical on married life and birth control, *Humanae vitae* ('Of human life'), he published no more encyclicals.

The Holy Year of 1975 (or year of special pilgrimages to Rome) multiplied demands on the ageing Pope. I attended the opening ceremony for the Holy Year, Midnight Mass at St Peter's 24/25 December 1974. Waiting outside in the square for an hour or so before the doors were opened, the immense and impatient crowd raised a little the chilly temperature of the night. An Italian nun leading a phalanx of other religious women had her shoulder down and was pushing against the legs of a tall man in front of her. He turned around and in a very English voice said: 'Would you *please* stop shoving me! You won't get in any quicker, and what's more, you are making me very angry.' The film director Franco Zeffirelli, who was still to make his *Jesus of Nazareth*, ran the television coverage that night. Zeffirelli's lighting of St Peter's was in keeping with his theatrical and operatic imagination. The illumination inside the basilica raised the heat, and it was no surprise when someone near me fainted and had to be carried out. The Pope tackled the never-ending Mass with his usual holiness and sincerity.

During the Holy Year itself, Paul VI personally ordained to the priesthood 363 deacons in the Square of St Peter's, on the Feast of Peter and Paul, 29 June 1975. That ceremony began on the late afternoon and ran for hours into the evening. As the light drained out of the sky, it created special, changing effects on the red vestments that the priests, bishops, cardinals, and the Pope himself wore to recall the martyrdom of two founding fathers of Christianity. All present remembered Peter and Paul, while very many honoured in their thoughts and prayers the sheer valour of Paul VI. Crippled with arthritis, he showed the faithful courage of a living martyr as he went through the four-hour ceremony.

A year or so later I volunteered to distribute Holy Communion at a Mass the Pope celebrated at St Paul's Outside the Walls. It may well have been on the feast of the conversion of St Paul, 25 January, a feast day which concludes something that was very dear to the heart of Paul VI, the week of prayer for unity observed by many Christians around the world. When the time came for the sermon, the officials led him to a chair in front of altar, supplied him with the microphone and then left him all alone — a frail figure, whose body seemed disintegrating with pain. His loneliness struck me, as he delivered the sermon in his normal plaintive tones.

When Pope Paul VI died on 6 August 1978, I was in Glasgow and had just finished leading a group of nuns on an eight-day retreat. We followed the Pope's funeral on television, a dignified ceremony on a sunny afternoon in St Peter's Square, which ended with spontaneous applause from the congregation when his coffin was lifted from the ground and carried for burial into the crypt of St Peter's. Little did I imagine that I would be in St Peter's Square less than two months later standing in the rain for the funeral Mass of Paul VI's successor.

Pope John Paul I

En route from Glasgow back to Rome, I stopped in London for a couple of days, and spent a memorable evening with Tom Burns, the editor of the London *Tablet*, in his apartment close to Westminster Cathedral. Wearing a shirt that hardly covered his stomach, Tom stood in front of his mantelpiece and put the question to his formally dressed guests: 'Who do you think will be the next Pope?' The guests included John Harriott, still a Jesuit but soon to depart the priesthood and marry, a British diplomat who had served in Italy, and some others. Various suggestions were put forward, and nobody seemed to accept Tom's own hesitant suggestion about Cardinal Albino Luciani the Patriarch of Venice; we had our papal candidates, and gave our reasons.

Back in Rome a few days later, I started putting together material for Tom Burns on the papal election. His regular Rome correspondent was still away on his summer holidays, and Tom had asked me to fill in for a couple of weeks. Since many professors, students and others had not yet returned to the city, I found the normal excitement of a papal conclave a little muted. However, the presence of the world's media stirred up gossip and speculation. Most of the experts failed to list Cardinal Luciani among their ten or so possible popes, and certainly didn't expect that anyone would be elected on the first full day of the conclave, Saturday 26 August 1978, when we learnt that the Cardinal Patriarch of Venice was to be Paul VI's successor.

That day I went out for a meal with an Australian philosopher, a friend who happened to be visiting Rome with his wife and children. 'There must have been a cosmic traffic accident,' he observed when we met at a 'trattoria' hidden away in a tiny square near the Pantheon. He explained: 'Just as we were about to cross the Corso, a dozen or more police vehicles roared past and turned right towards the river.'

I was so programmed to expect a long conclave that I failed to guess that the police already knew that a pope had been elected and were off to control the crowd which would quickly gather in St Peter's Square. The waiter took our orders, and suddenly disappeared with all the other waiters. I eventually went to see what had happened and found them gathered around the television! 'They've elected a pope,' I was told. A hour or so later when the new Pope appeared on the central balcony above the façade of St Peter's, he seemed to be so overcome that he simply gave his blessing, smiled, waved at the crowd, and disappeared inside.

The following day, Sunday 27 August, John Paul I delighted the crowd gathered in St Peter's Square for his midday blessing. Without any such address as 'My dear brothers and sisters,' he simply began: 'Yesterday, I went off to vote without a worry in the world, and suddenly I saw the danger.' His very first word, 'yesterday', drew applause from the crowd. What followed made them all feel that they were able to share with him the experience, almost in the spirit of 'yesterday a funny thing happened to me on the way to the forum. I became Pope.' At once I knew that the Catholics and the whole world were blessed in having a pope who knew how to communicate in ordinary language and introduce vivid stories.

In the weeks that followed people in Rome heard more of that lively, straightforward talk from him. He used the thirtieth anniversary of Georges Bernanos' death to recall how sixteen Carmelite nuns had been guillotined during the French Revolution.[14] As they went to the scaffold, they sang the 'Veni, Creator Spiritus (Come, Creator Spirit)'. Naturally, as the Pope pointed out, the singing grew progressively fainter as one head after another fell under the guillotine. He used

---

14 Bernanos immortalized the martyrdom of these French Carmelites in his 1948 *Dialogues des Carmélites*.

the week when Italian boys and girls returned to school to encourage them to study hard. He felt free to adapt for his purpose the famous words that the Duke of Wellington was supposed to have used long after the final defeat of Napoleon: 'The battle of Waterloo was won on the playing fields of Eton.' Repeating twice the two words which his Italian audience might have difficulty with ('Wellington' and 'Waterloo'), he told the young people that the victory at Waterloo had been prepared in the classrooms of Eton. A small boy put the Pope in an embarrassing position at a Wednesday audience, when John Paul I invited one of the children present to come up; this one made it to the dais first. On being asked by the Pope 'aren't you happy about going up to a higher class this year?,' the boy startled him by replying emphatically, 'No!' When asked why, he explained: 'I had a much better teacher last year.' The Pope tried to save the situation for the new teacher by murmuring something to the effect that 'we all have to adjust to new situations.'

For the open air Mass on Sunday 3 September, when the new Pope officially inaugurated his pontificate, I signed on as one of the many priests who were to distribute Holy Communion to the congregation. When we filed in behind the Pope, I was very happy to find myself right behind him. Across his shoulders I could take in a crowd that stretched beyond the end of St Peter's Square. One slight distraction was the Pope's haircut. Someone had trimmed his hair recently but without the usual artistry of an Italian barber. Whoever it was had left a slightly irregular line on the back of his neck. I wondered whether, before leaving Venice for the papal conclave, the Pope had asked his housekeeper or secretary to run the clippers over his head.

When he arrived in Rome for the conclave, Cardinal Luciani stayed with the Augustinians in the convent of St Monica, beside St Peter's Square. The Archbishop of Sydney, Cardinal James Freeman, also spent the last few days before the conclave as a guest at St Monica's. Cardinal Luciani suggested to his Australian colleague a trip to Venice after the conclave ended and before the new pope was installed: 'There will time for us to get up there and come back.' Another thwarted plan involved an English seminarian who arrived at the Beda College for late vocations (or mature aspirants to the priesthood) shortly after John Paul I died. This seminarian had, I think, been an officer in the British army. After retirement in his forties, he visited Italy. He was viewing Venice from one of the local motor boats, when he fell into conversation with a young lad. As they came ashore, the small Venetian insisted that his godfather would welcome the English stranger for afternoon tea. The visitor accepted the invitation and was amazed to discover that the godfather was the Cardinal Patriarch of Venice. Over tea Luciani asked the stranger: 'What do you intend to do now that you're out of the army?' 'I've often thought of becoming a priest,' was the reply. 'Why don't you do just that?,' suggested the Cardinal. The stranger returned to England, and a year or two later applied to study for the priesthood. He was accepted by an English diocese, and whilst still in England waiting to begin his studies at the Beda College in Rome in October 1978, he learned to his delight in late August that the Patriarch of Venice had been elected Pope. He wrote at once to John Paul I to offer his best wishes and promise of prayers, adding: 'You mightn't remember me. I'm the Englishman who came to tea with your godson one afternoon. I've finally taken your advice and am to study at the Beda.' This mature seminarian was astonished to receive a hand written letter from the Pope a few days later: 'Of course, I remember you. Please come and see me when you reach Rome.' It was not to be. The Englishman was driving down to Rome and had reached Switzerland, when to his great sorrow he heard the news about Pope Luciani's death. He told me the whole story when I was leading a retreat or week of prayer for the students of the Beda a year or so later. The only comment that occurred to me was: 'All of this means that you must become a truly great priest.'

During the month of John Paul I's pontificate, a group of forty or so American bishops and one Australian archbishop were attending lectures to update their theology. Although the Americans were not in Rome on their official, five-yearly 'ad limina' visit, which automatically involves a papal audience, they, nevertheless, requested a meeting with the new Pope and asked if they might bring along their lecturers as well. He agreed to see the bishops, but wanted to see them alone, so that he could talk frankly about the challenges he had to confront. They were delighted with their meeting and I was happy that it had gone ahead, but as one of their lecturers I was sorry not to have been allowed to join them. A few days later most of them had purchased large numbers of photographs of themselves with John Paul I. At the end of their meeting with the Pope, the official photographer had entered to take the formal photographs which are customary on such occasions, each bishop separately being welcomed by the Pope. The visitors packed these photos in their suitcases for the people at home, many of them leaving Rome on the very night the Pope died (28/29 September).

At breakfast on 29 September I heard the bells of a nearby church tolling, but imagined that it was for an early morning funeral. Then a Jesuit brother burst into the breakfast room with the startling news: the new Pope had died. It rained steadily on 4 October, the day of the funeral Mass held in the late afternoon for John Paul I. I found myself standing in St Peter's Square with a group of lay people from the Pope's small home town, Canale D'Agordo. Many of them had come south to Rome for the inaugural Mass that John Paul I had celebrated a month before under a warm sun in St Peter's Square. These men and women were very sad to be back so soon — on a wet afternoon for his funeral. I couldn't help thinking of their married life and the way Cardinal Luciani approached the question of birth control. In 1977, a year before he was elected Pope, he published with the other bishops of the Venice region a prayer book which contained a section on the sacrament of penance. The sub-section for married people encouraged them to show mature love and deep respect for one another. For those married adults about to confess their sins, there was a question which clearly recognized the evil of abortion. As regards birth control, the questions ran: 'In agreement with my spouse have I given a clear and conscientious reply to the problem of birth control? Have I prevented a pregnancy for selfish reasons? Have I lacked responsibility in bringing a child into the world?' And that was all. No questions were raised about methods of birth control.

Pope John Paul II

The conclave of cardinals to elect the next pope began on 14 October 1978, and this time they did not seem to be in a hurry. Every now and then black smoke poured out of the chimney next to the Sistine Chapel — a signal that an inconclusive ballot had taken place. The third day of the conclave coincided with the Mass in the Church of St Ignatius to open the academic year at the Gregorian. Our rector, Father Carlo Maria Martini, announced at the end of the Mass that white smoke had gone up. The new Pope had been elected at the eighth ballot. Students ran out of the church and reached St Peter's Square to join the excited crowd gathered under a full moon on that warm evening. Cardinal Pericle Felici, as the senior 'cardinal deacon', came out onto the central balcony to say with a somewhat sour expression on his face: 'Nuntio vobis gaudium magnum. Habemus Papam (I announce to you a great joy. We have a Pope).' The Catholic Church had a new Pope and he was not an Italian, as Felici obviously expected, but Cardinal Karol Wojtyla of Cracow, Poland.

I had previously agreed to attend a reception in the Doria Palace for some Anglican bishops who were visiting Rome. So it was in the Anglican Centre housed in the Doria Palace that I watched on television the announcement of the new Pope and his first appearance. One African Anglican bishop cried out with joy, when he took 'Wojtyla' — as pronounced by Felici! — to be an African name. I couldn't volunteer much information about Cardinal Wojtyla, although we had been together in Australia five years previously when he had flown out to Australia for the 1973 eucharistic congress in Melbourne.

Cardinal Wojtyla had attended some of the major functions of the congress, but his principal concern seemed to be with Polish migrants in Australia. After ordaining several Polish seminarians in Melbourne, he flew around the country and even down to Hobart to meet the Poles who lived in Tasmania. Before he left Melbourne, Cardinal Wojtyla had visited a wildlife sanctuary, where on another afternoon I had taken a guest, the eminent German theologian, Jürgen Moltmann. On a memorable evening Moltmann and Mother Teresa of Calcutta spoke in the Melbourne Town Hall, he on the theory and she on the practice of peace. A vast crowd heard and appreciated them both. 'Gerry,' Moltmann asked me afterwards, 'what were you trying to do?' I told him: 'I wanted to bring together the best Protestant theologian in the world with a Catholic saint. You simply can't go wrong that way.' I never asked Cardinal Wojtyla for his reaction to that evening. But at the wildlife sanctuary, however, where Moltmann and I kept our distance from the kangaroos and their dangerous back legs, Cardinal Wojtyla fed one. A photograph of him feeding a kangaroo went round the world, once he was elected pope a little over five years later. For years a copy of that photo hung in the office of the dean of theology at the Gregorian.

'Forgiving my Brother'

Less than three years into the new Pope's reign, Mehmet Ali Agca almost succeeded in assassinating John Paul II on 13 May 1981 in St Peter's Square. Although rumours ran rife, the theory of a Communist plot, which came from Moscow via Bulgaria and placed the intending killer in St Peter's Square, remains unsupported by any clear evidence.[15] The American journalist Jonathan Kwitny gives an excellent and apparently extremely accurate account of the assassination attempt. Two details deserve to be added to Kwitny's account.

The first relates to the following Sunday, when it was still not clear that the Pope would survive. He, nevertheless, insisted that he would not interrupt his custom of broadcasting a Sunday message, which he did from his hospital bed: 'My dear brothers and sisters, I know how you are united with me these days. I am deeply grateful for your prayers and I bless you all. I am especially close to the two persons who were wounded with me. I pray for the brother who struck me down, and I forgive him sincerely. United to Christ, priest and victim, I offer my suffering for the Church and the world.' The Pope spoke slowly, somewhat breathlessly, and with pauses that more than hinted at his pain. It was the most moving broadcast I have ever listened to.

The next detail relates to the day almost a month later when the Pope had left hospital and addressed the crowd in St Peter's Square at noon on Pentecost Sunday, 7 June. I made sure of being present, along with thousands of others. I expected some dramatic words from the Pope and vigorous applause from the crowd that would encourage him along the road to full recovery. Instead of saying 'Grazie, grazie, grazie' to all those who had been concerned with his well being, which would have evoked a moving response, the Pope seemed instead to

---

15 J. Kwitny, *Man of the Century: The Life and Times of Pope John Paul II* (New York: Henry Holt, 1997), pp. 288-90, 542-49.

be thinking anxiously of a delegation of Orthodox Christians visiting Rome for ceremonies in St Peter's (to commemorate the First Council of Constantinople of 381) and in St Mary Major's (to commemorate the Council of Ephesus of 431). He communicated anxiety about inter-church relations rather than grateful joy at being back at work.

Some days earlier I had sent John Paul II a collection of 'get well' cards drawn by some seven-year old children at an international school in Rome. On 12 June the Pope's private secretary, Father John Magee (later Bishop of Cloyne, Ireland), wrote to me as follows:

'It was with great pleasure that I showed the letters from Sister Brigid's class to the Holy Father and he was very much touched at the little ones' concern and very grateful for their prayers. Needless to say, we are very happy to have him back at the Vatican and to see the continuing improvement in his health.' In a letter I wrote a few days later to a nun, who was both a nurse and a missionary, I revealed my own hopes: 'The dear Pope has to start his second pontificate now. Please God it [the attempt on his life] will make him gentler and warmer. This may sound a bit scandalous. But I hope he had some nice nurses to tuck him in and give him a goodnight kiss in the hospital. How should a properly professional nurse behave with a pope?' What the Pope did to the Society of Jesus a little later that year made me wonder whether he had become gentler and warmer. I come back to this below.

Astonishingly Innovative

John Paul II proved astonishingly and persistently innovative. In a speech which I was to write for Cardinal Pio Laghi to deliver at a Chicago meeting at the end of 1996, I concentrated on the new things the Pope continued to do. John Paul II's courageous and breathtaking initiatives came so frequently that, sad to say, many people almost seemed to take them for granted. Despite being almost mortally wounded by the assassination attempt of 1981, facing major surgery on three subsequent occasions, and developing Parkinson's disease in his seventies, the papal initiatives hardly diminished with the years. I will mention later certain major innovations that affected the whole world. Some of them worked remarkably well in Rome itself.

On 31 December 1978 the new Pope renewed an annual papal custom, which had lapsed in 1870 with the loss of the Pope's temporal power over Rome and the surrounding territory, when he celebrated Mass on New Year's Eve in the Gesù. The first baroque church of Jesuits, it has been at the heart of Rome for four centuries. On New Year's Eve 1978 the city authorities made an appearance and presented the Pope with a chalice, presumably to symbolize their gratitude for what the Catholic Church does in Rome and to express their desire to collaborate on matters of common concern. A *Te Deum* was sung to thank God for the blessings of the year just ending. For several years I attended those New Year's Eve masses, partly, I confess, in order to be photographed alongside the Pope after the ceremony. I fancied collecting a series of photos showing us growing older together.

Those masses early in his pontificate were vividly memorable affairs. On one occasion a shepherd and shepherdess in charming costumes walked up the aisle of the Gesù at the offering of the gifts. They presented the Pope with a lamb which lay in its basket near the altar, managing to emit a faint 'baa' every now and then. When Mass ended and photographs had been taken in the adjacent residence, I went in search of the idyllic shepherd and shepherdess. When I found them I asked what the Pope had done with the lamb. Looking a little disconsolate, they told me that the Pope had given it to the Jesuits, 'and they've taken it off to their kitchen!' Fearing the worst, I slipped round to the kitchen, where I found the lamb still in one piece. It was snugly wrapped up near the stove and about to be sent off to pasture in the grounds of a Jesuit house up in the Roman hills.

Around the city the Pope proved an unfailing source of encouragement for the hundreds of parishes that make up the diocese of Rome. Pope Paul VI had visited parishes, but only during the six weeks of Lent. Whenever John Paul II was home in Rome and not away on one of his many pastoral trips, he tried to visit a parish every weekend and sometimes on feast days that fell during the week. He seemed to have deliberately started with the poorer parishes. Before he fell seriously ill and died, he had visited 317 of the 335 parishes of Rome. The Pope played a major role in strengthening the whole diocese and giving it what I had felt it lacked in 1974: a sense of its own identity and a feeling of common responsibility towards everyone, including refugees, the old, and victims of drug addiction.

The Pope's major initiatives included his visit in 1986 to Rome's Jewish synagogue: a striking gesture and a huge step forward, to say the least. John Paul II was probably the first Pope since St Peter to have visited a Roman synagogue, and one can't even be sure about Peter. He may have spent very little time in Rome; he might have been brought there as a prisoner to be martyred under the Emperor Nero.

John Paul II was totally lacking in the anti-Jewish sentiments that one, alas, still meets among some members of the Polish clergy. Over the years I have heard and read many criticisms directed against him; never have I encountered anyone who could accuse the Pope of anti-Semitism. John Paul's lifelong relationship with Jews provided the theme for at least one book.

I followed on television the Pope's visit to the synagogue, and took a little bet with myself that the president of the synagogue would make a reference which was at least mildly favourable to that scandalously immoral figure, Pope Alexander VI, the Borgia

Pope who reigned from 1492 to 1503. One may speak negatively of Alexander to everyone apart from the Jews or the Scots. The Jews recall with gratitude Alexander's willingness to accept into Rome the Sephardic Jews when they were driven out of Spain by Ferdinand and Isabella. The president of the synagogue did indeed make a favourable reference to Alexander on the occasion of John Paul's visit; so I won my bet.

The Scots remain grateful to Alexander because he helped to found the University of Aberdeen. In 1998 a Scottish scholar-priest admitted to me that Alexander VI 'would never be canonized for his chastity', but insisted that he had organized well the public affairs of the Church, including the holy year of 1500. Remembering the foundation of the University of Aberdeen, this priest felt justified in dismissing my complaint about Alexander VI's making his appearance on Vatican stamps. The Vatican post office had just issued a series of stamps to prepare for the Jubilee Year of 2000 by commemorating those popes who had invited pilgrims to Rome for holy years, ever since the first one of 1300.

On my desk as I write these lines is the first issue of a glossy journal, which advertises a film that 'contains very disturbing footage of John Paul II praying with heretics, schismatics, Jews, Muslims, and pagans'. The advertisement accuses him of 'direct participation with numerous false religions', and concludes with the judgement: 'All of John Paul II's actions as seen in this video have been forbidden and condemned by the Roman Catholic Church.' In 1986 religious fanatics expressed similar harsh views when the Pope headed north to Assisi on 27 October, the World Day of Prayer for Peace, in order to join non-Catholic Christians, Jews, Muslims, and representatives of other world religions in praying for our tortured world. Walking down a Roman street a few days later, I picked up a flyer which showed

John Paul II turning his back on Jesus and going off with Satan! I flung it into a garbage container, but now regret not having kept it in order to remind myself and others of something which sadly recurs. Religious conviction can turn sour and savage in those Catholics who think that following Jesus entails condemning and even hating others who not share all their views. Some Vatican officials were outraged at the Pope's courageous pilgrimage to Assisi. In his December 1986 address to the Roman cardinals the Pope defended his decision to pray for world peace in company with those of other religions. He refused to abandon his conviction that 'every authentic prayer is prompted by the Holy Spirit, who is mysteriously present in every human heart'.

John Paul II impressed me deeply by his courageous desire to put the record straight about Catholic relationships with Jews and indeed with all those who pray to God in faith. I was also enormously impressed by the Pope's decision to bring holiness home to the world by beatifying and canonizing so many heroic men and women. Before he died, John Paul II had canonized or declared to be saints 482 men and women, and had also beatified — a stage before possible canonization — a total of 1338. Many of those beatified or canonized died a martyr's death, including 103 Koreans whom he canonized on his visit to Seoul in May 1984. On 1 October 2000 he canonized 120 men and women who had been martyred in China from the seventeenth to the twentieth century. John Paul II was criticized for making so many blesseds and saints and often for a merely formal reason: sheer numbers must cheapen these honours. The critics point out that since the Congregation for the Causes of Saints, the Vatican office that deals with canonizations and beatifications, was set up in 1588, John Paul had made far more saints than all the Popes of the last four centuries put together. I beg to differ from these critics. Apart from three cases (of which more later), the men and women raised to the altars or solemnly approved for public veneration because of their lives of heroic virtue clearly deserved this recognition.

Two of those beatified by Pope John Paul gave me considerable personal satisfaction. The first was an early Jesuit, Brother Dominic O'Collins, whom the Irish, presumably for reasons of euphony, almost always call Collins — a fate that my own name regularly suffers in Ireland. My family have at times tried to claim Blessed Dominic as a distant relative, but it strikes me as doubtful. Dominic came from County Cork and my O'Collins ancestors from West Limerick. Born in Youghal near Cork, Dominic pursued a military career in France, before leaving the army as a captain at the age of thirty-two. He travelled to Spain and at Santiago de Compostela became a Jesuit brother. While becoming a full and permanent member of the Society of Jesus under the normal religious vows of poverty, chastity and obedience, he did not intend to be ordained a priest. In 1601 Dominic returned to Ireland to work as a religious missionary. He was captured the following year by English forces, and was hanged in Youghal on 31 October 1602 for refusing to deny his Catholic faith. He was the last Catholic martyr during the reign of Queen Elizabeth I, who died less than six months later. Dominic O'Collins was beatified in Rome by the Pope on 27 September 1992, with sixteen other Irish martyrs. It was the first such ceremony of beatification or canonization that I had ever attended.

I had waited eighteen years to attend a canonization or beatification ceremony, because I had hoped to make my first such ceremony the beatification in Rome of the Australian nun, Mary MacKillop. But when it became clear that the Pope would beatify Mother Mary in Sydney, I decided that Blessed Dominic should be my first.

Born in Melbourne in 1842, Mary MacKillop founded the Sisters of St Joseph of the Sacred Heart or Josephites, a religious institute which made its name by teaching poor children in parish schools, either in the working class areas of big cities or in the countryside. In Adelaide she fell foul of an unbalanced bishop; he excommunicated her in 1871. But then, full of remorse at what he had done, he lifted the excommunication and died — all within six months of his outrageous injustice against Mother Mary. The new bishop of Adelaide, after initially supporting her, allowed ugly calumnies to make him a bitter enemy of Mother Mary; he expelled her from the diocese of Adelaide in 1883.[16] The new Catholic Archbishop of Sydney, Patrick Francis Moran (created a cardinal on 27 July 1895), instructed her to step down as superior general of the Josephites and appointed in her place Mother Bernard — originally Grace Walsh, my great great-aunt. After Mother Bernard's death in 1898, Mother Mary was re-elected the superior general and remained in office until she died in 1909. John Paul II stopped in Sydney to beatify Mother Mary MacKillop in January 1995, as part of a whirlwind trip that first saw him beatifying a Filipino martyr in Manila and a Papua New Guinean martyr in Port Moresby, and ended with a beatification in Sri Lanka before he flew home exhausted to Rome.

An Australian Jesuit friend, Paul Gardiner, spent years in Australia, Rome and elsewhere doing the necessary research and writing in order to put together more than a thousand pages on the life and work of Mother Mary. This form of biography, backed up with photocopies of the relevant historical documents, is called in the official jargon a 'positio (position)'. It needs to be meticulously prepared for the committee entrusted with the task of evaluating a candidate for beatification and, possibly, eventual canonization. Copies of the

---

16 Some bishops and priests could not tolerate Mother Mary's vision of an institute of women whose educational mission, above all to the poor, was to make them somewhat independent of the local parish priest and local bishop. I suspect too that some male enemies found themselves threatened by her startling beauty and intelligence.

'positio' are submitted to about ten experts in church history and theology. If it happens, as is frequently the case, that one of these experts is on the staff at the Gregorian, he can give the volume or volumes to our librarian. The last time I looked, an entire room in our library was filled with 'positiones' of various holy men and women, not all of whom have made it in terms of subsequent beatification or canonization. When one of the experts had finished scrutinizing and commenting on Paul Gardiner's 'positio' of Mother Mary, he gave me the two fat volumes, which I sent out to my family in Melbourne. On my next visit home to Australia, my brother Jim gleefully reported the defeat of a sceptic at a dinner party held in my family's old home. When the sceptic had commented on the ease with which some Catholic could be beatified ('you only need a few good stories about the person, don't you?'), Jim excused himself and slipped out into the library. He returned with Paul's massive volumes, put them down on the vast mahogany dining table and remarked to his guest: 'You need to do a little research before presenting your candidate.'

Not everyone in Rome, not even every cardinal, relished the obvious desire of Pope John Paul II to beatify and canonize so many models of holy living, who illustrated the power of divine grace to raise up heroes and heroines from every part of the world and not simply from the traditional triangle of France, Spain, and Italy. I took the Pope's policy robustly for granted, and on the occasions when I checked the story of some new blessed or saint, I never found anything unseemly but rather a life of dedication to God and neighbour that called for admiration and imitation.

But the case of Saint Josemaría Escrivá (1902-75), the Founder of Opus Dei, a conservative organization dedicated to the sanctification of its lay and clerical members, left many people perplexed. Some who knew Escrivá during his lifetime remembered him not only as enormously dedicated to the quest for holiness but also as somewhat unforgiving, vain, and hungry for power in the affairs of both church and state — a power acquired on occasions by dubious methods. The secret manoeuvres of his followers were illustrated by the way in which, through taking advantage of the hot summer of 1982 to secure this provision, they succeeded in achieving relative independence from bishops and becoming a personal prelature or group presided over by its own bishop. This situation was brought about with the assistance of Cardinal Sebastiano Baggio (1913–93), despite the fact that many bishops in England, France, Italy, and Spain were strongly opposed to the move.

On the New Testament principle of 'by their fruits you shall know them', one would normally expect very much more time to elapse between the death of a founder and his or her beatification. A lengthy gap allows their followers the opportunity to establish that they belong to a healthy way of life that Jesus could approve of and Christians everywhere admire. Josemaría Escrivá was beatified only seventeen years after his death; this was a remarkable shortening of the usual time between death and the papal recognition of someone's heroic holiness, the more so as the case was controversial. Prior to his beatification in 1992, in modern times the briefest period between death and beatification had been twenty one years for Blessed Marie-Clementine Anuarite Nengapeta, a twenty-five year old nun martyred in the Congo in 1964 and beatified in late 1985 — a case that no one challenged because of her heroic death.[17]

The process leading to the beatification of Escrivá suffered from irregularities of procedure — a fact which Father Peter Gumpel of the Congregation for the Causes of Saints firmly pointed out to the

---

17 The modern record for speed of canonization belongs to St. Thérèse of Lisieux, who was declared a saint only twenty-three years after her death in 1897.

Pope before the beatification took place on 17 May 1992 and his canonization on 6 October 2002. The defensiveness of Opus Dei showed in their requirement that each expert who received a copy of the six thousand page long 'positio' return it after reporting on it. Despite repeated requests, no copy of the 'positio' was made available to the Bollandists, a group of Jesuit scholars in Belgium who since the time of John van Bolland (1596-1665) have dedicated themselves to scientific research into the lives of saints and blesseds, and could normally expect to have a copy of each and every 'positio' made available to them. The Bollandists too were left perplexed. Why, they asked, if the 'positio' was based on reliable evidence and showed convincingly the true sanctity of Blessed Josemaría, should it be removed from public circulation and scrutiny?

Perhaps my doubts are without foundation. But similar misgivings led ordinary folk around Rome to remark that the Pope had over-extended his right to grant dispensations. After dispensing from the requirement of a miracle to enable a Polish nun to be beatified, John Paul II was now dispensing Josemaría Escrivá from the requirement of sanctity. However, a French colleague of mine claimed that Josemaría's beatification, so far from scandalizing him, was a source of hope. 'If Josemaría could be raised to the altars, we might get there too.' Maybe that's the truth. A flawed character like Josemaría Escrivá kept trying; he died climbing towards God, whereas many others abandon the struggle. Moreover, whatever one's doubts, his teaching and example have clearly inspired many thousands to commit themselves to generous Christian living.

Only two other beatifications tested my admiration of the Pope's policy in raising to the altar large numbers of model Christians. The first was the case of Cardinal Alojzije Stepinac, Archbishop of Zagreb from 1937, who was beatified on 3 October 1998.

The Communist regime condemned Stepinac at a show trial in 1946; he was imprisoned, released under house arrest in 1951, and died in 1960. During the last years of his life, he did much to inspire people in their opposition to Communism. Although Pope John Paul II never raised the issue of the speed with which the beatification of Escrivá took place, he referred to the brief thirty eight years which separated 'us from the life and death of Cardinal Stepinac'. The problem, however, lay in the fact that Stepinac's beatification was almost entirely based on his opposition to Communism, his reputation being misused by Croatia's leaders who sought and seek to profit from it. The situation can be understood only in the light of Balkan history.

In 1941 Hitler's National Socialist government had established a Nazi puppet state of Greater Croatia, run by the Ustasha ('rebels') who aimed to create an exclusively Catholic nation. Their leader, Ante Pavelic, carried out systematic atrocities against Serbs, Jews, and other minorities. In the case of those Serbs who were Orthodox Christians, Pavelic advocated a policy of murder, eviction, and forced conversion to Catholicism, his motto being 'kill a third, drive out a third, and convert a third'. Stepinac himself, after initially supporting Pavelic's regime, denounced the atrocities and helped to save hundreds of Jews, Serbs, and others from being killed by the Ustasha. But he has remained indissolubly linked in Serbian memories with the savagery of the Croatian government during the Second World War. Moreover, the years since Stepinac's death in no way witnessed Croatian recognition of the crimes committed in the 1940s. In present Croatia, symbols of the Pavelic past have been restored and there is an attempt to mythologize the 'glories' of the past. The problem of the beatification lies not so much in the life of the heroic Cardinal Stepinac, but rather in the manner in which

Croatian leaders misuse and profit from the papal recognition of Blessed Alojzije Stepinac.

The third beatification that surprised and shocked many people was that of Pope Pius IX on 2 September 2000. Far from responding to any popular devotion, it seemed too much like a political move, designed to provide a conservative counterweight to the simultaneous beatification of John XXIII, the Pope who called the Second Vatican Council and was one of the most beloved popes of all time. What inspiring example could Catholics draw from Pio Nono, the Pope who reconstituted the Jewish ghetto in Rome, brought in anti-Jewish laws, and scandalized Europe by personally adopting Edgardo Mortara, a boy who had been kidnapped from his Jewish parents? Right until the fall of the papal states in 1870, Pio Nono used public executions to maintain public order and steadily opposed religious freedom and basic human rights. John Paul II's claim that we could and should venerate the virtues of Pio Nono left me deeply puzzled, above all because John Paul himself virtually rejected any legitimate use of the death penalty, championed human rights, and did at least as much as Pope John XXIII to heal the wounds in the relationship between Catholics and Jews. On the day of the joint beatification of Pius IX and John XXIII, the one hundred thousand people in St Peter's Square signalled the world's judgement by ecstatically applauding Pope John and remaining sullenly silent about Pio Nono.

Sermons and Addresses

Along with his mega-production of new blesseds and saints, John Paul II produced more documents, sermons and addresses than any of his predecessors, including Pius IX who reigned for thirty two years. The *Insegnamenti* (teachings) of Paul VI, who was pope for sixteen years, run to sixteen volumes; during his first sixteen years in the job John Paul II produced thirty-seven volumes of *Insegnamenti*.

Many of the texts written for his trips abroad and for his normal work in Italy were, of course, prepared by speech writers. But the Pope often indicated at least the broad outline of what he wanted, and obviously endorsed what was written when he used these texts. Very often his addresses and sermons for visits to Australia, Germany, India, the United States, and other countries were prepared locally and applied the good news of Jesus to the local situations of youth, the elderly, the sick, indigenous peoples, and so on. They are likely to remain enduringly valuable. Some papal documents appeared after much consultation and revision. The papal encyclical *Sollicitudo rei socialis* ('Concern for the social situation') of 1987 was believed to be the product of such consultation. It has already taken its place in the history of papal documents as a superb examination of social challenges and the application to them of Christian values.

I remain amazed that theologians, bishops, journalists, and other commentators regularly ignored two striking innovations to be found in the Pope's inaugural encyclicals: *Redemptor hominis* ('Redeemer of human beings') of 1979 and *Dives in misericordia* ('Rich in mercy') of 1980. Many articles and books evaluated and commented on these texts. Have I been the only one to point out how comfortable the Pope was with the theme of experience and with the idea of God's revelation in Jesus Christ *also* taking place here and now, not by adding new truths to what God definitively revealed in Jesus Christ but by making revelation a living reality today?[18]

Throughout the twentieth century many Catholic teachers, both bishops and theologians, have shied away from the language of experience, believing that it could lead to appeals which, distorting religious truth, would be emotional and 'merely subjective', if it is

---

18 See my essay 'John Paul II and the Development of Doctrine', in G. O'Collins and M. A. Hayes (eds.), *The Legacy of John Paul II* (London: Burns & Oates, 2008), pp. 1-16, at 2-7.

possible to be merely subjective. Even the texts of the Second Vatican Council, while addressing extensively our experiences as human beings and as believers, used the noun and verb 'experience' sparingly. John Paul II constantly used the language of experience. With a philosophical background that valued the experiential dimension of human existence, he had no inhibitions whatsoever with talk of experience. And rightly so. Whatever does not enter or at least impinge on our experience is simply not there as far as we are concerned. A non-experienced revelation of God would be a non-revelation. The divine revelation by definition means God taking the initiative to disclose to human beings some hitherto unknown truth and above all the personal Truth that is God. Thus revelation involves the human apprehension of the divine self-manifestation in what we experience.

When I drew attention to the Pope's way of speaking about revelation here and now, a colleague at the Gregorian dismissed John Paul's usage as 'loose and improper'! That may have been the feeling of some unknown Vatican employee whom I caught tampering with what John Paul II wrote. In November 1994 the Pope signed a common declaration on the teaching about Jesus Christ with Mar Dinkha IV, the leader of the Assyrian Church of the East. This group of separated Christians have often been called 'Nestorians', because they followed Nestorius (died after 451), the Patriarch of Constantinople who was alleged to have held that there were two separate persons in the Incarnate Christ, one divine and the other human. For the 1994 declaration English was the language of the official text, and whereas the Pope and the patriarch wrote of their 'experience' of being united in the same faith, the Italian translation offered by *L'Osservatore Romano* on 12 November 1994 declared: 'we confess ourselves united in the same faith.' The translator shied away from talk of 'experience', and felt free to change the text.

John Paul II's astonishing linguistic abilities and powerful dramatic presence always made him a star communicator. But an occasional penchant for abstract terminology was regrettable. One Good Friday evening I joined thousands of young people for the stations of the cross at the Colosseum. An actor read a beautiful commentary on the fourteen stations, recalling Jesus being condemned by Pilate and then carrying his cross to death and burial. The singing evoked deep religious feeling. And then came the Pope's homily. The body language was magnificent; his red and white vestments were splendidly theatrical as he stood on a height silhouetted against the ruins of an old Roman temple. But the sermon seemed full of tired old clichés that could not connect with the vibrant young congregation in front of him. The only saving grace was the presence of many non-Italians who would have understood few if any of his words, no matter what he said.

On a visit to Rome my sister Dympna attended one of John Paul's regular Wednesday morning audiences in the Hall of Paul VI, which can accommodate several thousand people. These meetings with the Pope gave visitors to Rome a chance to see him, listen to a talk in Italian, and often hear some words of welcome in their own language. On this occasion he was delivering one of a series of addresses on the story of Adam and Eve in the book of Genesis. Later in the day I met my sister for a meal. Dympna spoke Italian, and so I asked her what she had made of the Pope's address. 'Well,' she said, 'it was very abstract, like a boring university lecture. I couldn't get the point of much that he wanted to say, apart from the fact that he does seem to be in favour of human sexuality.'

Bishop Agnellus Andrew, a Scot who had worked very successfully with the British media, had been brought to Rome to improve communications for the Pope and the Vatican. Agnellus eventually told the Pope that his Wednesday addresses were going right over people's heads. But John Paul II proved unrepentant and explained: 'This is the only way a Pope can publish a book.' Those Wednesday addresses on Genesis came from a book, *The Theology of the Body*, which he had just finished writing at the time of being elected Pope. John Paul used chapters from the book for his Wednesday talks and published the book that way!

Agnellus did much to prepare the Pope for his visit to the United Kingdom in May 1982, a visit that was in doubt until the eleventh hour owing to the war in the South Atlantic between Argentina and the United Kingdom. Agnellus provided a crash course on English literature, culture and history, since John Paul had never previously been in Britain. Shortly before he left for London, he contacted Agnellus: 'Didn't you tell me that Shakespeare was the greatest English writer? I don't find even a single Shakespearean reference in the texts that have been prepared for me. Where should I quote him and what should I quote?' Agnellus proposed inserting something from Shakespeare into a homily to be given at Coventry airport, the closest place on the papal itinerary to Shakespeare's birthplace at Stratford-upon-Avon. He asked for a couple of hours to come up with an appropriate quote. When telling the story to a group of friends, Agnellus asked us to guess what he had proposed. Some, like me, suggested a passage from John of Gaunt's speech from *Richard II*, Act 2, scene 1: 'This royal throne of kings, this scepter'd isle' etc. Agnellus' brilliant choice was in fact totally appropriate to the fact that the United Kingdom was at war with Argentina. Agnellus picked some verses from Portia's speech in *The Merchant of Venice*, Act 4, scene 1: 'In the course of justice none of us/Should see salvation: we do pray for mercy, /And that same prayer doth teach us all to render/ The deeds of mercy.' The passage was doubly appropriate, given that the Pope's encyclical on divine mercy of 1980 was still fresh in the minds of many.

As Jesus' victory over death is the heart of Catholic faith and I have published extensively on his resurrection, Easter Sunday is the most important day of the year for me. Since the first Easter of John Paul II's pontificate in 1979, I watched his Easter addresses to the huge crowd in St Peter's Square on television. The spectacle was always breathtaking, not least because the Easter greetings he offered in forty or more languages went down so well with his audience. After listening to his address in 1979 and again in 1980, I found it relentlessly heavy. John Paul was failing to connect and to take advantage of a unique chance for proclaiming the great news of Jesus' resurrection from the dead. I decided to write a text for him and sent it off on 1 March 1981 — in good time for Easter. His secretary, John Magee, wrote to assure me that he had given my proposed Easter address to the Pope and to thank me on John Paul's behalf for my 'kind thought'. Monsignor Giovanni Battista Re of the Secretariat of State also wrote:

The Holy Father wishes me to express his gratitude for your gift of an Easter Sunday address, and for the accompanying offprint of your most recent article on the resurrection. He very much appreciates your devoted sentiments. His Holiness asks God to sustain you in the grace and love of our Lord Jesus Christ, and to fill you with his peace.

But I didn't see any evidence of my efforts in the Pope's 1981 Easter address in St Peter's Square.

However, nearly fifteen years later I was specifically asked to prepare a papal address for the thirtieth anniversary of the proclamation of the final (and longest) document of the Second Vatican Council, *Gaudium et spes* ('Joy and hope'). I decided to concentrate on such themes as the dreadful inequality between the rich and the poor, the scourge of war, Jesus as the answer to the deepest hungers of the human heart, and the rights and dignity of women. My text for this address in November 1995 was a little too long, and needed to be cut. It was interesting to see what was trimmed. I had taken the opportunity to link the Pope's major initiatives to the great themes of *Gaudium et spes*, a document which he had helped to prepare when he took part as a bishop in the Second Vatican Council. Perhaps papal modesty led to the omission of these links. A second major omission concerned the rapid growth in world population from three billion to well over five billion which occurred between 1965 and 1995. Since *Gaudium et spes* treated the mission of the Church in the modern world, I thought it appropriate to recognize this change and some other dramatic changes in the world which had taken place during those thirty years. Other changes to which I had drawn attention, which included such things as space trips and heart transplants, remained in the address delivered by the Pope, but my reference to the dramatic rise in world population was struck out. The text as delivered by John Paul II was reproduced in *L'Osservatore Romano* for 10 November 1995 and elsewhere.

Lunch with the Pope

In the early 1990s John Paul II had invited the rector of the Oriental Institute to bring together a team of theologians for a series of seminars in the Pope's own apartments. I was invited to participate in the meeting on redemption as a representative of Western, Latin theology. The meeting took place shortly after Easter 1993, with the Pope sitting at the head of a long table. I summarized the theory of satisfaction which was developed by St Anselm, Archbishop of Canterbury from 1093 to 1109, and which interpreted human redemption primarily as Christ's making amends for the offence to the divine honour caused by sin. I argued that, despite its great and long-lasting influence in the West, this theory of satisfaction cannot be taken to be anything like defined doctrine. I then enlarged on a way of understanding redemption as *the* great work of divine love.[19] The other participants concentrated on representative writers from Russia and other parts of Eastern Christianity. The Pope said very little during the session, and at the end of it he gathered up our summaries and led us in to lunch.

I found myself sitting on his right. The previous day John Paul had made a lightning visit to Albania, now relatively free after years of appalling tyranny. Over the meal I fished for his reactions to that visit and got nowhere. Albania was yesterday's business. Today's business was with us and then with another group he was to meet in the afternoon. He wanted to continue the seminar discussion over the meal and had much to say about the nature of redemption.

I had long been aware that the Pope constantly emphasized the role of St Peter as leader, and thought that this might be my only opportunity to encourage him to present Peter's role as witness to the resurrection, something underlined by Luke 24: 34, St Paul (1 Corinthians 15: 5), and the opening chapters of the Acts of the Apostles. I asked John Paul to give that Petrine Easter witness a chance, because people had forgotten it and theologians highlighted unilaterally the leadership themes of Matthew 16: 18-19, Luke 22: 31-32, and John 21: 15-17. 'I promise not to do that again,' the Pope replied teasingly. But the three leadership texts were to receive the primary emphasis once again two years later in the papal encyclical on Christian unity *Ut unum sint* ('That they may be one').

Since the lunch took place only a few weeks after Easter, I remarked: 'Holiness, you had competition this last Easter Sunday from a German

---

19 See my *Christology: A Biblical, Historical, and Systematic Study of Jesus* (2nd edn; Oxford: Oxford University Press, 2009), pp. 306-14.

golfer, Bernhard Langer. On Easter Sunday he, too, announced the good news of Christ's resurrection to millions.' 'Langer? Golf?,' the Pope knew nothing of all that. So I explained that in the previous year on his last putt Langer had lost the Ryder Cup for the European team. The following year he had, so to speak, come back from the dead to win the Master's tournament at Atlanta (Georgia) and told the public of his joy in winning on Easter Sunday, 'the greatest day in the year, the day when Jesus rose from the dead'.

During the meal we also talked about the May 1986 encyclical on the Holy Spirit, *Dominum et Vivificantem* ('Lord and Giver of Life') and difficulties which Greek and Russian Orthodox Christians have with the way Catholics talk (or fail to talk) about the Holy Spirit's place in the life of the tripersonal God and in the work of human redemption. I said how glad I had been to see the expression 'God's Self-communication' turning up repeatedly in the encyclical. 'I didn't take it from Karl Rahner,' the Pope replied, perhaps suspecting that I expected an acknowledgment of the great Jesuit theologian, who had written repeatedly on the divine self-communication. John Paul II explained: 'I used that personal term about the Holy Spirit to build a bridge to the Orthodox.'

In *Man of the Century* Jonathan Kwitny identified the same intention (p. 549). Sensitive to the Greek and Russian Orthodox complaint that 'Catholics made the Holy Spirit subsidiary in the Trinity', the Pope reached out to them in the hope of healing the rift. Anticipating the 'ugly religious clash' that was to come in what was then the USSR and the 'countless lives lost in what was then Yugoslavia', the Pope stressed the importance of the Holy Spirit and expressed the hope for a ecumenical unity 'to restore religion's force in life'. What I heard from the Pope in 1993 supports Kwitny's comment, but two points should be added. The 1986 encyclical *Dominum et Vivificantem* completed the Pope's trinitarian project. His 1979 encyclical *Redemptor Hominis* reflected on God the Son; the 1980 encyclical *Dives in Misericordia* reflected on God the Father. By treating the third divine person, God the Holy Spirit, *Dominum et Vivificantem* completed the project. Further, 'God's Self-communication', despite some background in the patristic period, is a term that emerged through the work of Friedrich Schleiermacher and Georg Wilhelm Friedrich Hegel. Although this means that it arose under the auspices of Liberal Protestantism and German Idealism, the term does not carry difficult memories from a thousand-year-old debate with Orthodox Christians about the Holy Spirit.

Three Shadows

After pages of warm appreciation, it is not inappropriate to draw attention to three shadows upon John Paul's pontificate: the continuing over-centralization of the Church; his tensions with Jesuits; and his attitude vis-à-vis liberation theology.

(1) The centralization of the Catholic Church is now more pronounced than at any other stage in its history, and in no small part due to the Code of Canon Law promulgated by Pope Benedict XV in 1917. Such centralization makes a mockery not only of the old saying 'Rome rule means home rule', but also of the principle of subsidiarity. But more of this in the next chapter.

(2) As a Jesuit I have been more intimately concerned with a shadow over John Paul II's relationship with the Jesuits; so I will write about this at greater length. Soon after the election of John Paul II, Jesuit houses around the world received copies of a photograph of the Pope blessing the kneeling Jesuit general, Pedro Arrupe, who is pledging to the Pope the service of the Society. Arrupe exudes calm serenity, but the expression on the Pope's face can only be described

as fierce. It is no secret that some Jesuits had been distressed by Father Arrupe's visionary policies in facing a new world, and had gone behind his back to denounce him to Paul VI and then to John Paul II. At some point between late 1978 and mid-1981, Fr Arrupe had offered his resignation to the Pope and requested his permission to make the arrangements for a successor to be elected. But John Paul refused the request.

In August 1981 Arrupe visited the Jesuits in the Philippines. On his way back to Rome he stopped in Bangkok to visit refugee camps, exhort the Jesuits working in Thailand about collaborating more closely with the local bishops, and plan future studies for the first Thai Jesuit. On 7 August during his flight back to Rome, Arrupe fell asleep and woke up a couple of hours before touchdown. Father Bob Rush who was travelling with him told Father Arrupe: 'There's a really good movie coming, *Breaker Morant*, and they don't charge for the

With Blessed John Paul II, New Year's Eve, 1978, and Fr Pedro Arrupe SJ on the left

headphones.' The film ended as the plane entered its final approach to Rome's airport. While he and Bob Rush were waiting for their bags to come off the carousel, Father Arrupe suffered a massive stroke.

Back in Rome and very much incapacitated, Father Arrupe nominated a vicar general who was to take charge of the Jesuits (as the Society of Jesus is usually known) and to make the preparations for a general congregation, a meeting of Jesuit representatives from around the world, who would elect a new general. That was all in accordance with the Society's constitutions. But a few weeks later, on 5 October, the Pope intervened to postpone the general congregation; he also appointed his personal delegate, Father (later Cardinal) Paolo Dezza (1901-99) himself a Jesuit, to run the affairs of the Society. From his sickbed Father Arrupe wrote to all members of the Society of Jesus saying that he accepted the Pope's decision with full loyalty and expected his brother Jesuits to do the same. I thought instantly of Nelson's famous message before the battle of Trafalgar: 'England expects that every man this day will do his duty.'

In *The Man of the Century* (pp. 402-05) Jonathan Kwitny tells the story of Father Dezza's appointment. A few (minor) inaccuracies can be corrected by checking Kwitny's account with what was written some years later by a first-hand witness, Father Vincent O'Keefe.[20] When I received the news about the Pope appointing Father Dezza his delegate to the Society, it left me feeling very upset until I walked out the main door and met a poor woman with an invalid husband whom I knew to be threatened with eviction by their landlord. Then I went to say Mass in the church of the Reparation Sisters, who sang a particularly lovely Alleluia before the Gospel. The first incident spoke to me of the millions of people in our world who have no legal redress, starve, have to flee from armed conflicts, and live in refugee

---

20 V. T. O'Keefe, 'Arrupe, Pedro', *New Catholic Encyclopedia*, vol. 19 (1996), pp. 22-27.

camps, and that was not my condition as a well-fed, well-housed Jesuit. The second incident reminded me that Jesus' resurrection is such good news that no bad news could ever count against it.

That day and later I heard other Jesuits passing comments on the Pope's decision. One recalled how Giuseppe Garibaldi, when receiving some imprudent order from his king, replied with the message, 'I obey, your majesty (obbedisco, Maestà).' Another Jesuit remarked: 'We have talked a lot in recent years about poverty and chastity. It's about time we put in some work on obedience.' Yet another Jesuit referred to the fact that Father Dezza would be turning eighty shortly and said with a smile: 'Life begins at eighty.'

It struck me how dramatic some elements in the whole story had been. On the last stage of his flight back to Rome in August, Father Arrupe had watched the film *Breaker Morant*.[21] Just before he was led out to be executed, Morant was asked by a chaplain if there was anything he wanted. 'Nothing,' he said. 'But you can put Matthew 10:36 on my tombstone.' The text reads, 'And a man's enemies will be those of his own household.' I could not help wondering whether the Pope had been 'got at' by rigid Jesuit critics of Father Arrupe? Or had others such as members of Opus Dei supplied denunciations of our General, his policies, and the activities of Jesuits? Or was it more Christian to avoid all such speculations?

When I learned of Father Arrupe's stroke, I also wondered whether the Pope would now feel some regret about preventing Arrupe from going ahead with a general congregation and submitting his own resignation, when he first raised the matter with John Paul. Would Arrupe have been under less strain and not have suffered his stroke?

---

21 An English-born, Australian hero, Harry Morant was nicknamed 'Breaker' because of his legendary skill at riding and breaking in horses. He was executed as a scapegoat during the Boer War.

I imagined the scenario which could have followed, if the Pope had given the green light when Arrupe first raised the question of his resignation: a general congregation of Jesuits from around the world in mid-1981, Father Arrupe there in reasonably good health, and a moving speech from him at the end of his stewardship, followed by an intense and long ovation from the delegates. It would all have been a nice human story, the proper ending to sixteen years of office. Instead, something much more Christ-like had happened to him.

On 6 October the Pope's Secretary of State or chief executive officer, Cardinal Agostino Casaroli, came from the Vatican across St Peter's Square to the Jesuit Curia, and, standing at Father Arrupe's bedside, read to him a letter from the Pope announcing the appointment of the papal delegate. Was this a case of hitting a good man when he was down? Arrupe asked at once to be taken to the chapel. Through his secretary he asked us all to accept the Pope's decision in 'a spirit of full and filial obedience'. If we Jesuits truly loved Pedro Arrupe, now was the time to show it. For years he had put up with many criticisms and accusations against his Jesuits — unfair ones as well as charges based on fact. He had suffered on our behalf, shielding and encouraging us. Now we were asked to suffer a tiny bit of humiliation and uncertainty with him and, in a sense, for him.

The Pope's decision implied three judgements: (a) Father Arrupe's leadership had been defective; (b) the Society was not yet prepared spiritually for the congregation to elect Arrupe's successor; (c) the Pope lacked confidence in our four elected general assistants, (and, very specifically, in the Vicar-General, the American Father Vincent O'Keefe), to run our affairs and prepare for the next general congregation. I prayed hard that the Pope's action would not divide the Society of Jesus, and/or make us wrongly introspective and forgetful of the world's needs.

From the history of our founder, St Ignatius Loyola, I remembered how he limped into Rome in 1537 and had a visionary experience at La Storta, a tiny village on the northern outskirts of the city. He heard some words from God: 'I will be favorable to you (plural) in Rome.' Ignatius rightly took the words to mean that he and his companions should expect persecution, along with success, in the papal city. When I got back to Rome from Australia on 10 September, I kept wondering for a month or more whether I was simply limping along in my spiritual life. After turning fifty in June, where was I heading? Would my existence be just a holding operation until death in my sixties, seventies, or eighties? The answer to all that came on the evening of 23 October when the Pope celebrated Mass for the ecclesiastical institutions on the occasion of the opening of the academic year. He was thin, a bit apprehensive, and without his normal extraordinary vitality. At the collect, the first major prayer in the service, he paused a long time with his hands joined in front of his face before praying to God for the grace 'to know what is pleasing to you, so as to carry it out in unity and harmony'. I really joined in that prayer for the Holy Father, for myself, and for other Jesuits.

That year (1981) we happened to celebrate the centenary of the birth of several men who did their best work for the church and humanity in old age (Pope John XXIII, Cardinal Augustin Bea, and Marc Boegner) and of one who did his best work after death (Pierre Teilhard de Chardin). That struck me as a happy omen, with Father Dezza beginning his new job less than two months short of his eightieth birthday. In Rome, the scene of martyrdom for Sts Peter and Paul, one could not miss the symbolism as Jesuit life continued under Pedro (Peter) Arrupe (still legally general) and Paolo (Paul) Dezza.

But, for all that, they were still difficult years from late 1981 until normal Jesuit government resumed with the Pope allowing a general congregation to meet in September 1983. Father Dezza was the personification of kindness and encouragement during those two years. As a young member of the philosophy faculty of the Gregorian, he had been the first professor to teach in our present main building on the slopes of the Quirinal and served as our rector from 1941 to 1951. He had been confessor to Pope Paul VI for years and to Pope John Paul I for the brief month of his pontificate. Dezza, along with Johannes Hirschmann from Germany and Mario von Galli from Switzerland, was the best Jesuit speaker I have heard during my years in the Society of Jesus. Dezza was a master of rhetoric, choosing precisely every word and delivering his speeches and sermons without notes.

Dezza's most unforgettable sermon during those two years as the Pope's delegate was delivered in February 1982. On the eve of the three hundredth anniversary of the death of a seventeenth-century Jesuit, Saint Claude de la Colombière, Dezza preached to a packed congregation in the Church of the Gesù on a phrase from Pope Paul VI, 'the culture of love'. The sermon contained not a word about or from Pope John Paul II. Dezza remarked that Saint Claude had 'observed scrupulously the constitutions of the Society'. It seemed a clear hint to the packed congregation of Dezza's desire to be allowed to call a general congregation, secure the election of a new superior general, and so lead us back to normal Jesuit government. In September 1983 the thirty-third General Congregation of the Society of Jesus elected Father Peter-Hans Kolvenbach as successor to Father Arrupe.

(3) A third shadow over John Paul II's pontificate was his antipathy to liberation theology. This is largely a Latin American movement inspired by the Old Testament calls for freedom and justice and by Jesus' proclamation of God's kingdom; it has struck deep roots where structures of injustice continue to oppress masses of poor people.

Some newspapers and journalists of wealthy countries aided and abetted death squads in Latin America, who murdered hundreds or even thousands of those working for the poor and oppressed. In a kind of knee-jerk reaction such journalists talked or wrote blandly of Jesuits toting guns with the Latin American guerillas. Challenged by Father Arrupe or others, they could only come up with one or two names of *former* Jesuits.

Some people fed the Pope distorted talk about liberation theologians following Marxist solutions rather than the message of Christ. John Paul II knew the evils of Communism and was Pope for eleven years before the Communist empire collapsed in 1989. What could he be expected to think or do? The Brazilian Leonardo Boff was, to say the least, an embarrassing colleague for those two great liberation theologians, Gustavo Gutiérrez and Jon Sobrino. The saddest aspect of the Pope's Latin American policy, with its reservations concerning liberation theology, was his lack of support for Archbishop Oscar Romero of El Salvador, who was to be shot dead when saying Mass on 24 March 1980. Jonathan Kwitny, a former journalist with the *Wall Street Journal*, told the whole story in *The Man of the Century* and concluded: 'John Paul's treatment of Archbishop Romero, and his continued treatment of Romero's memory, are an injustice like no other he has done anyone' (p. 354).

When a military death squad in El Salvador murdered six Jesuits, with their housekeeper and her daughter, one night in November 1989, many Catholics expected that John Paul II would have personally celebrated a requiem Mass for the dead in St Peter's basilica, or would have asked a top cardinal to do so on his behalf. But no such papal gesture was forthcoming. A huge crowd jammed into the Church of the Gesù for a Mass of extraordinary intensity. One person who came remarked to me afterwards: 'If the military had dragged six priests

out of their beds in Poland and shot them in their garden, we would
be hearing about it from the Pope for weeks. But those six priests in
El Salvador made the mistake of endorsing and practising liberation
theology!'

Friend of the Young

The next chapter will tell the story of John Paul II's final sickness,
death and burial — events in which young people participated in
a striking way. Let me introduce that story by detailing briefly its
background. As no other world leader of his generation, the Pope
reached out to young people everywhere, and not least through the
World Youth Days he initiated in 1986. His personal charism with
the young was unequalled. Millions of them were drawn to Denver,
Manila, Paris, Rome, and other large cities that hosted those Holy
Woodstocks, which, despite the name of World Youth Days, ran for
the better part of a week. Well over a million young people came to
Rome, for example, to celebrate the jubilee year with John Paul II in
the summer of 2000 (15-20 August). The city of Rome hung banners
and flags along the main streets leading to the major churches and
most significant monuments (like the Colosseum). Special posters
and tapestries adorned the Cathedral of St John Lateran and St Peter's
Basilica. The celebration ended with a mega-gathering: an all-night
vigil and a Sunday morning Mass with the Pope in the grounds of a
university on the outskirts of Rome.

   A friend of mine who joined a group of students from a British
university at the 1997 World Youth Day in Paris recalled what John
Paul II had said to the vast crowd of young people: 'My friends, I
want you to know that Jesus loves you. My friends, I want you to
know that the Pope loves us.' 'The impact', my friend remarked, 'was
enormous. No wonder that they kept chanting "John Paul II, we love

you.'" Then my friend added: 'The words he used were very simple, but true and effective. I've never heard any bishop or priest saying just that to his congregation.' Part of the impact came from the way in which the Pope delivered his lines. Sir John Gielgud, an outstanding

With Blessed John Paul II, New Year's Eve, 1978

actor on the stage or in films, remarked about John Paul II: 'I have never heard anyone deliver his lines with better timing.'

Some sour critics have dismissed the impact of the World Youth Days and other such gatherings. The young, they assure us, loved the messenger, but not the message. Millions of young people flocked to hear his words and enjoy his acting. But his influence on their moral and religious compass was minimal. I beg to differ from this negative evaluation. My own experience of John Paul II's impact on young people leads me to think otherwise. Let me give one example, the story of Kathryn, an Irish girl who married my cousin Tony.

Receiving rosary beads from Blessed John Paul II

En route to the United States in September 1979, the Pope stopped in Ireland and spoke to a huge crowd in Phoenix Park, Dublin. Kathryn (aged fifteen) and many of her school friends were there. The enthusiasm John Paul II generated led them to take up the idea of riding bicycles to Rome and visiting the Pope the following summer. Serious practice on shorter rides got them into shape for the long ride across Europe. In August 1980 they cycled to Rosslare (the port of Wexford) only to learn that French fishermen were on strike and blocking the access of boats to France. After days of camping at Rosslare, they managed to get on board a boat to Rotterdam and reach Paris by train. Then they cycled down France and Italy, taking two weeks to arrive in Rome — only just in time for an appointment that his Irish secretary, John Magee, had arranged with the Pope at Castel Gandolfo. In shorts and t-shirts, the group of teenagers (with Kathryn one of the seven girls among them) took to the Via Appia for the final thirteen-mile ride, up hill to John Paul II's summer residence. They arrived hot and sweating to meet him and receive rosary beads from him. When he came to Kathryn, the first girl in the line, the Pope put his hand on her cheek and said with a look of surprise: 'You look very young, only about twelve'. The young Irish boy next to her cut in at once and said in his thick Dublin accent: 'Ahh, no, Father, she's sixteen.'

In her twenties Kathryn married Tony, and they suffered a tragic loss when their first child died after a difficult birth. When they buried the tiny baby, Kathryn put into his coffin one of her most precious possessions, the rosary beads she had received from John Paul II. Many years and two other children later, Tony brought Kathryn back to Rome for her fortieth birthday. Over dinner in a Roman 'trattoria' I heard for the first time of the epic ride to Rome and the meeting with John Paul II. John Magee had long since left Rome to serve as a bishop in Ireland. But through a Polish friend I managed to provide Kathryn with another set of rosary beads blessed by the Pope. Undoubtedly it is difficult to assess the impact of any one person on another. But, in the light of the way her life has unfolded, it would be a false insult to dismiss as minimal John Paul II's influence on Kathryn's moral and religious compass.

6

The Death of John Paul II

Many readers of this book will have watched on TV or followed by radio the events unfolding in Rome from 1 February 2005, the night when John Paul II was rushed to hospital. After some days, he returned home to the Vatican, but then had to be taken back again to hospital for an emergency operation.

The Final Days of the Pope

During both of his last stays in hospital, a hillside right outside the clinic was packed with the stands of TV or radio networks. They looked right across at the fifth floor of the hospital where the Pope was confined to bed. The world's media wanted to be there and cover the last few weeks in the life of John Paul II, someone they had come to know very well and cherish deeply. He was a world celebrity, among the best known faces around the globe. About a half an hour before he went home from his first stay in the clinic, I was being interviewed around 7 p.m. by a tall Australian blond who ended by asking how he would go back to the Vatican. 'Diana', I assured her, 'he's not going to return home in his pajamas and dressing gown. He's going home dressed like the Pope and sitting up.' He did just that and was driven back to the Vatican in his popemobile, a special vehicle with big windows. John Paul II could wave to people along the road, and the Romans could show how much they cared for him and were emotionally involved in his last sickness. On a Sunday during the Pope's second stay in hospital, I was interviewed around midday by a BBC presenter. When he appeared at the window of his hospital room to wave to the crowd below and bless them, the presenter was very moved. She had to wipe some tears from her eyes.

At the end, John Paul II went home to the Vatican for Holy Week and Easter. But he was unable to preside at or even attend the ceremonies. He could not even speak when he was moved to the window of his apartment to give the Easter Sunday blessing to the vast crowd gathered below in St Peter's Square. Parkinson's disease had finally reduced him to silence, and I thought: 'That's it. He will be ready now to go home to God.'

The following Saturday, 2 April at 9.37 p.m., John Paul II died at home in the Vatican Palace. Below his apartment thousands of young people had been keeping vigil: holding candles, singing hymns, and praying in various languages. Some were weeping, others rejoicing that the 84-year-old Pope had been delivered from so much pain and could finally leave his suffering behind and enjoy eternal happiness with God.

From the TV platform of the BBC, up on the Janiculum hill which overlooks St Peter's Square, I followed this very public death and heard the huge, ten-ton bell tolling the passing of the Pope. They were amazing days to be in Rome. A flood of people poured into the city. Above all, there were hundreds of thousands of young people who spontaneously converged on Rome. They wanted to pay their last respects to an old friend whom they loved very much. Reportedly the last whispered message from John Paul II before he fell unconscious was for the young: 'I went looking for you. You came to me, and for that I thank you.'

The Pope died on a Saturday evening. On the Monday afternoon, he was carried out of the Vatican Palace and through St Peter's Square, held up high in an open casket so that all the crowd could see. He seemed like a Viking king being carried through the midst of his people to his last rites. They placed his body in front of the main altar of St Peter's Basilica — to lie there in state for the world to visit.

From the Monday evening through to Thursday, a gigantic column of people queued up for ten or twelve hours or even more, before they could enter St Peter's and file past the catafalque to pray and pay their last respects. The column, which moved along between wooden barriers, was at least twenty-five people across and ran back for more than a mile. Up to two million people came to visit John Paul II lying in state.

The Funeral and Conclave

On Friday, 8 April, the world stood still for the last rites of the Pope. There has never been a papal funeral like that one. On TV, two billion people followed the funeral Mass, guided brilliantly by the master of ceremonies (Archbishop Piero Marini) and presided over with dignity and devotion by Cardinal Joseph Ratzinger, the dean of the College of Cardinals. In Rome itself half a million packed into St Peter's Square and the adjacent streets. In other squares around the city, huge screens let two million more people follow the ceremony.

There were numerous touching moments in the funeral Mass and the concluding rites. At the time for Holy Communion the first in line to receive Communion from Cardinal Ratzinger was a white-haired, 90-year-old man in a wheel chair, Brother Roger Schutz of Taizé, an ecumenical centre in France that has become a powerful place of pilgrimage for young people.[22] For many of us the most moving moment during the papal funeral came right at the end, when the coffin bearers raised the simple wooden coffin from the ground in front of the altar, and carried John Paul II slowly and solemnly past the rows of presidents, monarchs, princes, prime ministers and other powerful political leaders of our world. As he was being carried out past all those celebrities who enjoy lives of pomp and circumstance, it was as if John Paul II was preaching his last sermon to them and saying: 'You too are mortal. You too must face death and go home to God.' When those bearing the coffin reached the top of the steps and were about to disappear through the huge doors into St Peter's Basilica, they paused and turned the coffin around to face the huge crowd. It seemed as though they were giving John Paul II one final look at Rome and at the world he loved so much. Then they took him inside and buried him in the crypt of the Basilica, right next to his immediate predecessors, Pope Paul VI and Pope John Paul I, and near the tomb of Queen Christina of Sweden.

The funeral was over and the political and religious leaders of the world began moving away from the steps of St Peter's. At the end only one solitary figure remained standing there, alone in the section reserved for special guests: Rabbi Elio Toaff of Rome. The old rabbi, a Holocaust survivor, stood there in his black hat, praying for his friend, John Paul II. Then a young cleric slipped along the row of seats to take the rabbi's arm and accompany him into St Peter's and out the back to his car.

---

22 As a young bishop during the Second Vatican Council, John Paul II got to know Brother Roger and other monks of Taizé through praying and eating with them in their small apartment in Rome. During summer, the fields surrounding their monastery fill up with tents, and young men and women learn to love the meditative music of the eighty or so monks. At evening prayer in August 2005 a deranged person stabbed Brother Roger to death.

That was Friday 8 April. After days taken up with further Masses and preparatory meetings, the conclave began on Monday 18 April and 115 cardinals were locked up in the Sistine Chapel to elect a successor to John Paul II. I was on camera with the BBC when they filed into the Sistine Chapel and took an oath to preserve secrecy about the proceedings. I could not help remarking to Brian Hanrahan, the presenter, 'Brian, there are 115 cardinals going in to vote, and 44 of them studied at the Gregorian University or at least taught there. It's about time the papacy came back to the Gregorian.' In the event, the papacy did 'come back' to the Gregorian; as a visiting professor Joseph Ratzinger taught an optional course on the Eucharist in the autumn of 1972. In 1977 Paul VI named him archbishop of Munich and three months later a cardinal. When John Paul II called Ratzinger to Rome in November 1981 to become the prefect of the Congregation for the Doctrine of the Faith, I suggested to the dean of theology at the Gregorian, René Latourelle: 'Why don't we invite Cardinal Ratzinger to teach an optional course each year? I'm sure he would like to keep his hand in as a theology professor.' Latourelle nodded agreement but then paused to say: 'A good idea. But it would make other cardinals jealous.'[23]

It was a privileged experience to work for the media during those weeks of the funeral and the conclave and, especially, to be with BBC World when white smoke came out of the chimney above the Sistine Chapel at 5.55 on the afternoon of Tuesday 19 April. Originally the white smoke was a signal for a cannon to be fired from Castel Sant' Angelo. In the days before radio and TV, that was an efficient way

---

23 When I became dean of the theology faculty in 1985, I might have invited Cardinal Ratzinger to teach an optional course each year at the Gregorian. But two documents (of which more in the next chapter) had dampened my enthusiasm: the 1984 'Instruction on Certain Aspects of the Theology of Liberation' from the Congregation for the Doctrine of the Faith, and the 1985 *Ratzinger Report* edited by Vittorio Messori.

of letting all the people of Rome know at once that a new pope had been elected. This time round the white smoke was meant to be accompanied by bells ringing out across Rome to announce the papal election. But it took about ten or fifteen minutes before the bell ringers were reached and the bells of St Peter's and of other major churches began to ring out the message: 'Habemus papam (we have a pope).' The reason for the slight delay was this. The key to the phone in the Sistine Chapel for contacting the bell ringers was in the pocket of the dean of the College of Cardinals, Cardinal Joseph Ratzinger. He had just been elected Pope, and had slipped into a small room next to the Sistine Chapel and was changing into his white garments.

Between the time the white smoke first emerged from the chimney above the Sistine Chapel, it was going to be about 45/50 minutes before the senior Cardinal Deacon could appear on the central balcony of St Peter's and announce the name of the newly elected Pope. The people of Rome took to the streets to get to St Peter's Square to hear the announcement and have their first glimpse of the new Pope. It had been over 26 years since the last papal election. The Romans wanted to be there in front of St Peter's to see and greet the next Bishop of Rome. People surged down the streets; it made it impossible for any taxis, cars or buses to get through. In less than an hour, at least 100,000 people had gathered to hear the name of the new Pope and then to welcome him when he came out on the balcony.

A huge burst of noise welled up from St Peter's Square to the BBC stand on the Janiculum hill when the Cardinal Deacon announced the name of the new Pope. The presenter caught the name at once: 'It's Ratzinger.' 'Oh no', said a young priest next to me on the platform, and at once drew the camera on himself. I had a couple of minutes to compose my thoughts before Hanrahan swung back to me 'Father O'Collins, Pope Benedict is 78 years old. Do you think he will retire at

80?' 'Give him a chance, Brian', I retorted. 'He hasn't even started yet.'

I had proved satisfactory to the BBC by predicting a few days earlier in an interview that the new Pope, whoever he was going to be, would take the name of Benedict XVI. 'Before he even appears on the balcony of St Peter's and opens his mouth, he will have delivered his first message through the choice of his name. If he adopts the name of a very recent pope and calls himself John XXIV, Paul VII or John Paul III, he could be creating all kinds of presuppositions and expectations that he may not want. There could be too much baggage brought by those names. It would be better to go back to Benedict XV and call himself Benedict XVI.' I explained what was so attractive about Benedict XV (pope 1914-22): 'Benedict stood for peace and strongly opposed World War I. When the fighting stopped, the winners never involved him in the 1919 Treaty of Versailles. It had awful consequences and proved to be one of the worst peace treaties in human history.' I had further reasons for hoping that the new Pope would call himself Benedict: for instance, the strong interest Benedict XV showed in promoting better relations with the Orthodox and other Christian churches of the East. But it seemed more understandable to talk about him as a pope of peace.

Not wanting to clash with the Orthodox celebration of Easter on 1 May, the new Pope scheduled his inaugural Mass for Sunday 24 April — just five days after he had been elected. The closing words of his homily echoed and reaffirmed the heart of what John Paul II had preached: 'If we let Christ into our lives, we lose nothing, nothing, absolutely nothing of what makes life free, beautiful and great. Do not be afraid of Christ. He takes nothing away, and he gives you everything. When we give ourselves to him, we receive a hundredfold in return. Yes, open, open wide the doors to Christ, and you will find true life. Amen.'

The Legacy of John Paul II

That was my experience, that was the world's experience, in those dramatic weeks from February to April 2005 when John Paul II faced the last stages of his illness, died and was buried, and his successor was elected and began his work as Benedict XVI. Until his beatification, the body of John Paul II was to lie in a grave down in the crypt of St Peter's Basilica. Around the world, his published teaching fills shelves in the libraries of universities, colleges and seminaries. He left well over 70,000 pages of official teaching, not to mention the books he published as a 'private' person. Many of the bishops he appointed are still alive and in office. During the year celebrations of the Eucharist recall the 482 saints he canonized or the 1338 men and women he declared to be 'blessed' and worthy of veneration. How might one pull together and evaluate John Paul II's legacy? At least six points seem to be worth mentioning.

(1) First, he left a lasting mark on Europe and its life. He played a major role in the largely non-violent downfall of Communism in central and eastern Europe. His role in that peaceful transformation was recognized when Mikhail Gorbachev, the President of the Soviet Union, and his wife Raisa flew in from Moscow to visit John Paul II in December 1989. Among the most memorable photographs from the Pope's life was that snap of him dressed in his white garments and standing between Gorbachov in a dark business suit and Raisa in a bright red dress.

Right from his election in 1978, John Paul II worked to unleash the power of faith and truth to mobilize the Polish people in their resistance to Communism. The end of the Communist regime in Poland helped to trigger the collapse of Communism in Czechoslovakia, Hungary, East Germany, and elsewhere. But the demise of Communism across central and eastern Europe has not brought a political, social, and economic paradise, nor a religious paradise either. The new Europe, through the nineties and into the third millennium, has experienced a steady erosion of religious practice and beliefs, both among Catholics and other Christians. There has been a marked decline in Sunday worship and in the endorsement of Christian values. In some ways the new Europe seems to be living off its religious and moral capital. Did John Paul II, so to speak, win the war but lose the peace? Obviously high on the agenda for Benedict XVI, right from the start of his pontificate in April 2005, was the religious future of Europe. Yet there are now more Catholics in Africa than in the whole of Europe.

(2) Second, as the leading apostle of peace in the world's public arena, John Paul II stood out for his firm opposition to war, right down to his clear 'no' to the invasion of Iraq in 2003. In an address that he delivered in January 2004 to the diplomats accredited to the Holy See, he once again expressed his conviction: 'War never resolves conflicts among peoples.' He constantly defended the culture of life and freedom, against the anti-culture of oppression and death. That stance set him against war as the tempting but false solution to international conflicts. His Gospel of life also set him against abortion, euthanasia, and capital punishment as tempting but false solutions to other human challenges and problems. John Paul II's consistent ethic of life aimed to promote the well being of families, and to save and support millions who suffer from extreme poverty, disease, hunger, and even death by starvation.

He was like his predecessors, Paul VI, John XXIII, and other popes, in opposing war, calling for peace and justice, and defending an ethic of life. But John Paul II did so in a comprehensive way and with great vigour. He also wanted an end to the war against our planet. Unlike his papal predecessors, he was deeply aware of the threats to our fragile ecological systems, and pleaded for peace with our earth.

(3) Third, John Paul II continued the work of his predecessors by encouraging better relationships with other Christians and, in particular, the work of the Council for Promoting Christian Unity. In Cardinal Edward Cassidy and Cardinal Walter Kasper, he appointed outstanding leaders to head that Council and oversee numerous dialogues with Anglicans, Lutherans, Methodists, and other Christians. One can read much of what the Pope did in Cardinal Cassidy's book *Ecumenism and Religious Dialogue*.[24]

Where John Paul II broke new ground ecumenically was in his personal gestures and initiatives. In 1983, on the occasion of the 500th anniversary of the birth of Martin Luther, he preached in the Lutheran church in Rome; he was the first pope ever to preach in any Lutheran church. In 1997 a group of Anglicans came to Rome to recall Pope Gregory the Great sending a group of monks to England. One of them founded the see of Canterbury in 597, and entered history as St Augustine of Canterbury. The 1997 Anglican group was headed by Archbishop George Carey, the then Archbishop of Canterbury. In a ceremony to mark the occasion, John Paul II gave Archbishop Carey a cross, the pectoral cross worn by bishops.

In January 2000, as part of the services for the start of the great Jubilee Year, the Holy Door in the huge and ancient Basilica of St Paul's Outside the Walls was to be opened. John Paul II wanted the ceremony to express and further the cause of unity between all Christians. When opening the door, he was flanked by Metropolitan Athanasios (representing the Ecumenical Patriarch Bartholomew I) and by George Carey, still Archbishop of Canterbury and head of the Anglican Communion. At the ceremony itself the Pope invited the Orthodox leader and Archbishop Carey to do something which

---

24 Mahwah, NJ: Paulist Press, 2003.

was not on the programme. The three of them pushed together in opening the Holy Door, a vivid symbol of their common effort towards unity among all Christians.

Four months later, in May 2000, John Paul II led a prayer service at the Colosseum, the place where tradition places the death of many early Christian martyrs. The Pope wanted to recall the much larger number of Christians who in the *twentieth century* had suffered and died for their faith. That ceremony recalled with honour Dietrich Bonhoeffer, Oscar Romero and numerous other men and women, Anglican, Catholic, Protestant, and Orthodox, who around the world had witnessed to their common Christian faith through suffering and death.

The ecumenical gestures that consistently marked John Paul II's years as Pope brought an unprecedented result: the large number of Anglican, Protestant, and Orthodox leaders who attended his funeral Mass. No previous papal funeral had ever drawn such an ecumenical gathering. In life John Paul II had shown himself their friend and brother. They came to pay him their respects in death.

(4) Constantly reaching out to Jews, Muslims, and those of other faiths also characterized the papacy of John Paul II — my fourth point. One can understand why the Simon Wiesenthal Centre, a Jewish human rights organization based in the United States, awarded him its 2003 Humanities Award for his 'lifelong friendship with the Jewish people' and for his efforts to promote Jewish-Catholic understanding. In his teaching, he insisted that the special covenant made through Moses with God's chosen people had never been revoked. The subsequent covenant inaugurated by Christ's death and resurrection has not rendered obsolete or inoperative the earlier covenant. In his actions and gestures, John Paul II constantly showed his friendship with the Jewish people and total rejection of any anti-

Semitism. In April 1994, he hosted a Holocaust memorial concert in the Paul VI Audience Hall of the Vatican. The Royal Philharmonic Orchestra came from London and was conducted by Gilbert Levine, a Brooklyn-born American Jew. John Paul II sat with the chief rabbi of Rome, Elio Toaff, who had brought with him his congregation. The concert was part of the Pope's personal mission to keep alive in the centre of the Catholic world the memory of the Holocaust. He also arranged for the Kaddish, the traditional Jewish prayer for the dead, to be recited. The visit John Paul II made in 1986 to the main synagogue in Rome was highly significant (see last chapter). He was probably the first pope to visit and pray in a synagogue since the early days of Christianity.

He was certainly the first pope to pray in a mosque, as he did in Damascus in 2001. Years earlier, when returning from a 1985 visit to Zaire, Kenya, and some other African nations, John Paul II went home to Rome via Morocco. At the invitation of King Hassan II of Morocco, he spoke to a crowd of over one hundred thousand young Muslims about the religious and moral values common to Christian and Muslim faith. Since the days when Muhammad launched Islam more than 1,300 years ago, no pope has ever been invited by a Muslim leader to do anything like that.

More than ninety times (actually 94 times) John Paul II acknowledged the grave sins and errors committed by Catholics against others. He asked pardon from Jews and Muslims, as well as from Protestant and Orthodox Christians. He proved an outstanding role model in trying to reconcile people. Saying 'sorry' does not automatically solve everything, but it is always a step in the right direction.

An outstanding inter-faith act of John Paul II was his 1986 trip to Assisi with the Dalai Lama and other heads or representatives of the world's religions. They met to pray for peace in our time and in our world. Some people (as we saw in the last chapter) sharply criticized the Pope over that Assisi meeting. But in a speech to the Roman Curia two months later, John Paul II insisted: 'Every authentic prayer is called forth by the Holy Spirit, who is mysteriously present in the heart of every person.' Four years later, in his encyclical letter *Redemptoris missio* (the mission of the Redeemer), the Pope developed further this line of teaching. He wrote: while manifested 'in a special way in the Church and her members', nevertheless, the Holy Spirit's 'presence and activity are universal'. 'The Spirit's presence and activity affect not only individuals but also society and history, peoples, cultures, and religions' (no. 28). John Paul II had a vivid faith in the Holy Spirit, present in every human heart and prompting genuine prayer whenever and wherever it goes up to God. That stress on the Holy Spirit was one powerful way in which the Pope contributed to the progress of doctrine and encouraged inter-faith dialogue, or dialogue between various religions.

Another major way in which he broke new ground was through encouraging the followers of all religions in their common responsibility for human welfare. His 1995 encyclical letter *Evangelium vitae* (the Gospel of life) called for 'the concerted efforts' of 'all those who believe in the value of life'. They must promote together human life as 'everyone's task and responsibility'. This is a common service shared by Christians and 'followers of other religions' alike (no. 91). In this encyclical letter and on other occasions, John Paul invited Christians and those of other faiths to make common cause and act together on their shared values in advancing human rights and human dignity.

(5) Fifth, along with 'Pope', John Paul II had various other titles such as 'Bishop of Rome' and 'Patriarch of the West'. These other titles included 'Roman Pontiff' or 'Supreme Pontiff', with

'pontiff' coming from the Latin word 'pontifex', which originally meant 'bridge-builder'. As we have seen above, John Paul II was an exceptional 'bridge-builder' with young people. He also built bridges in a remarkable way to the Italian people, even though he was Polish and his fluent Italian maintained Polish cadences until the end. Right from his first words he won the hearts of the Romans. Speaking in Italian to the crowd gathered in St Peter's Square right after his election in October 1978, he said: 'Please correct me when I made a mistake in your, no our, language.'

As we saw in the last chapter, John Paul II quickly revived an old custom of celebrating a Mass on New Year's Eve with the city authorities in a downtown church of Rome. Eventually the city council invited him for a formal visit to the Campidoglio or town hall — the first such visit any pope had made to the Campidoglio since the Italian government took over the papal states in 1870. The mayor and other city authorities made John Paul II an honorary citizen of Rome — an honour very rarely granted to a foreigner. He struck up a close friendship with several Italian presidents and in November 2002 was invited to address the Italian parliament — another first for any pope. On that occasion, he disarmed everyone by ending his speech with an apt quotation from Dante, the great Italian poet who is a point of reference for everyone ('this Rome where Christ is Roman', *Purgatorio*, 32. 102). When John Paul II died, it was no wonder that the Italian government and the civil administration of Rome performed brilliantly in playing their part. They wanted to show their friendship for him by ensuring that everything went smoothly and safely for more than two million people who flooded into Rome.

(6) My sixth and final point concerns his tireless missionary work that made him a papal Billy Graham, a mega-evangelist who made an extraordinary effort to bring the good news of Christ to the whole

world. As we recalled at the start of the last chapter, he made over one hundred journeys outside Italy and visited at least 130 countries, even if denied the chance of visiting China and Russia. He tried to help Christians and others to see how Jesus Christ is the centre and source of life for every individual and for the whole human race. The words with which Benedict XVI ended his homily at his inaugural Mass sum up what John Paul II preached in season and out of season: 'If we let Christ into our lives, we lose nothing, nothing, absolutely nothing of what makes life free, beautiful, and good.'

The final part of this chapter was entitled 'the Legacy of John Paul II'. It was an attempt to sum up his achievements or at least something of what he managed to do during more than 26 years as pope. There was a greatness there, a greatness that reminds me of William Shakespeare's words about Julius Caesar: 'He hath bestrode the narrow world like a colossus.'

Greatness, of course, is not the same as perfection. In the story of John Paul II, there were also shadows, imperfections, and unfinished business. But, beyond question, there was greatness and great achievements. Such achievements can and should turn into a lasting legacy, a legacy that continues to have a life of its own. But that depends on Catholics and others, who are still very much alive. Recalling what John Paul did, we might ask ourselves: Do we consistently stand *for* the culture of life and *against* the culture of death? Do we show real love and understanding towards other Christians? Do we cherish Jews, Muslims, and those of other faiths? Above all, do we centre our lives on Jesus Christ, and help as many as possible to let Christ into their lives and find through him a life that is true, beautiful, and great? To the extent that we do these things, the achievements of John Paul will become a living, fruitful legacy.

7

The Vatican

'They wouldn't like that in Rome.' Over and over again I have tried patiently to point out that no one in their right senses would make a similar remark about other large capital cities. Who ever says, 'they wouldn't like that in London or in Madrid', when in fact he or she wants to refer to the Prime Minister and his cabinet, or to the civil servants? When critics talk of things that 'Rome thinks' or 'doesn't like', they presumably mean the Pope and his close advisors, or some particular Vatican office like the Congregation for the Doctrine of the Faith (hereafter CDF).

What do the millions of people who live in Rome think about any single issue? I would be loathe to ascribe to them a collective mind and will. The same goes for the Vatican. The four or five thousand people who work in Vatican City may be, more or less, united in a desire to serve the Pope, the universal church, and the whole world. But it would be ludicrous to allege that they share one monolithic opinion on any single issue. But that seems to be the presupposition of those who talk glibly about 'what the Vatican thinks'.

When the *Catechism of the Catholic Church* appeared in 1992, one dear friend, a highly educated professor who lives far from Rome, sent me the draft of a lecture he was about to give in which he presumed that the work was the product of 'the Roman schools of theology'. Would that our Gregorian faculty of theology had been able to see the text and help revise it before it appeared! During the years when the *Catechism* was being prepared, I served as dean of the Gregorian's theology faculty and, as far as I know, none of our resident professors ever had anything to do with its preparation. The only time I ever saw any text connected with it was on the desk of a visiting American professor, Avery Dulles, who was labouring through a big pile of proposed emendations, presumably on behalf of the American bishops.

At times it seems that 'Rome', 'the Vatican', and 'Roman theology' can be convenient labels for things some people don't like. But enough of this gripe. I shall become boring if I keep on writing in this vein and avoid the thoroughly fair question: 'What do you think about the Vatican after nearly thirty years in Rome?'

On the one hand, I feel blessed by having shared the city with some saintly servants of God like Cardinal Eduardo Pironio, Cardinal Agostino Casaroli, Pope Paul VI, Pope John Paul II, Father Pedro Arrupe, and several women of outstanding courage, devotion, and breadth of vision, who spent years either working for the Vatican or living in the city in the head office of their religious institutes. But, on the other hand, there are less than edifying things to report.

Christian Unity

My contacts with Vatican officials began seriously in Australia in early 1973 — through being involved with the ecumenical preparation for the eucharistic congress held in Melbourne. Cardinal Jan Willebrands, President of the Vatican's Secretariat for Christian Unity, came to Melbourne as one of our principal speakers, and I was greatly impressed by him and also by Tom Stransky, an American Paulist priest, who had been among the founding members for the Secretariat. As soon as I came to live full time in Rome, I determined to do anything asked of me by the Secretariat of Christian Unity.

In June 1977 Monsignor Bill Purdy of the Secretariat telephoned to ask whether I would be willing to serve on the team for the official Catholic-Methodist dialogue, and I agreed. I went to the United States and home to Australia for the summer, and returned to Rome in September. Bill phoned to tell me with some embarrassment that the Vatican's Secretariat of State had crossed my name and that of Tom Stransky off the list of Catholic participants. I was never told what had made me unacceptable, and I didn't know whether Tom was any the wiser as to why he too had been turned down.

There was an ironical aftermath eighteen years later. In 1995 an official of the Secretariat of Christian Unity, now called the Pontifical Council for Promoting Christian Unity, asked me to evaluate the document on revelation and faith which the Catholic-Methodist dialogue had finally produced. When writing my report and drawing attention to limitations and weaknesses in the text, I couldn't help wondering whether I could have helped to produce a better document. It is hard to tell. But my life would certainly have taken a rather different direction if I had joined the Catholic-Methodist team. Instead of spending my summers lecturing in Australia, England, India, Ireland, Japan, New Zealand, Singapore, South America, the United States, and elsewhere, I would have been meeting the team of Methodists and Catholics in Venice, Moscow, and other exotic places. I certainly missed out on the opportunity for an annual discussion with two friends on the team who were excellent Methodist theologians, Geoffrey Wainwright of Duke University and Norman Young of the United Faculty of Theology in Melbourne.

During my Roman years the main service that I could offer the Pontifical Council for Promoting Christian Unity office took the form of welcoming groups of Anglicans and Protestants who wanted to hear about theological education in Rome. They frequently came to the Gregorian to hear me and others speak. Some came year after year, particularly those completing an inter-church course outside Geneva at Bossey.

Other Offices of the Curia

In late 1974 I sent an article on the making of Easter faith to the Jesuit journal, *Civiltà Cattolica*, which enjoys a semi-official status as a mouthpiece for Vatican views and comes under the direct supervision of the Vatican's Secretariat of State. The editor of *Civiltà Cattolica* accepted my text, and had it translated into Italian and typeset before sending it up to the Vatican. It was rejected by the censors at the Secretariat of State because I had not been hard enough on one Protestant scholar, Willi Marxsen, while being too critical of another, Wolfhart Pannenberg. Also my notion of faith was considered 'insufficiently clear'. I was happy for my work to be assessed by the editor of *Civiltà* and his advisors but found it unpleasant to receive similar attention from anonymous Vatican censors. The following year the Jesuit journal *Rassegna di teologia* published the piece and for some years I was one of their regular contributors, but I did little for *Civiltà Cattolica*.

In the autumn of 1975 with a small group of professors from Roman institutions, I took part in some informal discussions under the auspices of the Vatican's Justice and Peace Commission, now the Pontifical Council for Justice and Peace. The group was asked to prepare a paper on religious life and liberation, and I vigorously asserted the Commission's right to use 'liberation theology' language, when a Dominican professor of theology condemned such language. I never knew what happened to the paper my group drafted, but that was the last time I was asked to do anything for the Council for Justice and Peace.

The Congregation for Bishops is responsible for the nomination of bishops all over the world. My involvement with them was minimal, but, like many others, I have been occasionally consulted about the appointment of particular priests. On one such occasion I wrote a long letter explaining why I thought it better to delay episcopal appointment for the candidate in question. Nonetheless, the priest had friends in high places, and two years later he got his bishopric. On another occasion God's providence put me next to the official from the Congregation for Bishops who handled appointments in Australia and some other countries. We were in the line-up of priests about to take part in a major ceremony at the North American College. Knowing that I was Australian, he whispered that they would be soon making a recommendation to fill the vacancy in the Sydney archdiocese. He then mentioned the name of his chosen candidate. I was horrified: 'You couldn't do that to the good people of Sydney.' The priest looked extremely embarrassed, and in the event the see went to someone else, Archbishop (later Cardinal) Edward Clancy. I never told Cardinal Clancy about the meeting at the North American College which I believe to have been providential.

The Congregation for Education

When I came to the Gregorian in 1974, the head (or prefect) of the Vatican's Congregation for Catholic Education was the former Archbishop of Toulouse, Cardinal Gabriel-Marie Garrone, who was also ex-officio the chancellor of the Gregorian. As chancellor he had a voice in such matters as the promotion of professors. Around the time of my nomination as 'extraordinary' (= associate) professor in 1976, our affable and open-minded rector, Father Hervé Carrier, told me that Cardinal Garrone had received complaints about my views on revelation and the resurrection. I asked if the Cardinal could be more specific. Revelation and resurrection are large topics and it impossible to deal with a general complaint. Had someone objected to a something specific I had written? Unless I knew a bit more, it would be impossible to correct any error there might be. Carrier asked me to write him a letter making these points. I did so and that was the last I ever heard of this particular matter, although I was on the receiving end of other criticism from time to time.

In late 1976 an American Jesuit drew my attention to an article in the *The Critic* written by Monsignor George Kelly in which he referred to me as 'Collins' and fired some shots against me in a wild caricature of my book *Has Dogma a Future?*, describing it as 'a direct thrust at the heart of Catholicism'. I was in distinguished company since the same article described the famous Redemptorist theologian Bernard Häring as 'stamping his feet with temper whenever a papal position is used to contradict his own theological position'. I talked with Father Carrier about the appropriate reaction. He warned me that I should do something at once, because people like Kelly 'shoot to kill'. It occurred to me to ask my niece, Joanna Peters, by then a Philadelphia lawyer and about to move to Wall Street, to send Kelly a letter requiring retraction. Carrier, however, thought that would be overkill. In the end I wrote a letter to *The Critic* listing the ways in which Kelly had misrepresented my book.

However, before it was published I received out of the blue a letter from Cardinal John Joseph Wright, the most prominent American ecclesiastic in Rome and head of the Sacred Congregation for the Clergy (1969–79). Obviously someone had tipped him off about my reaction to Kelly's article. The Cardinal was ailing and his signature was very shaky when he wrote to me:

I happen to agree with many of the things written by Msgr. George A. Kelly, but I had thought that the day had passed when anyone would be disturbed by an article written on any side of any question for publication in *The Critic*. Heaven knows ... who will read it. Because you are interested in this particular article, however, I shall make it a point to find it and read it. Thank you for bringing it to my attention. It is eight years since I have seen a copy of *The Critic*. That was when they were polishing me off about something or other.

Despite Wright's playing things down, Carrier's advice was preferable. I did not appear among the villains attacked by Kelly in his 1979 book *The Battle for the American Church*. Presumably he suspected that I would take him to task, even legally, if he kept up his attacks.

The specific opposition may have been based to some extent upon my ecumenical commitment. In the mid-seventies an unidentified group, rumoured to consist of certain Mexican bishops, 'got at' Paul VI on the grounds that they had been scandalized to learn that the Gregorian's theology faculty invited one or two non-Roman Catholic, visiting professors each year. As I mentioned earlier (Chapter 2), the Pope was prevailed upon to direct that such invitations be discontinued. The professors who had been coming to us had to be approved by the Congregation for Education, and were nothing if not thoroughly Christian in their beliefs. When the distinguished Anglican theologian, Dr Eric Mascall, taught a course for us in the spring of 1976, a thoroughly conservative Catholic priest who had come out to Rome for some (very necessary!) updating assured me in a loud voice and in Mascall's hearing: 'Dr. Mascall is the only orthodox professor teaching at the Gregorian.' After the death of Paul VI and with the election of John Paul II, the theology faculty repeatedly tried to have the papal veto officially lifted, so that we might once again invite non-Catholic professors — always, of course with the approval of the Congregation for Education.

Eventually the green light came on again, and our first visiting, non-Roman Catholic professor after a break of eight years was the Greek Orthodox theologian John Zizioulas, whose course on the Holy Spirit in the spring of 1984 drew a most appreciative audience. Already a prominent figure in inter-church dialogue. Zizioulas subsequently became an Orthodox bishop. The following years we enjoyed the presence of Jürgen Moltmann from Tübingen and Owen Chadwick from Cambridge.

Shortly after I became dean of theology in 1985, an American friend introduced me to Eugene and Maureen McCarthy. Through their family foundation they agreed to fund a chair for visiting professors. These visiting academics were frequently non-Roman Catholics. I was glad to be instrumental in putting our provision for world-ranking figures on a sound economic basis.[25] Just as before, invitations to non-Roman Catholic professors needed the approval of our chancellor, the head of the Vatican's Congregation for Education. The McCarthy Family Foundation went on to endow similar chairs for visiting professors for our faculty of philosophy and at the Biblical Institute. Eugene and Maureen became great friends of mine, and we began meeting at their home in New York as well as in Rome.

In their quiet, loving way Eugene and Maureen encouraged me to include among the requirements for the visiting professor a special public lecture to be followed by a reception for all those who attended the lecture and then by a dinner at a restaurant for fifteen or so invited guests, including the McCarthys themselves. They always flew over

25 Up to the last McCarthy professor in theology (2008), they were (in chronological order): William Henn, OFMCap, George Lindbeck, James Dunn, Bishop Eduard Lohse, Dietrich Ritschl, Ulrich Luz, Sergei Averintsev, Geoffrey Wainwright, Harding Meyer, Janet Martin Soskice, Gavin D'Costa, Ulrich Kuhn, Eamon Duffy, Bishop Tom Wright, Robert Wilken, Lord Carey of Clifton (former Archbishop of Canterbury), James Charlesworth, Metropolitan Kallistos Ware, Oliver Davies, Turid Karlsen Seim, and Susan Wood.

from New York to attend the public lecture, bringing with them a beautifully executed scroll to be presented to their guest professor at the end of the question period and just before the reception. The McCarthys also suggested that the text of the public lecture be published subsequently in our quarterly, the *Gregorianum*. All this helped to make the presence of the visiting McCarthy Professor one of the highlights of the academic year for the theology faculty.

Here I need to backtrack a little to explain my rocky road to becoming dean of the theology. In 1979, after what I understood to have been a heated debate, the ordinary or full professors of the theology faculty voted in favour of my promotion from the rank of extraordinary professor to ordinary professor. Juan Alfaro told me after the meeting that he and others had supported the promotion and only a few diehards voted against it on the grounds of doubts about my orthodox faith. The dean of the theology faculty then passed the results on to the rector and the request for my promotion went up to the office of our chancellor, Cardinal Garrone. And there the matter stuck. Those who disapproved of my presence at the Gregorian may have expected that I might turn disgruntled and leave Rome to teach elsewhere. I was happy with the situation, however. Promotion to ordinary professor carried with it the increased risk of being chosen to be dean of the theology faculty, with all the administrative and organizational headaches that would involve. (When the faculty voted for a dean, an 'extraordinary' professor could be elected only on a two-thirds majority, instead of the simple majority required for the election of an ordinary professor.) As extraordinary professor I was a full member of the faculty, could teach to my heart's content, and did not have to attend too many meetings.

No professor at the Gregorian, apart from the dean, ever commented on my odd situation, and I heard nothing directly from the Vatican. The students of the German College were probably more intensely interested in matters of promotion than our other non-Jesuit seminarians. Every now and then one of them dropped a hint which showed that they were in the know. I had a fantasy of myself going home to Australia at seventy and in the departure lounge of Rome's Fiumicino Airport finally receiving a piece of paper announcing my promotion to ordinary professor.

My unpromoted situation did, however, bother Father Gilles Pelland, the Canadian dean of theology (1976-82); he wished to see the situation adjusted and discussed the matter with me. In order to provide him with ammunition I collected letters of support, including one from the distinguished American theologian Avery Dulles in praise of my *Fundamental Theology* (Ramsey, NJ: Paulist Press, 1981). Part of the problem apparently concerned doubts which had again been expressed concerning my views on revelation, Christ's resurrection, and dogma. I was also 'guilty' of an act of inter-communion in Ghana in 1974 before my arrival at the Gregorian.

When Carlo Martini left the Gregorian in early 1980 upon his appointment as Archbishop of Milan, I wrote a long letter to Father Simon Decloux, Martini's interim successor as rector, and explained how baffled I was about difficulties people might have with my writing and teaching on revelation and the resurrection. I pointed out that in 1974 and 1978 I had lectured on the resurrection to groups of bishops from the United States, who had seemed quite happy with what had been presented. As regards dogma and other issues in fundamental theology, I remarked that George Kelly had gravely misrepresented me in his article in *The Critic* and drew attention to my published response. On the issue of inter-communion, I told Decloux that, when in Ghana, I had indeed communicated at a Eucharist celebrated by a non-Catholic priest — an Orthodox as far as I could recall. But I was unclear as why the point had been raised, because I did not teach sacramental theology, neither did I practice inter-communion, nor did I encourage others to receive communion at non-Roman Catholic eucharists.

Nothing further happened until 1982 when our new rector, Father (later Cardinal) Urbano Navarette, decided to take up the case with the current Prefect of the Congregation for Education and former Archbishop of Washington, Cardinal William Baum. A large-minded canon lawyer, Father Navarette joked about the hyper-orthodoxy of the faceless men who had problems with what I published and taught: 'Some of them won't be satisfied with less than four persons in the Trinity.' I don't know the full story but in the spring of 1982, while I was away from Rome on a sabbatical semester in Nuremberg, Navarette wrote to tell me that the Congregation for Education had approved my promotion to ordinary professor and suggested that I write to thank Cardinal Baum.

In the spring of 1985, without much fuss, the faculty voted me in as dean of theology. Administration proved a headache, but I tried to put into practice Navarette's advice 'deal with letters instantly'. I flung myself into the task of recruiting new professors, improving public relations, and bringing faculty members together for days of study and social events. Over the next six years I had quite a lot to do with Cardinal Baum's successor at the Congregation for Education, Cardinal Pio Laghi. I remember with gratitude his concern over the case of one professor, whose promotion to extraordinary professor was being blocked. In his case the block was the fact that he had not published a book since his earlier nomination as adjunct professor, one down from extraordinary professor. The professor in question had in fact published several major articles in learned journals since his nomination as adjunct professor. The Gregorian's statutes, approved by the Congregation for Education itself, required 'learned writings' as one necessary condition for promotion; they did not prescribe the form these writings should take; they could be published as a book or its equivalent in articles. One official at the Congregation was bent on applying to the Gregorian standards which the Congregation had approved for *other* universities, namely that promotion depended on the publication of a new book. Cardinal Laghi sat down with me and let me clarify for that official the difference between our statutes and those of some other institutions. The professor was promoted and became my friend for life.

Cardinal Laghi marked the end of my six-year stint as dean of theology by kindly encouraging the organizers of the symposium to invite me, along with Bishop (later Cardinal) Walter Kasper and Father Raymond Brown, to speak at an October 1991 meeting hosted by the Josephinum, a theological centre in Columbus, Ohio. In a lecture entitled 'In the End Love', I explored the possibility of using love as the key for understanding what God promises to do at the end of history for human beings and their world. During the talk I enjoyed startling the audience with the news that 'eschatology' or the study of the last things had entered the English language through George Bush, 'a nineteenth-century author and not your President!'

The Congregation for the Doctrine of the Faith (CDF)

My first contact with the CDF took the form of a request to check part of a draft of the National Catechetical Directory for the Catholics of the United States, which eventually appeared in 1979 as *Sharing the Light of Faith*. Specifically I was asked to examine the section on God's revelation through Jesus Christ. I found that the text distinguished between the climax of God's self-disclosure in Christ by calling it Revelation (in upper case) and using revelation (in lower case) for the present realization of that self-disclosure in the lives of believers.

Although I prefer to distinguish between 'foundational revelation' which came to an end at the time of Jesus and his first followers and 'dependent revelation' which happens now, I found the terminology of the American document to be well based and helpful. I put in my report, was sent 15,000 lire (about twenty dollars at the time), and never again asked to read anything for the CDF.

I had obviously been expected to disapprove of anyone speaking of revelation happening now. The old inhibition was still at work— the fear that using revelation in the present tense was tantamount to alleging that God continued to reveal new truths. The closed nature of revelation must be preserved at all costs. That inhibition comes through the terminology of the Second Vatican Council. Except for one footnote in the Decree on the Church's Missionary Activity, *Ad gentes* ('To the nations', 3, n. 2), the conciliar documents studiously avoid the noun 'revelation' or the verb 'reveal' when referring to God's living voice speaking now to believers. As we saw in Chapter 5, John Paul II had no fear that we might be 'increasing' the content of what was revealed once and for all through Jesus and the Holy Spirit, if we recognized that God's enlightening word encounters us now. When the American Catechetical Directory was published as *Sharing the Light of Faith*, I saw that somebody (presumably the CDF) had made the authors describe what happened in the history that culminated with Jesus and his apostles as 'revelation', whereas God's word to us now was 'manifestation'. Along with John Paul II, above all in his November 1980 encyclical, *Dives in misericordia* ('Rich in mercy'), I take 'revelation' and 'manifestation' as broadly synonymous, and, more importantly, I fail to see how acknowledging God's present self-revelation to us must involve false claims about new revelations occurring and previously unheard of truths enlarging the original 'deposit of faith' or foundational revelation through Christ.

Perhaps the problem with revelation comes from a widespread sense that it always happened (or happens) dramatically — through visions and other very special phenomena. Back in 1967, when I was writing *Theology and Revelation*, a fellow wedding guest kindly enquired about my current activity. I told her that I was writing a book on revelation. Her immediate response was: 'Have you had any yourself?' I have constantly tried to remind my readers that divine self-revelation *also* took place and continues to take place in the most ordinary of ways and that it is not limited to extraordinary events and remarkable episodes.

One of the very few times, perhaps the only time, that I saw all but one of the theology faculty united by a sense of outrage happened in late 1979. A Belgian theologian Edward Schillebeeckx had been summoned to Rome by the CDF to answer questions about his views on the priesthood and his depiction of Jesus in a huge volume first published in 1974: *Jesus*. Jonathan Kwitny tells the story accurately in his *Man of the Century: The Life and Times of Pope John Paul II*,[26] apart from describing the local villain as a Frenchman. He was in fact a French-speaking Belgian on the CDF's team which was to examine Schillebeeckx's views. The villain had attacked Schillebeeckx as a heretic on Vatican Radio only a few days before Schillebeeckx arrived for the hearings.

The Belgian critic was also a professor on our theology faculty. Within a day or so, a transcript of his remarks on Vatican Radio was circulating around the Gregorian. Some colleagues wanted him censured or even dismissed from the faculty. Fortunately for him, events conspired to distract general attention and save him from censure or dismissal. The Pope paid a visit to the Gregorian, and shortly thereafter named our rector, Carlo Martini, the next Archbishop of

---

26 New York: Henry Holt, 1997, p. 348.

Milan. And Schillebeeckx himself retained his teaching position in the theology school of Nijmegen University, although some of his views on the priesthood were declared to be 'at variance with the teaching of the Church'. Beyond question, the Belgian critic's attack on Vatican Radio had backfired by swinging public sympathy (and also that of John Paul II) towards Schillebeeckx. What the critic had said on Vatican Radio prompted the Pope into sending a message to the CDF about giving Schillebeeckx a fair hearing. The critic subsequently alleged that when he had spoken on Vatican Radio, he had not yet been invited onto the CDF team, and told the Australian reporter Desmond O'Grady that his work on the Schillebeeckx case had been 'a duty, not a pleasure'.

Cardinal Ratzinger

In 1981 the Pope appointed fifty-four-year-old Cardinal Joseph Ratzinger, the Archbishop of Munich, to succeed the aging Cardinal Franjo Seper as Prefect of the CDF. I had lived next door to Professor Ratzinger in Tübingen and attended his lectures at the local university. I remember remarking to his sister who kept house for him that I liked the book her brother had published with Karl Rahner on revelation and tradition. 'Never heard of it,' she replied. Although Fräulein Ratzinger shared her brother's love for music, she seemed uninterested in theology, despite the fact that the enormously successful *Introduction to Christianity* (German original, 1967) would help to pay for a house they were to share.

It is significant in terms of some of Cardinal Ratzinger's subsequent concerns as prefect of the CDF that it was Rahner and not Ratzinger who wrote the chapter on revelation for their joint book. Many years later, when examining a thesis written by a student at the Gregorian on Ratzinger's theology, I was able to verify the way he had persistently paid little attention to two themes, one of which was divine revelation. In essays and books he treated related themes such as faith and tradition but had very little to say about God's self-disclosure, or the divine word speaking to us, judging us, and calling us into question. Ratzinger's limited grasp of the ins and outs of divine revelation was to affect *Dominus Jesus*, a declaration he issued in 2000, and his investigation of the work of Jacques Dupuis; we return to all that in the next chapter. The other theme which seldom appeared in Ratzinger's writings over the years was that of human evil and human suffering. Ratzinger did not place his theology in a world torn by war, oppression, hunger, violence against women, and the rest. In this he differed from Jürgen Moltmann and resembled much more Wolfhart Pannenberg, a Lutheran theologian just a year younger than Ratzinger himself. Pannenberg, despite living through the Second World War and its aftermath likewise failed to examine in any depth the terrible cruelty and evil that human beings can inflict on one another and on their world.

The inspired scriptures are closely associated with divine revelation, as its record and interpretation. Back in his days at the University of Tübingen (1966-69) Professor Ratzinger left me uneasy with his seeming disdain for biblical scholarship, much as I admired his lectures for their content and their aesthetic shape. Years later I imagined he might have become more open to scriptural scholarship when I learned that he had agreed to visit New York in January 1988 to take part in a frank dialogue with Raymond Brown on the interpretation of the Bible. The proceedings were edited by Richard Neuhaus and published by Eerdmans in 1989 as *Biblical Interpretation in Crisis*. But then I was saddened by Cardinal Ratzinger's remarks during a scripture symposium at the Gregorian in April 1992 when he gave a keynote lecture. The first part of his lecture traced with accurate fairness the history of Catholic biblical scholarship up to the Second Vatican Council, which closed in 1965. But he continued with the inflammatory statement: 'After the Council, Catholic exegesis capitulated to the world.' I was sitting with a Spanish biblical scholar. We both began writing down the names of leading Catholic commentators on the Bible who had apparently 'capitulated to the world': Raymond Brown, Joseph Fitzmyer, Joachim Gnilka, Xavier Léon-Dufour, Carlo Maria Martini, Roland Murphy, Rudolf Schnackenburg, Heinz Schürmann, Albert Vanhoye, and other great and distinguished scholars. After the symposium ended, I tackled the Cardinal's secretary: 'What on earth was that about?' 'He was only trying to be provocative,' was the loyal if lame response.

An ironical aftermath came with the superb and very well received 1993 document by the Pontifical Biblical Commission (PBC) on 'The Interpretation of the Bible in the Church'. As prefect of the Congregation for the Doctrine of the Faith (CDF), Cardinal Ratzinger was automatically president of the PBC and wrote the preface. But the slim volume also contained the text of a beautiful and very positive address given by the Pope on the occasion of the document's presentation. The address had been prepared for John Paul II by the secretary of the PBC, Father Vanhoye, one of those post-conciliar exegetes who had 'capitulated to the world'.

Many Latin American students — and others — were upset by the 1984 'Instruction on Certain Aspects of the Theology of Liberation', issued by the CDF and condemning liberation theology. The document often seemed to caricature a theology which is in fact deeply committed to justice. Cardinal Ratzinger put his case against any and all attempts to distinguish Marxist analysis from Marxist ideology. When he accused the liberation theologians of preferring justice to faith, he appeared to be supporting faith without justice.[27] None of us were aware that the Pope, too, became dissatisfied with the negative tone of the August 1984 instruction and asked Cardinal Roger Etchegaray, the head of the Pontifical Commission for Justice and Peace (later the Pontifical Council for Justice and Peace), to draft a second text to counterbalance the first.[28] Two years later the CDF published a friendly, positive document, 'Instruction on Christian Liberty and Liberation'.

As a result of the new document I was asked to record a programme in Italian and English for Vatican Radio answering the questions: 'Do your professors think of themselves as speaking for the poor? What would it mean, if they did?' I had to admit that few of the professors thought of themselves as speaking for the poor, and if they all decided to do so, it would mean a revolution in theology at the Gregorian.

Vatican Radio

Up to 1985 I had contributed regularly to the English language section of Vatican Radio. Sometimes I did the broadcasts alone, especially on the major feast days such as Christmas and Easter. For several years I shared a weekly programme with three others: an Australian nun, an American layman, and an English laywoman. I found myself persistently taking a central position alongside the laywoman, Mary Venturini, while the nun's views were often to the left and those of

27 Somewhat late in the day, in September 1993, when speaking in Riga (Latvia), John Paul II used some Marxist terminology and spoke of 'Marxism's kernel of truth', in that it analysed with partial correctness the social and economic situation, even while proposing unacceptable solutions.

28 See Kwitny, *Man of the Century*, pp. 514-18, 718. A journalist with good contacts assured me that the initiative for the 1986 instruction came from Etchegaray himself, supported by three Brazilian cardinals. They persuaded the Pope to commission and accept this second, more favourable, document.

the layman to our right. Mary taught in the social communications programme at the Gregorian; we co-authored a book on the Apostles' Creed, *Believing*, and she has remained a treasured friend. Life in the dean's office meant that I had to abandon regular work for the Vatican Radio in the summer of 1985.

In 1987, however, I was invited to comment on Vatican Radio on a perceived public disagreement between Cardinal Giuseppe Siri of Genoa and myself. The incident occurred during a press conference in the Hotel Columbus (on the Via della Conciliazione and near St Peter's Square) arranged by the publishers of the Italian translation of Jürgen Moltmann's book on creation. The press conference had been planned to coincide with the period of Moltmann's lectures at the Gregorian, and I went along to the Hotel Columbus to support our distinguished visiting professor. The journalists and others present seemed bored by Moltmann's urgent message to the Italian public about the environmental crisis. The question period had almost ended when, out of the blue, a journalist in the front row quoted what Cardinal Siri had just said on AIDS as a divine punishment for sexual immorality: 'What do you think about that view, Professor Moltmann?', he enquired. 'And I also want to know what Father O'Collins thinks.' I didn't hear what Moltmann had to say, as I was too busy framing my own response: 'Don't blame God. We smoke too much and die from cancer of the lungs. We drink too much and suffer from cirrhosis of the liver. Sexuality is God's gift to us, but we can use it irresponsibly.' Next day *La Repubblica* and *Corriere della Sera* both ran prominent articles: 'Dean of the Gregorian disagrees with Cardinal Siri.'

Later that same day I was asked to repeat what I had said for Vatican Radio in both English and Italian. 'Please, say just what you said, but don't mention Cardinal Siri by name.' I tell the story in part to put the record straight concerning David Willey's allegations that Cardinal Siri had given 'Rome's view' on AIDS.[29] To describe AIDS as divine punishment was utterly alien to the pastoral love which the Pope showed in the United States and in Africa to those suffering and dying from AIDS. In this matter, as in others, Cardinal Siri was an embarrassment rather than an official spokesman.

A couple of weeks later, however, I received a mild but deserved rebuke for the way in which I had expressed my views. Sergio was a retired engineer who lived like a hermit in a tiny apartment just off the Piazza del Popolo. Every evening he came out to eat at a nearby trattoria. Every now and then I would simply turn up there about seven to join him for a pizza and some spiritual conversation. Following the incident at the Hotel Columbus, Sergio almost barked at me over our pizza: 'You're a typical Jesuit!' 'How's that?,' I asked. 'The problem with Cardinal Siri is his false image of God, and, for all your talk about the greater glory of God, you Jesuits think in terms of human beings.' Sergio was on target. In the Hotel Columbus it had never even occurred to me to frame my reply in terms of God. 'The journalists wouldn't have understood that,' was my weak reply.

The Ratzinger Report

In 1984 the Italian magazine *Jesus* featured several interviews with Cardinal Ratzinger in which he expressed his views on a wide range of topics to Vittorio Messori. The Cardinal had to tone down some remarks in the resulting book, *The Ratzinger Report* (English trans.; San Francisco: Ignatius Press, 1985). Bishops and other American Catholics had let him know their displeasure at some of his remarks in the original interviews: for instance, Ratzinger's claim that biblical

---

29 See D. Willey, *God's Politician: John Paul at the Vatican* (London: Faber and Faber, 1992), p. 178.

scholarship in the USA was simply derivative from European (read German) scholarship. So much for the work of such great American scriptural scholars as Raymond Brown, Joseph Fitzmyer, and Bruce Metzger! Before I left Rome for the summer of 1985, the editor of the London *Tablet* insisted that I review the *Report*, which had appeared in Italian but not yet in English. For various reasons, not least because I was about to start work as dean of theology, I asked him to agree to my remaining anonymous and on that basis wrote about 'Ratzinger's sad book'.[30]

I then left Rome for a summer visit to Australia and travelled via the United States where I was to give a series of lectures. In New York the director of the Gregorian Foundation (a fund raising operation for the Gregorian University, the Biblical Institute, and the Oriental Institute) took the opportunity of my visit to arrange a press conference — in the spirit of 'come and meet the new dean'. Inevitably Ratzinger's book came up in the question period. The fact that I took my distance from it was widely reported, and I had no hesitation in making it clear that Ratzinger's point of view differed substantially from that of the Pope and that the book had saddened many people in Rome.

I flew on to Melbourne, Australia, where I received an invitation to visit the Apostolic Pro-Nuncio in Canberra, Archbishop Luigi Barbarito. My comments at the New York press conference had already reached him. When I met him, I was pleasantly surprised by his positive reaction. I was even more surprised when we moved onto the topic of liberation theology. Far from being nervous about this characteristic brand of Latin American theology, Archbishop Barbarito, speaking out of his diplomatic experience of representing

---

30 The review appeared in the *Tablet* for 13 July 1985.

the Vatican in Latin America, described liberation theology as 'a necessary inoculation against Marxism'.

However, on my return to Rome at the start of September 1985, I found a letter waiting for me from the Jesuit general, Fr Peter-Hans Kolvenbach, in which he told me that he had received a number of complaints about what I said in the New York press conference from bishops and other church officials. But by that time the Pope had publicly distanced himself from the *Ratzinger Report*. Speaking to journalists during a trip to Africa in the first half of August, John Paul II had commented: 'what Cardinal Ratzinger said is his own opinion (parere suo)', and added: 'He is free to express his opinion.' But the Pope made it quite clear that he himself did not share the Cardinal's decidedly one-sided and negative assessment of the Catholic life in the aftermath of the Second Vatican Council. This defused the situation for me. Over lunch with Fr. Kolvenbach I undertook to be more discreet, noted that the Holy Father's comments had come at the right time, and added: 'However, I do agree with the old axiom, *quod licet Iovi non licet bovi* (what's ok for Jupiter is not ok for an ox).'

Going to the Top

Pope Pius XII, a centralizing figure if ever there was one, taught that what could or should be dealt with at a lower level in the life of the Church should remain there.[31] But going straight to the top seems to have become rather common in the church, judging by what I have been told by archbishops, bishops, and others. Too often the first intimation of an objection to some event or course of action within their diocese comes in the form of a letter from the CDF or another Roman office. Some of the 'loyal' flock have decided to take matters

---

31 For those interested in Pius XII and the issue of subsidiarity, see my *Living Vatican II: The 21ˢᵗ Council for the 21ˢᵗ Centtury* (Mahwah, NJ: Paulist Press, 2006), pp. 156-58.

into their own hands, and instead of tackling the bishop about what is distressing them, they have written direct to Rome.

Let me, with his permission, tell a couple of stories about the similarly negative experiences of the Society of Divine Word Father John Fuellenbach, a part-time Gregorian professor who also taught at Regina Mundi, an international institute for religious woman. In 1987 within the German-speaking section of the institute, John was teaching a course on religious life. The course was part of a renewal programme for German nuns, but far from being renewed by what he had to say, two of the sisters took offence at his remarks on 'charisms' or spiritual gifts within the life of the Church and, in particular, at his quoting the Brazilian theologian, Leonardo Boff, who had suffered some run-ins with the Vatican.

One might have expected the two sisters first to have expressed their misgivings and objections to the German sister in charge of that section, if not to Fuellenbach himself. If they were dissatisfied with her handling of their problem, they could then have taken their complaints to the sister-president of Regina Mundi. Instead through their mother general they made an 'end run' straight to the head of the Congregation for Catholic Education, Cardinal Baum, who was ex officio chancellor of the Gregorian University and as chancellor of the Gregorian responsible for its affiliate, Regina Mundi. The first that Fuellenbach knew of the charges filed by two members of his Regina Mundi class was the four pages of accusations which reached him from Cardinal Baum's office. Fuellenbach asked his Redemptorist friend, the Irish moral theologian Sean O'Riordan, to write a defence for him which he signed and sent to the Congregation for Catholic Education.

But Baum referred the case on to the secretary of the Congregation for Religious and Secular Institutes, Archbishop (later Cardinal)

Vincenzo Fagiolo, who ran an office with responsibility for hundreds of thousands of consecrated men and women around the world. Fagiolo not only mailed Fuellenbach exactly the same list of accusations as Baum, but also took the matter to the CDF. A month later Cardinal Ratzinger sent a letter to John Fuellenbach's superior general.

What puzzled and grieved Fuellenbach was Cardinal Baum's initial failure to deal with the two German sisters by asking why they hadn't discussed the matter with the sister in charge of their section. If dissatisfied with her response, they could then have taken their complaints to the sister-president of Regina Mundi. If still dissatisfied, they could have approached the dean of theology (myself) or the rector at the Gregorian to which Regina Mundi was affiliated. Then, *and only then*, should the charges have been brought to Cardinal Baum of the Congregation for Education, accompanied by written evidence that they had previously approached the sister president, the dean, and the rector.

When Fuellenbach learned from his superior general of the letter from the CDF, he requested a personal meeting with Cardinal Ratzinger, so that they could have it out German to German, or dark-haired Rhinelander to white-haired Bavarian! The interview began with a ten-minute discourse from Ratzinger on the work of theologians. In fact, the particular lecture at which the two sisters had taken offence was based on Fuellenbach's own article, 'What is it to be a theologian?' When John asked what was wrong with the article and his subsequent lecture, Ratzinger responded: 'You have to be careful how your message comes across.' Assuring him that he was not under investigation, the Cardinal went on to praise the views of religious life expounded by Hans Urs von Balthasar as opposed to those expressed by Karl Rahner. 'But, unlike von Balthasar, Rahner at least remained a religious,' objected Fuellenbach, referring to the fact that, while remaining a priest in good standing, von Balthasar had left the Jesuit order. 'Just a minute,' Ratzinger broke in. 'Who is being accused, you or I?' At the end Ratzinger seemed glad that their meeting had taken place. He had taken action; positions had been clarified. Fagiolo and Baum could rest assured that Cardinal Ratzinger had investigated!

As Fuellenbach stood up to leave, the Cardinal had a request to make: 'Please don't take it out on Father Herron.' 'I never bear a grudge,' Fuellenbach assured him. Father Thomas Herron, one of the Cardinal's collaborators, had used spare time at the CDF to write a thesis on the dating of the Letter of Clement, an epistle written by Pope St Clement I late in the first century and a work on which Fuellenbach was a world expert. Fuellenbach was Herron's director; the dissertation defence took place a few days later, with Herron receiving a 'magna cum laude'.

A few months later, without indicating or even hinting at the authorship, Fuellenbach gave copies of his own article on the work of theologians to the members of his third-year seminar at the Gregorian, along with the four page criticism from Cardinal Baum's office. He asked the students to read both texts and write brief evaluations. Their responses were uniformly negative: 'The author of the criticisms is right off the point; he has no idea what theology is about.'

Should two cardinals and one archbishop, top persons in the Church's organization, allow or even encourage such end runs by self-appointed vigilantes? What is happening when a couple of disgruntled students can go straight to the top in that way and waste the time of three church leaders, responsible, respectively, for Catholic education, religious men and women, and sound doctrine throughout the world? Pius XII was surely right in upholding the principle of subsidiarity, which demands that matters that can be dealt with at a lower level should not be allowed to go directly to a higher one?

In early 1998, after some function Fuellenbach's superior general happened to give a ride home to the archbishop who was Cardinal Ratzinger's second in command at the CDF. The archbishop surprised the superior general by pulling out of his pocket an article published by Fuellenbach three years previously ('On the Five Basic Realities of Our Time') with a page of objections to Fuellenbach's reflections. The page carried neither a date nor a signature; the objections were not even written on the official stationery of the CDF! Fuellenbach's superior general took the proffered page, mulled over it for some days, and submitted a vigorous defence of the great work Fuellenbach was doing for seminarians, nuns, priests, and others (including bishops) through his theological and spiritual teaching. Nothing further was heard from the CDF, but the episode saddened Fuellenbach, not only by the very unprofessional way of communicating objections about his ideas to his superior general but also by the patent silliness of the charges. He was accused, for instance, of having nothing to say about God, Christ, and prayer. And yet he had written repeatedly on Christ's preaching the Kingdom of God, and in the 'offending' article itself included repeated references to God and Christ and began with a reflection on the Bible as the book of prayer. The whole episode left me wondering how many of the staff members at the CDF are able to read and understand texts put in front of them. Some months later, as we will see in the next chapter, my concern was rekindled and very much more dramatically.

Flawed Procedures

Beyond question, the Catholic Church needs a theological conscience and a last court of appeal in matters of faith and morals. But it does not need an organization that functions too often as a secretive, first court of doctrine in a manner unaccountable to the world-wide Church led by its bishops. Can the CDF be left to monitor its own activities? It grieves many bishops and others that anonymous critics around the world denounce to the CDF what they themselves see as false or dangerous. Often a bishop's first knowledge of such criticism is a letter from the CDF which privileges the voice of right-wing dissidents. Should the charges not be sustained, the CDF never apologizes to bishops for passing on false accusations.

In his treatise *On Consideration* St Bernard of Clairvaux (1090-1153) addressed his fellow Cistercian and former student, Eugenius III (pope 1145-53). Bernard acknowledged faithfully the authority of the Pope, but deplored the injustices committed by the Roman curia. In 1139 Bernard had written even more vigorously to Innocent II (pope 1130-43) about the lack of justice and, in particular, about the lack of respect for the role of the bishops who were leading dioceses:

Episcopal authority is being treated with utter contempt, so long as no bishop is in a position to avenge promptly injuries done to God, or is allowed to punish illicit acts of any kind even in his own diocese. Cases are referred to you and to the Roman curia. You reverse, so it is said, what has been rightly done; you confirm what has been wrongly done. Shameless and contentious people from among the clergy, even men expelled from monasteries, run off to you. On their return they boast and bluster to the effect that they have found protectors, when in fact they ought to have felt the punishment of an avenger.

In *On Consideration* Bernard showed how worried he was that the authority of local bishops was being undermined by improper appeals to the pope and his curia:

Appeals may result in being positively pernicious, unless as a system they are used with utmost moderation. They are addressed to you from every quarter of the globe. That of course is a tribute to your unique primacy. But you, if you are wise, will rejoice not in your primacy but in its good fruits...appeals are addressed to you and would that the results were as fruitful for good as the appeals are necessary. Would that when the oppressed [the bishops] cry out, the oppressor [the delators] were made to suffer.

St Bernard suggested a practical remedy, which could find its counterpart today.

In my opinion a man ought to be made to suffer himself when he has brought an appeal without due cause ... an appeal unlawfully brought should neither be to the advantage of the appellant nor damage the respondent. For why should a man [the respondent] be worn out on no good grounds at all? How just it is that a man [the appellant] who wants to injure his neighbor [by appealing] should injure himself! To have appealed without good grounds is to do a wrong; to have appealed wrongly and also with impunity is an encouragement to groundless appeals.

The *Oxford English Dictionary* defines a 'witch hunt' as 'a single-minded and uncompromising campaign against a group of people with unacceptable views or behaviour'. The definition fits the actions of some right-wing vigilantes, whose denunciations and campaigns, conducted with impunity, have regularly activated the CDF. But by no means always. For years the vigilantes (known to some as the 'spot it and stop it brigade') targeted Father Raymond Brown, one of the world's greatest New Testament scholars. Denunciations against him must have filled several mailbags at the CDF. But as far as I know, the CDF never took any action against him. When Brown died at the age of seventy, he was serving a second term as a member of the Pontifical Biblical Commission. Apparently in some instances the CDF was well aware that accusations were without foundation.

It is perhaps the very nature of its work which distorts the CDF's view. What happens to people whose daily task it is to scrutinize texts for heresy and/or near-heresy? Add, too, the fact that during the eighties the CDF was also given the unwelcome task of handling applications from priests who wished to be dispensed from their ministry. One would like to think that this task deepened the spiritual insight and sensitivity of the CDF staff members handling these cases. But it struck me at the time that they had to bear a doubly negative burden which could have regrettable psychological repercussions.

Over the years I have come to know a number of members of staff of the CDF. Some have been well balanced human beings and theologically well educated. But at least a few seemed to me to be unhappy individuals, discontented with themselves and with their neighbours. Some of those who came to work at the CDF without a doctorate never took advantage of their time in Rome to write a doctoral dissertation. Even if a doctorate in theology may not be essential for sharp theological judgement, the successful defence of a doctoral thesis is generally considered to indicate some expertise.

I was saddened by the use made of the *L'Osservatore Romano* as a vehicle for attacking theologians who were unable to respond, because *L'Osservatore* did not publish letters from readers. In late 1998 the American theologian Frank Sullivan, who had taught ecclesiology or the doctrine of the church at the Gregorian for thirty six years (1956–92), had to turn to the London *Tablet* to defend himself against such an attack in *L'Osservatore* from the pen of a leading CDF staff member.[32] When the CDF published in *L'Osservatore* a warning against ambiguities in the work of a deceased writer, the Indian Jesuit Anthony de Mello, and, in addition, included in *L'Osservatore* a lengthy, unsigned article directed against his work, one could not but feel that

---

32 See *L'Osservatore Romano* for 11 July 1998 and London *Tablet* for 26 September 1998.

the official journal of the Catholic Church was disregarding fair play.[33] The reform of the CDF cannot arrive too soon.

Vatican City

The Vatican City has around 3,500 employees. My contacts with those who work there were almost uniformly pleasant. Those who man the exceptionally busy post office set a far better standard of courtesy and efficiency than their counterparts in the Italian postal system. And I always found the Salesian Father Nicolò Suffi, former director of the Libreria Editrice Vaticana (LEV) or the Vatican publishing house, to be both professional and precise in his work. Occasionally he called on me for advice about books to be published or translations to be followed. But I was normally the one seeking help. The LEV published Italian translations of four of the books I authored, co-authored, or co-edited: *A Concise Dictionary of Theology* (1991), *Retrieving Fundamental Theology* (1993), *Experiencing Jesus* (1994), and *The Resurrection* (1997). Before publication Suffi let me check the Italian text, with a view to idiomatic English expressions which might have been inaccurately rendered into Italian. He seemed particularly happy to put on the back cover of the translation of the *Dictionary* a tribute I received from John Paul II himself, who had expressed the wish that 'the volume would enjoy a wide distribution as a precious instrument in the study of the Science of God'.

Another friendly Salesian, who not only worked at the Vatican but also lived in the large Governor's Palace within Vatican City, was the Venezuelan Cardinal Castillo Lara, whose nephew Raul wrote a doctoral dissertation under my direction. When I first met him, the Cardinal was already governor of Vatican City and in charge of its plumbers, builders, gardeners, security guards, and all the other

---

33 *L'Osservatore Romano*, 23 August 1998.

personnel who keep the tiny city state running. At our first meal together, he assured me with a smile that he was setting out to corrupt me on behalf of his nephew! I assured him that corruption was totally unnecessary — Raul was highly intelligent and likely to produce a first class dissertation which would gain its just reward! Raul was back in Venezuela when he completed the first draft. As his family never lacked connections, he gave the text to a pilot of the national airline. So it travelled in Rome under the pilot's seat! And the thesis was first class, as I had anticipated.

My experience with the Swiss Guard was almost always agreeable, apart from the occasion when I wanted to show my sister-in-law Posey and her daughter Victoria round the Vatican Gardens. An older looking and extremely gruff guard more or less made us stand to attention before allowing us into Vatican City. This was a few months before the tragic death of the commander of the Swiss Guard and his wife in May 1998. Both were shot dead by a corporal who then committed suicide. It quickly emerged that the Swiss Guard were both undermanned and underpaid, and that the corporal had allowed himself to become unbalanced as a result of the actions of his commanding officer, Alois Estermann. After the tragic deaths I wondered whether my gruff Swiss guard might in fact have been Alois Estermann. Whoever he was, he showed clear signs of the stress the corps were experiencing in early 1998.

Following the shootings the Vatican press officer, Dr Joaquin Navarro-Valls, rushed to assure journalists that the corporal in a fit of madness had shot his commanding officer, his commanding officer's wife, and then himself. Everything was totally clear. End of story. If Navarro-Valls had only said, it *appears* that this is what has happened. However, proper police investigations must take place before things can be clarified with any assurance.' As it was, the world's tabloid press went ballistic. Theories popped up like mushrooms: a love triangle, involving homosexual activity, connections with the Swiss banks — then under fire for taking Nazi gold in the Second World War — or even links with the recent visit to the Vatican of the Cuban leader Fidel Castro. After all the wife of the commander spoke Spanish and was a Latin American, even if her Venezuelan origin failed to put her very close to Cuba.

La Repubblica suggested espionage. The commander may have been Swiss but his native language was German. He *could* have been engaged in spying for East Germany. Hadn't a Jesuit [of course!] unearthed an East German spy in the Vatican? *La Stampa* retaliated by interviewing the legendary East German spy master, Markus Wolf, who dismissed the espionage theory as bunk. East Germany had indeed placed an agent in the Vatican but he was long gone and would have been over eighty if still alive.

The prize for journalistic fantasy must go to the French journalist who suggested a contract killing on behalf of one or more 'liberal' cardinals! The commanding officer had spent twenty years or more on duty in Vatican City and was a member of Opus Dei. He had been keeping a record of the suspicious comings and goings of liberal cardinals, and would have been in a position to spill the beans on them at the next papal election and thus force the election of a conservative cardinal! He had to be eliminated.

For once the Vatican press office story was correct. A young man had flipped out of his mind and killed two other people before taking his own life.

8

The Dupuis Case

Our lives contain too many characters for even the thickest novel. Hence I have limited severely the list of people recalled in this book. But the international stature of the Belgian theologian Jacques Dupuis (1923-2004) and the enormous stress and uncertainty with which the CDF (the Congregation for the Doctrine of the Faith) burdened him in his late seventies justify not only mentioning him but also making his experience the theme of this chapter.

Before the Storm

I first met Father Dupuis early in 1971 when I spent time with him at a Jesuit theological college (St Mary's, Kurseong) in north India near Darjeeling, where he had been teaching theology since 1959. After a semester as a visiting professor at Weston School of Theology in greater Boston and a month's study in Rome, I had broken my flight home to begin a new academic year in Melbourne (Australia). I had been asked to teach an intensive course on the theology of hope in Kurseong, one of the most beautiful places in the world, with its astounding views across rich forests and tea plantations to the majesty of Kanchenjunga rising to 28,000 feet. Besides his work as a professor of theology, Dupuis helped with Tibetan and other refugees along the frontier of India. A luminous intelligence shone through the glasses perched on his oval face. Wiry and tireless, despite bouts of bad health, he was most energetically hospitable. On our free days he took me to meet a wide variety of people, including the Sherpa Tensing, who shared in 1953 with the New Zealander Edmund Hillary the first proven ascent of Everest; in the early seventies Tensing headed a mountaineering school. As Dupuis raced his Yugoslavian motorcycle along the narrow roads of the Himalayan foothills, I clung to him for dear life, and prayed not to fall down the sheer precipices so close to our wheels. When his theological college shifted to Delhi later in 1971, Dupuis rode his motorcycle right across northern India to his new home.

A strong friendship had been forged with 'Jim', as I have always called him — the name by which he was known in India. Dupuis came to the Gregorian for a few weeks as a visiting professor. He seemed to enjoy the experience and in 1984 he left India and joined our theology faculty. Dupuis quickly made his mark as a first-rate teacher in our two-year, 'second cycle' in theology; his classes often drew well over two hundred students. He was not unknown in Vatican circles, not least because he had attended as an interpreter two synods or international meetings of bishops (in 1974 and 1983), and was also to work as an interpreter for the synods of 1985 and 1987. For ten years (1985–95) he acted as an official consultant on the Pontifical Council for Interreligious Dialogue, and played a key role in drafting a document jointly produced with the Congregation for the Evangelization of Peoples, *Dialogue and Mission* (May 1991). This document broke new ground by reflecting on the relationship between dialogue with other religions and the Christian mission to proclaim Jesus Christ. In 1985 he became the editor of our scholarly theological and philosophical quarterly, the *Gregorianum*, and we collaborated closely on the journal.

With the approval of the superior of the Jesuit community at the Gregorian, Dupuis asked me to be the in-house censor for *Who Do You Say that I Am?*, an introduction to Christian doctrine on Jesus

(1994). it followed his much acclaimed *Jesus Christ at the Encounter of World Religions* (1991). Both books appeared in English, French, Italian, and Spanish; *Who Do You Say that I Am?* easily proved itself the best seller in the fifteen volume series of basic texts in which it appeared. His next project was the sixth edition of doctrinal documents of the Catholic Church, *The Christian Faith* (1996). He had co-edited the five previous editions with a team of colleagues working in India, and the sixth was prepared with the help of eight other professors at the Gregorian. With that project off his hands, Dupuis set himself to complete his trilogy on Christ's person and redemptive mission by writing a major work on interreligious encounter.

Well ahead of time he asked me, again with the agreement of the community's superior, to take on the task of reading and censoring this third volume, on behalf of the Jesuit community at the Gregorian. He fed me the chapters over a period of three or four months, and I read the text closely, not only to check his theology but also to correct on occasions his English. Although French is his native tongue, after years in India he preferred to write in English. The result was the 447-page *Toward a Christian Theology of Religious Pluralism*, which appeared more or less simultaneously in English, French, and Italian at the end of 1997. While Orbis Books (Maryknoll, NY) were preparing the English edition, Dupuis had already passed on his manuscript for translation into Italian and French by the publishing houses of Queriniana (Brescia) and Cerf (Paris), respectively. The book was to appear also in Portuguese (1999) and Spanish (2000).

In October 1997 Dupuis flew off to the Catholic Institute of Paris for a presentation and a debate on the French edition of the book, which had been chosen as number 200 in the renowned *Cogitatio Fidei* series. The Italian publishers, together with the Italian Theological Association (ITA) and the rector of the Gregorian, Father (later

Archbishop) Giuseppe Pittau, also wanted to honor the appearance of this magisterial work with a solemn launch. This happened in the largest hall of the Gregorian on the late afternoon of 22 November 1997. The large crowd of students, the speeches from Fr. Pittau, the secretary of the Pontifical Council for Interreligious Dialogue (Bishop Michael Fitzgerald), the president of ITA, and myself, followed by a carefully crafted response from Dupuis, made it an unforgettable event.

In 1998 Dupuis learned that *Toward a Christian Theology of Religious Pluralism* had won an annual award from the Catholic Press Association in the United States. Numerous reviews were appearing in English, French, and Italian — the first, a very positive review, in the 22 November 1997 issue of *Avvenire*, which is owned by the bishops of Italy. My review was published by the London *Tablet* in January 1998, and Dupuis began composing an article for the Naples-based *Rassegna di teologia*, as he wanted to be in dialogue with his reviewers.

At Easter 1998 a tiny cloud appeared — in the shape of a very negative article published by *Avvenire* in its issue for 14 April. The author, a theologian who taught in Milan and was a world expert on the work of St Anselm of Canterbury (d. 1109), vigorously misrepresented and misreported Dupuis. The most charitable judgement was that the piece resulted from a rapid and careless reading of the book. Dupuis later learned that someone in the Vatican had commissioned that article. Meanwhile the theological public puzzled over the paper running a second piece on Dupuis's book after giving it a long review some months previously. Dupuis himself prepared nine pages of notes on the April article for our rector, Fr. Pittau, who promised to write a letter to *Avvenire*. But no such letter setting the record straight ever appeared; the editor of the paper subsequently denied that it had reached his desk.

Meantime, without waiting for Dupuis's theological peers to continue evaluating his new ideas, the CDF had gone into action against his book, prompted partly by secret denunciations coming from two professors of the Gregorian itself. At meetings held on 30 March and 4 April, strong criticisms were levelled against the book, especially by one consultor, who was a fellow member of the Gregorian's theology faculty. A further instance perhaps of a man's enemies being those of his own household (Matthew 10:36)? A second CDF meeting on 10 June 1998, an 'ordinary congregation' as they describe it, included a number of cardinals, one of whom afterwards admitted that he had never read Dupuis's book. Those present at that ordinary congregation voted in favour of taking action against the book, a step that would involve securing the Pope's permission, which was forthcoming a week later.

But Dupuis knew none of this at the time. When I returned to Rome from the United States in early August, he was out of town but had left for my comments the article he had prepared for *Rassegna di teologia*, in order to continue the dialogue with his reviewers. Another review, this time a highly significant one, had appeared a few weeks earlier, in the 18 July issue of *La Civiltà Cattolica*.[34] written by one of that journal's staff members. In a letter dated 14 July, the editor had informed Dupuis in advance about this review and told him that the censors at the Secretariat of State had introduced some 'modifications' into it, evidently the pointed questions that fill the concluding pages of the review. (Had these modifications and questions come from CDF staff members acting as censors for the Secretariat of State?) The editor added without naming names: 'They told me that they would be very glad if an article in reply from you could dissipate

---

34 Published by Italian Jesuits, *Civiltà Cattolica* has a close relationship with the Holy See, and Vatican censors check issues before their publication.

the misunderstandings, so that the affair could work itself out in the context of a theological debate.'

The Storm Breaks

Before publishing his response to that and other reviews with *Rassegna di teologia*, Dupuis had decided to wait for comments not only from me but also from Monsignor Luigi Sartori, an outstanding Italian theologian with whom he had also shared the draft of his article for *Rassegna*. In a letter dated 12 October 1998 Sartori forwarded two pages of precise and constructive comment. But by that time Dupuis had been stunned by a communication which had reached him from the CDF on 2 October, via the Jesuit superior general, Father Peter-Hans Kolvenbach.

A nine page, single-spaced document developed fourteen theses challenging *Toward a Christian Theology of Religious Pluralism*. A covering page explained that the CDF found in this work by Dupuis 'serious errors or doctrinal ambiguities on doctrines of divine and Catholic faith concerning revelation, soteriology [teaching on salvation], Christology and the Trinity'. They acknowledged his 'good intentions' and the fact that the book contained 'valid aspects'. But, for good measure, he was also accused of 'serious errors and doctrinal ambiguities' regarding truths concerned with the Kingdom of God, the Church, and the inspiration of the Bible. The page ended by naming several 'dangerous affirmations' that 'cannot be safely taught', such as the application of 'Mother' to the first Person of the Trinity. Dupuis was given three months to reply. Fr. Kolvenbach suggested his dropping the optional course (for which over two hundred Gregorian students had enrolled) and also a seminar that Dupuis was due to begin teaching on 19 October. This would ensure more time and greater peace in which to write his response to the CDF.

Dupuis began by spending two weeks in hospital. As a chronically sick man, this may have been inevitable. But the stress he experienced under the quite unexpected onslaught from the CDF unquestionably played its part. At the time I was away, enjoying a sabbatical semester as a visiting professor at Marquette University in Milwaukee. On Dupuis' behalf the dean of theology phoned me with the bad news, asking me to act as the one adviser the CDF allowed Dupuis. I faxed Jim immediately to say: 'you have not only my affectionate sympathy but total support — as consultor or whatever you want me to do in this affair with the CDF.'

I was particularly astonished and scandalized at the poor quality of much of the material contained in the fourteen theses prepared by the CDF which Dupuis sent on to me by special courier. I faxed back nine pages of comments on the theses, which repeatedly attributed to him views that he had not only never expressed in the book but also had in several passages explicitly rejected: for example, the bizarre notion of different heavens for the followers of different religious traditions. Thesis one attacked him for interpreting the Bible along the very lines recommended by the Pontifical Biblical Commission's 'The Interpretation of the Bible in the Church' (1993), the document for which Cardinal Ratzinger had himself written the preface! A number of the theses demonstrated a regrettable inability to attend to language and terminology: where Dupuis spoke of 'distinction', the CDF repeatedly accused him of 'separation' — an utterly vital matter, for example, in the theology of the Trinity: the three divine persons are distinct but not separate. There were further examples of the inability to catch basic linguistic nuances. Where Dupuis wrote of X being 'symbolized' by Y, the CDF charged him with 'identifying' X and Y. Running through their theses was a deep reluctance to acknowledge that the human condition assumed by the Second

Person of the Trinity is limited, unlike his divine nature. The thesis-writers were alarmed by Dupuis' references to the First Person of the Trinity as 'Father-Mother', even though he normally named God in the traditional way as 'Father, Son, and Holy Spirit' and made much of Jesus' relationship to 'Abba' or 'Father dear'. The CDF had forgotten how, during his less than five weeks as pope, John Paul I managed to talk of God as both Mother and Father (on 10 September 1978). They were presumably distressed at John Paul II using similar language at a public audience on 8 September 1999, when he said that God contains in himself 'all the characteristics of fatherhood and motherhood'. Of course, the perfect reader does not exist. One would, however, have expected competence from the CDF in at least correctly reading and interpreting what Dupuis had written. Far from being obscure, his meaning was clarified by repetitiveness in his writing.

Throughout my four months in Milwaukee I was in constant touch with Dupuis, and by the end of my sabbatical semester was already receiving the first sections of his draft response to the CDF. I urged him to break up his paragraphs and insert as many headings as possible. He had no guarantee that those who showed themselves incompetent readers of his book would miraculously become competent readers of his reply. On the last Sunday before leaving Milwaukee, I went off to a very cheerful Mass in a Black American parish; the effect of those hours of singing, praying, and clapping was to make me remember an editorial and compose a letter, 'In defence of Fr Dupuis', which appeared in the London *Tablet* for 12 December 1998:

> Sir, Your editorial on the case of Fr Jacques Dupuis (*The Tablet*, 21 November) was very welcome. Instead of his latest book, *Towards a Christian Theology of Religious Pluralism*, being strangely misinterpreted, he should be winning accolades everywhere for having now published six

editions of *The Christian Faith*, a collection of documents
from the teaching of the popes, councils and bishops
arranged thematically. The latest edition of 1996, which
takes the reader from the earliest creeds down to John
Paul II's 1995 encyclical *Ut Unum Sint*, has no equal in
any language. No one else in Christian history has ever
edited such a collection six times and thus performed
an extraordinary service for the official teaching of the
Catholic Church. The orthodox faith of a theologian who
has repeatedly and most generously dedicated himself to
such a task should be beyond question.

In *The Tablet* on 4 January 1998 I called Fr Dupuis' new
book on the theology of religious pluralism a "superb
contribution to inter-religious dialogue and theology."
What has struck me since writing that review is the way
he develops at theological length themes that come from
the Pope's teaching and example: for instance, the need
for inter-religious dialogue (which is definitely not the
same thing as a falsely tolerant pluralism), God as the
only One who is truly absolute, the maternal face of
God (see the 1980 papal encylical *Dives in Misericordia*),
the living actuality of the divine self-revelation whose
fullness will appear at the end (*Fides et Ratio*, 2 [John Paul's
encyclical on faith and reason of 14 September 1998]),
the obligation to interpret the inspired Word of God in
the specific contexts of today, a patently deep respect for
all "the treasures of human wisdom and religion" (*Fides
et Ratio* 31), and a special interest in Indian "religious
and philosophical traditions," to be drawn from with
discernment and sound criteria (*Fides et Ratio* 72). These

are all major themes of Fr Dupuis' book. Like John Paul II, Fr Dupuis recognises those treasures of religion through which millions of non-Christians will, we may confidently hope and pray, find salvation and be united with all the redeemed in the coming kingdom of the glorious Son of God. To condemn Dupuis' book would, I fear, be to condemn the Pope himself.

My last remark was no subtle piece of Jesuitry. I wondered then and still wonder now whether some Vatican officials were 'going after' John Paul II by 'going after' Dupuis. My suspicions were fed by the bigoted reactions to the Pope's meeting at Assisi on 27 October 1986 with leaders of other world religions. (Years later, when that Assisi meeting was repeated on 24 January 2002, certain curial cardinals were notably absent.)

Once back at the Gregorian before Christmas 1998, I carefully read the whole of the 190 page response which Dupuis had prepared for the CDF; I marvelled again at his theological culture and acumen. He had hardly handed the response over to Fr Kolvenbach for presentation to the CDF before matters took a distinct turn for the better. On 16 January 1999 the London *Tablet* carried a two-page article, entitled 'In Defence of Fr Dupuis', written by Cardinal Franz König, the retired Archbishop of Vienna, a prominent personality at the Second Vatican Council (1962–65), a longtime advocate of interreligious dialogue, and someone who was reputed to have played a major role in the election of John Paul II. The Archbishop of Calcutta and some other Catholic leaders had already expressed their support for Dupuis, but König's powerful advocacy could not be ignored. The Cardinal explained how he had been 'fascinated' by Dupuis 'latest masterly work', to which he had been alerted by my review of the book in the Tablet. This led some people in Rome to spread the rumour that this article in defence of Dupuis had been written by me for the Cardinal's signature. The style was said to betray my authorship. When König followed up his *Tablet* article with a long interview in the February issue of the Italian monthly *Trenta Giorni,* I took pleasure in pointing out how successful I had become in masquerading as a cardinal in his nineties and fooling the interviewer. The *Trenta Giorni* interview startled the CDF, above all because *Trenta Giorni,* then edited by the former Italian prime minister Giulio Andreotti, was considered to be safely conservative, at least in Church doctrine.

Shortly after that interview appeared, the *Tablet* carried an English translation of an open letter addressed to Cardinal König and signed by Cardinal Ratzinger, who had invited the London weekly to publish it. Ratzinger began by expressing his 'astonishment' and 'sadness' about the article König had published, and then went on to claim that the CDF's action 'had consisted simply in sending some confidential questions to Fr Dupuis and nothing more than that'. He rejected König's statement that the CDF 'may well suspect him [Dupuis] of directly or indirectly violating the Church's teaching'. I read these assertions with both sadness and astonishment. What Dupuis had received from the CDF included much more than 'some confidential questions'. The document that they sent Dupuis via Father Kolvenbach did contain *some* questions. But it began with fierce charges about the orthodoxy of Dupuis's book; he was explicitly accused of directly violating Church teaching. It made me sad that Cardinal Ratzinger (or, presumably, someone at the CDF writing in his name) could be so economical with the truth in a public letter to a very notable cardinal.

The use of the word 'dialogue' also astonished me. The letter to König repeatedly referred to the CDF's desire to 'dialogue' with Dupuis and to 'consult him personally'. 'If this is dialogue,' I thought,

'I would hate to see confrontation!' One had to work very hard to describe what had happened, or rather not happened, as 'dialogue'. Cardinal Ratzinger had never met Dupuis nor contacted him personally by phone or letter, let alone asked to sit down with him for a discussion. The initial set of theses against Dupuis' book were delivered to him indirectly — by the Jesuit superior general. When Dupuis submitted, again via his general, his lengthy response, he received no acknowledgment from the CDF.

Months of silence followed, and that played on Dupuis' nerves. In February 1999 he fell ill, and had to cancel a lecture trip to India and Japan — something to which he had been looking forward greatly. It did not seem to cheer him up when I assured him: 'Jim, you would never have been so famous but for the CDF's intervention. Your book is selling very well in three languages, and look at all those invitations you are receiving.' After Dupuis recovered, the Dominicans at Montpellier flew him to southern France to talk about his book. He also spoke in England at Douai Abbey to Benedictine leaders from around the world. Dupuis was the only theologian asked to give a paper at a remarkable meeting in Ferrara, which featured Claudio Abbado conducting Verdi's *Falstaff* and Jonathan Miller directing a play. The organizers of a joint meeting of Italian associations that represent various theological disciplines requested Dupuis' participation at their meeting scheduled for November 1999. In a courageous and well argued book, which the Urbaniana University Press had published in late 1998, a Roman biblical scholar, Giovanni Odasso, provided strong biblical underpinning for Dupuis's positions on salvation for non-Christians. Supportive letters poured in from such notable figures as René Latourelle, who had been dean of the theology faculty at the Gregorian for twelve years and was now living in retirement back in Montreal. When I noticed that publishers and journalists from the United States, Latin American theologians such as Gustavo Gutiérrez and Jon Sobrino, and scholars from Europe, Asia and the Middle East were regularly turning up at Dupuis's door. I assured him: 'Jim, you are becoming a shrine that pilgrims to Rome must visit.' Dupuis may have agreed with me in his mind, but not in his heart. He wanted to be loved by Mother Church, for whom he had given his life and energies with a tenacity that took my breath away. I failed to cheer him up when I told him that his critics did not truly represent Mother Church.

Another factor also played on Dupuis' nerves: our Jesuit general decided that Dupuis should postpone publishing in *Rassegna di teologia* his response to the Italian reviews of his book and in *Louvain Studies* his response to reviews that had appeared in English and French. Father Kolvenbach wanted to avoid irritating the CDF. Some of the reviews, for example, a long one in *Louvain Studies*, had entered into critical dialogue with Dupuis in a way that was admirable; others like an equally long piece in *Revue Thomiste* seemed a bizarre going back to a dead past. He was forbidden to respond and I could do little, apart from the case of one attack on Dupuis — in the May 1999 number of *Seminarium*, a journal published by the Vatican's Congregation of Catholic Education. The author, Fr Angelo Amato (later Cardinal Amato), whom Dupuis and I had known for years, lumped him together with a number of contemporary writers who drastically reduce the role of Christ as Saviour of the world. I wrote at once to Amato and said how 'saddened and scandalized' I was at a blatant misinterpretation of Dupuis. I explained exactly where the writer had misread the book, and sent copies of my letter to Cardinal Pio Laghi (the prefect of the Congregation of Education) and to his newly appointed deputy, Archbishop Giuseppe Pittau, the former rector of the Gregorian. I felt sick at heart that a Vatican publication could contain such unfounded criticism of Dupuis, when no defence was allowed.[35] The previous year the CDF had insisted that another Vatican publication, the bulletin of the Pontifical Council for Interreligious Dialogue, drop an article by Bishop Michael Fitzgerald, the secretary of that Council, who had written up the friendly and intelligent criticisms which he made at the November 1997 presentation of Dupuis' book. (Eventually this article was published in 2001 in bulletin 108 of *Pro Dialogo*.)

When I flew off to the United States and Australia to teach during the summer of 1999, Dupuis was about to take a holiday in Naples before a lecture tour in Bangladesh and India. In Melbourne on 30 July I received a fax from him to say that he had finally received a response from the CDF to the text he had handed over at the start of January; once again the response had not come to him directly but through our Jesuit general. The July response began with a letter which welcomed the clarifications offered by Dupuis' long document of December 1998, but naturally said nothing about the many places where he had shown the CDF's theses to be mistaken. The July document from the CDF included a shorter list of points detailing propositions which were considered 'erroneous or ambiguous or insufficient'. There were one or two new and bizarre elements in this communication from the

---

35 Back in March 1995 at a congress in Loreto, Dupuis publicly expressed his disagreement with what Amato had just said in his paper on 'the incarnation and the inculturation of the faith'. They were together again at a meeting of ITA held in Sicily (September 1997) on the theme of 'Christianity, Religion, and Religions'. Amato gave a major paper and stated his opposition to some of the things Dupuis had written in *Toward a Christian Theology of Religious Pluralism*, which had just been published. Dupuis was loudly applauded when he remarked: 'You wouldn't think that way if you had spent some time in India.' Amato evidently thought that there was nothing unethical about attacking Dupuis in his 1999 article in *Seminarium*, even though the Dupuis case was still *sub iudice* and Amato himself was deeply involved with it, both as a CDF consultor and as a major author or editor of *Dominus Iesus* (2000), the CDF declaration aimed, at least in part, against Dupuis.

CDF: for instance, the claim that a *question* Dupuis raised was contrary to faith. They appeared to have forgotten that questions as such can never be true or false. If questions can be against the faith, St Thomas Aquinas would have to be rejected as heretical, since he like many others raises numerous questions dealing with matters of faith. But, all in all, Dupuis thought the second document he received from the CDF more balanced and intelligent than its predecessor.

But there was bad news of Dupuis' health: he had been hemorrhaging and had been rushed to hospital. It turned out that he was not, as he feared, suffering from any cancer in his prostate or his kidneys. But he had to drop the trip to Bangladesh and India that had been scheduled to begin in late July.

Once again the CDF gave Dupuis three months to reply, but their requirements about confidentiality were not so strict this time. As well as sharing with me the second communication from the CDF, he was able to send copies of it to Cardinal König and Monsignor Sartori for suggestions. The embargo on his articles for *Rassegna di teologia* and *Louvain Studies* was lifted, and both articles appeared at the end of October 1999.

Dupuis's skirmish with the CDF was making me cry out for more love and more justice in the church. Primarily for love.[36] The CDF's misgivings about his book might have been solved by a phone call or by a personal invitation to join Cardinal Ratzinger over afternoon tea

---

36 Significantly the CDF declaration *Dominus Iesus* (of which more below) uses the terms 'truth'and 'true' 45 times, but the term 'love' only four times. Repeatedly the declaration quoted or referred to John Paul II's 1990 encyclical *Redemptoris missio* (the mission of the Redeemer), but the papal document differs significantly, not least because it uses 'love' 31 times and 'truth' 25 times. The statistics more than hint at the way the Pope appreciated how knowing (the truth) and loving mutually condition each other. The contrast between his mindset and that the CDF emerges even more strikingly if we recall his 1999 apostolic exhortation *Ecclesia in Asia* (the Church in Asia), a relevant document to which *Dominus Iesus* merely refers once. *Ecclesia in Asia* introduces 'love' 54 times and 'truth' 22 times.

for a serious, face-to-face discussion. They never met until September 2000 (of which more below), and they lived less than three miles from each other! When Dupuis fell ill in October 1998, half jokingly I suggested he should send the CDF his bill for hospital expenses. When he fell ill again in July 1999, I felt deeply saddened that it had never occurred to anyone at the CDF that a get well card, a phone call, or even a visit to Dupuis in hospital might be something Jesus would expect of them. No one at the CDF ever expressed any sympathy over his sicknesses for which they had some responsibility. One of them even made light of Dupuis's time in hospital describing it as a 'pyscho-somatic' affair.

And the need for more justice. Justice begins at home, the Washington-based Jesuit Ladislaus Örsy argued,[37] and he demonstrated that the procedures to which the CDF subjected Dupuis were not in accord with proper principles of justice: for example, the right of the accused to be present, to know his accusers, to defend himself (or to be represented by someone of his own choice) right from the time when his case begins to be heard. Far from being anything new to the Catholic Church, these provisions were laid down at the Fourth Lateran Council (1215) by Pope Innocent III:

He who is the object of an inquiry should be present at the process, and, unless absent through contumacy, should have the various headings of the inquiry explained to him, so as to allow him the possibility of defending himself; as well, he is to be informed not only of what the various witnesses have accused him but also of the names of those witnesses.

<hr>

37 Örsy's famous article on this theme written and published in German before the Dupuis affair, was fully translated into English for *Doctrine and Life* 48 (1998), pp. 453–65, and appeared in summary form in the *Tablet* for 16 January 1998 to accompany a piece by Cardinal König. Born in Hungary, Örsy taught for a number of years at the Gregorian University before moving to the United States. I cited Örsy in my article on reforming the CDF ('Art of the Possible') in the *Tablet* for 14 July 2012.

This stipulation calls to mind the warning made by St Bernard (1090–1153) almost a century earlier to one of Pope Innocent's predecessors: 'the murmuring of the churches' would not stop 'unless the Roman Curia ceased to give judgement in untried cases and in the absence of the accused' (*Letter* 48).

Perhaps the saddest irony of the whole Dupuis affair lies in the fact that in the very month he received word of the harsh charges against him (October 1998), John Paul II's desire to have the Catholic Church undertake a general 'examination of conscience' had brought together in the Vatican an international group of scholars for a symposium on the sins of the Inquisition, from which the CDF is the latter-day descendant. When making some archives of the Roman Inquisition available to scholars, Cardinal Ratzinger commented dryly: 'We know all the sins of the Church. And I hope more will not be added to them.' Pope John Paul II wanted the CDF to apologize for past wrongs and here they were perpetuating new ones!

The Storm Ends

As the city of Rome continued to collaborate generously with the Vatican in making the Great Jubilee Year of 2000 a holy and festive occasion, Dupuis immediately noticed one or two straws in the wind. In January the CDF held a plenary assembly, a meeting which occurs every two years and brings together its members from around the world. The address which Cardinal Ratzinger prepared for the Pope to deliver on 28 January placed a one-sided stress on the historical revelation communicated by Jesus Christ in the incarnation. No attention was paid to the other half of the truth — the revelation which will be completed at the end of history. Thus Vatican II's constitution on divine revelation was cited to show that Christ's first coming brought 'the fullness of all revelation', but there was no reference to what that document teaches two paragraphs later about 'the public revelation' that is to be 'expected' at 'the glorious manifestation of Our Lord, Jesus Christ'. In the same way the discourse cited a 'safe' passage from the Gospel of John, but overlooked the persistent New Testament theme that our present knowledge of God (even as Christians) is limited. We 'see through a glass darkly' as St Paul puts it in 1 Corinthians 13: 12, not 'face to face' as we shall do: 'now I know in part, but then I shall know even as I also am known.' The language of revelation in the New Testament is strongly angled towards the future.

In his 1998 encyclical on the relationship between faith and reason, *Fides et Ratio*, Pope John Paul II followed St Paul by speaking of 'that fullness of truth which will appear with the final revelation of God'. But the discourse delivered to the plenary session of the CDF on 28 January 2000 chose not to dwell at all on the mystery or the cloud of unknowing in which we all walk. In a second leader on 26 February the London *Tablet* noted the one-sided nature of the address put into the Pope's hands and added: 'Cardinal Ratzinger is said to be preparing a longer document on God's self-revelation in Christ. So we can surely look to that for a balanced account of the whole truth expressed by the Scriptures and teaching of the Church.'

The editor of the *Tablet* did not suggest any names when describing the context of the papal address: 'There is no Catholic enterprise which is more risky at present than dialogue with the world's great religions, and some of the theologians who have engaged in it most closely have retired hurt. This is because of the discouragement they have received from the Congregation for the Doctrine of the Faith.' Other journalists went further to specify the precise targets: Asian theological views of world religions and Dupuis himself. Without naming him personally, the CDF wanted to express its misgivings about his theological formulations.

When I left the Gregorian at the end of June 2000 to lecture in the United States and return to Rome via Australia, Dupuis was still waiting for any reaction to the sixty-page reply (which he had submitted the previous November) to the second document received from the CDF. In the middle of August he contacted me by fax in Melbourne with the news that the CDF had prepared a 'declaration' (*Dominus Iesus*) on Christ's unique and universal impact as Saviour and a 'notification' on his book. Cardinal Ratzinger had invited him to a meeting scheduled for 9.30 a.m. on Monday 4 September, the day before *Dominus Iesus* was to be published.

On Friday 1 September, I returned to the Gregorian and found that Dupuis had just received that day copies of the 15 page 'notification' on his book and the 32 page text of *Dominus Iesus*, both officially approved by the Pope the previous 16 June. We had the weekend to digest the two documents and prepare our comments. We knew that the CDF intended to publish *Dominus Iesus* on Tuesday 5 September and the 'notification' against Dupuis later in the same week. When rejecting 'certain' false views about Christ and other religions, *Dominus Iesus* provided no names. But following up its publication within a few days by also publishing the 'notification' would indicate that Dupuis was *the* target or at least a major target of *Dominus Jesus*. He was to be hit twice within the same week.

On the morning of Saturday 2 September, rather than let Dupuis and myself make our way to the Jesuit Curia or headquarters up near the Vatican, Fr Kolvenbach came for a briefing session at the Gregorian. A week earlier, before flying out of Melbourne for London and Rome, I had gone for another briefing session — over supper with a red-haired nephew of mine, an outstanding Australian barrister. 'You'll be facing a Star Chamber,' he remarked, when I explained that on 4 September the members of the CDF would be accusers, jury, and judges all in one.[38] 'My advice,' he added, 'is not to get into a fight. Take things with them in the spirit of "there's a problem here; let's work out our solution".'

The morning of the meeting in the CDF building (facing what is still called 'the piazza of the Holy Office') turned out to be oppressively hot. Cardinal Ratzinger sat in the middle, with Fr Kolvenbach, Dupuis, and myself on his left and Archbishop Tarcisio Bertone (secretary of the CDF) and Angelo Amato (as a CDF consultor) on his right. Copies of Dupuis' book were spread around the table. But there were no bottles of water available, nor was any tea or coffee ever made available. After some opening words from the Cardinal, Fr Kolvenbach briefly pointed out that the 'notification' against the book of Dupuis made numerous accusations but provided no page references from the book itself. He knew that I would take up this issue in full detail. When Ratzinger asked Dupuis to speak, he seemed a little surprised when Dupuis said that I would be speaking on his behalf.

The Cardinal gave me nearly an hour to go through the 'notification' and show how various false positions it listed were simply not found in the book of Dupuis. For example, Dupuis never wrote of the redemptive 'work' of the eternal Son of God being *separated* from the human activity of Jesus. Dupuis *distinguished* the 'operations' of the divine nature of Christ from those of his human nature, as did the Council of Chalcedon in 451 and, even more clearly, the Third Council of Constantinople in 680/81. But Dupuis never proposed *separating* the divinity and humanity of Christ, which would be equivalent to

---

38 Starting in the late 15th century, the Court of the Star Chamber sat in an apartment of the royal palace of Westminster, which was said to have gilt stars on the ceiling. In the service of the Crown's interests, this court became an instrument of tyranny and was abolished in 1641.

proposing two persons at work for the salvation of human beings: the eternal Son of God and the historical Jesus of Nazareth. Likewise, Dupuis never alleged that the Holy Spirit enjoys a sphere of operation which is separated from that of the crucified and risen Christ. Nor did Dupuis ever write of the Church as merely 'one way of salvation' and of non-Christian religions as 'equivalent ways of salvation'. The Cardinal heard me out, with Archbishop Bertone and Fr Amato never interrupting me to say: 'But Fr Dupuis does hold that opinion. See page so and so in his book.'

I drew attention to the fact that the 'notification', more or less blatantly, accused Dupuis of holding views about Christ, the Holy Spirit, and the Church, which are contrary to Catholic faith and doctrine. After six of the eight positive propositions which it contained, the text added some such phrase as 'hence it is contrary to the faith of the Church to hold' such and such a opinion. In this context, the inevitable and unjust implication was that Dupuis held such false views, even though no incriminating passages from his book were ever cited or even referred to. (In the event my protest over this 'style' failed, as the third and final text of the 'notification', for all its modifications, was to maintain this unjust style of implied accusation.)

To press home my defence of Dupuis, I illustrated my unease about the inaccurate and even false use of biblical references and quotations in the 'notification'. Without any discussion, the 'notification' quoted, for instance, John 1: 9: 'the Word is the true light which illuminates every human being coming into the world.' Dupuis, however, had appealed to some notable biblical scholars who find a different meaning in the verse: 'the Word was coming into the world, that Word which illuminates every human being'. This translation respects more clearly the distinct and enduring divine activity of the eternal Word of God. Like the speech put into the hands of the Pope the previous January, the 'notification' ignored key texts of the New Testament to insist unilaterally on the completeness of the revelation brought through the incarnation of the Son of God.

After giving details of these and further examples of the way the scriptures were misused in the 'notification', I suggested, in conclusion, that the CDF might reduce the text to the eight positive propositions which it had already listed: for instance, that Jesus Christ is the universal mediator of salvation for all human beings. 'All of us here, starting from Fr Dupuis,' I said, 'could happily subscribe to this list.' I had typed out the eight propositions on one page, ready for everyone's signature. For good measure, I added: 'We all know that the Congregation for the Doctrine of the Faith has a negative public image. To publish a set of positive formulations on which Fr Dupuis and the Congregation agree would end the affair happily, surprise the media, and do some real good.'

When I finished, Cardinal Ratzinger commented: 'Father O'Collins, I see that you share the views of Father Dupuis.' I thought it neither the time nor the place to reply: 'Eminence, a lawyer is not his client.' The Cardinal was obviously impressed by my protests over the misuse of scripture: 'Let's drop all the biblical references and leave the discussion to the exegetes.' It was also clear that he could not go ahead and publish the 'notification' as it stood.

Before adjourning the meeting, Ratzinger asked Dupuis whether he would help the CDF improve the text of the 'notification'. 'But I have already sent you 260 pages of answers to your questions,' Dupuis protested. He looked amazed when the Cardinal then retorted: 'You can't expect us to read and study all that material.' Ratzinger then asked Dupuis: 'Would you agree that your book should be understood in the light of *Dominus Iesus?*' 'You are asking too much, Eminence,' Dupuis replied.

With that, the meeting ended after more than two hours, and the 'notification' was not published. A document approved for publication by the Pope the previous June was quietly dropped.

The following day, as planned, the CDF published the declaration on 'the uniqueness and saving universality of Jesus Christ and the Church', *Dominus Iesus.* Right from the press conference which presented it, the document with its repeatedly negative tone raised a storm of protests, especially about the relations of the Catholic Church to others. Various Christians, including such leaders as the head of the Anglican Communion, Archbishop George Carey, felt that some unfortunate remarks the document included about what it called 'ecclesial communities' undercut progress made through ecumenical dialogues. Muslims and others were upset by a passage about 'followers of other religions' being in 'a gravely deficient situation' (art. 22). Jews were offended by the way it glossed over their special relationship to the Church. A day of dialogue in Rome between Jews and Christians scheduled for 3 October was cancelled. *Dominus Iesus* upset followers of world religions and Christians concerned with interreligious dialogue by distinguishing between the 'faith' proper to Christians have and the mere 'belief' which followers of other religions profess. In a private letter to the editor of the London *Tablet*, I wrote:

> Surely, wherever human beings respond to the divine initiatives, there is faith. What about Hebrews 11, which offers a wonderful vision of the faith that exists before and beyond the call of the chosen people? How can *Dominus Iesus* cope with the salvation of others, if it is

impossible to please God without faith? Will mere belief do the trick? DI's distinction between faith and belief is false and dangerous: 'We have faith, but those poor chaps can only have belief.' This is naked triumphalism.

That same letter also remarked on a deep inconsistency in the document. On the one hand, it seemed to interpret the religions as resulting from a purely human quest for God (art. 7). But, on the other hand, it went on (art. 8, 12, 21) to follow the lead of John Paul II by recognizing that the treasures of spirituality in the world religions come from the divine initiative. If God takes the initiative, these religions cannot be 'dismissed' as resulting from a human quest. The work and saving plan of God are always much more important than any human efforts or failures.

There was a widespread concern about the negative impact of the CDF's declaration on the relationship between the Catholic Church and the world religions and the other Christian Churches. The Pope felt it necessary to assure Queen Elizabeth II when she visited him that there could be 'no turning back' from the ecumenical course.

Cardinal Edward Cassidy, the president of the Pontifical Council for Promoting Christian Unity, and his number two, Bishop Walter Kasper, who had little or nothing to do with the preparation of the document, were clearly distressed at the negative results from *Dominus Iesus*. They were doing their best to mend bridges. But, when I wrote to both of them on 3 October, my concern was with the Dupuis case:

> On 4 September, as seems to be widely known, I spoke for Fr Dupuis as an informal meeting of the CDF, apropos of a 'notification' (seemingly now postponed) on his book, *Toward a Christian Theology of Religious Pluralism*. Enclosed are the outlines, which I used and left with

Cardinal Ratzinger at the end of the meeting; they may be of interest to you. What bothered me in the 'notification' (which I received only two days before the meeting) was not its eight positive formulations (gathered on p. 3 of my notes); they are more than acceptable to Fr Dupuis and any other orthodox Catholic. I was and am concerned about what came after six of these formulations. What followed formulations 2–6 and 8 denounced and rejected some false views. In the context of the 'notification', this clearly amounted to attributing to Dupuis these false views; and he simply has not and does not defend these false views. In brief, he seems to be accused of things that one cannot find anywhere in his book. He happily accepts the eight positive formulations, but he can hardly retract (false) views which are attributed to him but which he has never endorsed.

Since both Cassidy and Kasper were members of the CDF, I thought it might help to spell matters out very frankly for them. On different Sundays before Christmas, they came as my guests to lunch at the Gregorian.

But by that time Dupuis was troubled by a new, if much shorter (only 7 instead of 15 pages), version of the 'notification' which the CDF sent him through Fr Kolvenbach. The three pages of background information in the new text made no reference either to the first version or to the meeting of 4 September. It had been approved for publication by the Pope in an audience with Cardinal Ratzinger on 24 November. Dupuis was asked to sign at once without any further discussion. Every scriptural reference and much else had been dropped — in particular, some strange pages which had played down the role of the Holy Spirit in the work of human redemption.

But the new version maintained the unjust style of adding after six of the positive formulations 'hence it is against Catholic faith to hold' so and so — with the (unproved) implication that Dupuis held such a false view. However, this new text, instead of speaking of 'errors and serious ambiguities', had softened matters to 'serious ambiguities and difficulties', while adding that, 'independently of the author's intentions', the book could lead readers to adopt 'erroneous or dangerous opinions'. Despite his misgivings about the way the CDF would interpret his signature, in mid-December Dupuis signed this second version of the 'notification'.

When the CDF finally published the 'notification' on 26 February 2001, it turned out to be a third version, officially approved by the Pope a month earlier and somewhat different from the text Dupuis had signed before Christmas. Several pages had been dropped, and some points softened: 'serious ambiguities and difficulties' on points of doctrine had become 'notable ambiguities and difficulties', even if — as before — these ambiguities could lead readers to 'erroneous or dangerous opinions'. What distressed Dupuis, however, were four new lines in the document: 'with his signature of the text the author has committed himself to agree with the theses set out [in the notification] and in his future theological activity and publications to follow the doctrinal contents indicated in the notification, the text of which will have to appear in reprints, new editions or translations of the book in question.' After Dupuis had signed the document, it seemed an abuse to add such a passage without his knowledge.

On 27 February fifteen journalists (American, British, German, French, Italian and Spanish speaking) came to the Gregorian and met Dupuis at a conference which I chaired for him. Alexandra Stanley of the *New York Times* was there and wrote an article which appeared in her paper on 1 March. Curiously no one attended from any of the major Italian daily papers. Richard Boudreaux of the *Los Angeles Times* had phoned me the night before, and on 27 February itself was the first into print with his article, 'Vatican has "Difficulties" with Jesuit's Book on Pluralism'.

The London *Tablet* for 3 March ran a leader ('the Church and Other Faiths'), reprinted the final version of the 'notification', and quoted my account of its significance. I was 'glad to find' that the CDF 'had not included any sanctions whatsoever' against Dupuis nor asked him 'to change a single line in subsequent editions of the book'. Dupuis, I insisted, accepted 'the eight positive affirmations which constitute the heart of the notification'. He also agreed with the CDF 'in rejecting the false opinions which are also indicated'. But Dupuis 'could not retract these opinions, as he never held them'. The CDF seemed to 'agree with Fr Dupuis's continued insistence on this, since the notification 'did not include any page references to his book, let alone quotations from it, for any of these false opinions'.

The Final Years

With what he called 'a sense of recovered though limited freedom', Dupuis returned to his writing and lecturing. In September 2001 the Brescia publishing house of Queriniana put out his *Il cristianesimo e le religioni* (Christianity and the Religions), a shorter version of the book which the CDF had investigated. Dedicated to Cardinal König, this new book, which had been completed by March 2000, added a few more arguments in support of distinguishing between the human and divine activity of the incarnate Son of God and modified some terminology. For instance, Dupuis had accepted a suggestion from me and now described the relationship between the Church and other religions as one of 'asymmetrical complementarity'. He wrote this new book in Italian, in response to Queriniana's long-standing request to provide a work which could be more accessible to interested but non-theological readers. (It was to take a year for this book to be translated into French and English and be published in late 2002 by Cerf and Orbis, respectively.)

Dupuis continued to accept invitations to lecture in various centres in Italy and elsewhere. In May 2001 he flew to Brussels to speak on 'The Word of God, Jesus Christ and the religions of the world'. The editor of *La nouvelle revue theologique* asked for the text and printed it in the last number for the year. In September Dupuis was in Poland for a congress organized by the Catholic University of Lublin; his paper, 'Unity and Pluralism: Christianity and the Religions', was published in the proceedings of the congress, which were available for the participants on their arrival. In October Dupuis flew to London and delivered the *Tablet* open day lecture, 'Christianity and other religions: from confrontation to encounter', which was published by the *Tablet* in three installments (20 and 27 October, and 3 November 2001).

At the end of the year Dupuis took up again the declaration *Dominus Iesus* and the subsequent 'notification' on his *Toward a Christian Theology of Religious Pluralism*. Shortly after those two documents appeared, he had subjected them to some detailed and scorching evaluation, but his Jesuit superiors judged it wiser not to insert these pages as epilogues in his new book, *Il cristianesimo e le religioni*. Now over Christmas and New Year he revised his comments, and his serene tone showed up even more devastatingly the weaknesses of the two documents. Until recently only one or two colleagues like myself had read his forty pages. Now they have been published by William Burrows.[39]

But in mid-January 2002 Dupuis's new found serenity was shattered by a letter, signed by Cardinal Ratzinger and prompted by

---

39 William R. Burrows (ed.), *Jacques Dupuis Faces the Inquisition: Two Essays by Jacques Dupuis on Dominus Iesus and the Roman Investigation of His Work* (Cascade, OR: Pickwick, 2012).

someone 'denouncing' to the CDF the chapter Dupuis contributed to
the proceedings of the recent Lublin congress and his recent article in
La revue nouvelle théologique. Strangely, nothing was said about his new
book, even though the papers he delivered in Brussels and Lublin
more or less reproduced sections from that book, which had been
available in Italian bookstores for several months. The Cardinal was
'disturbed' by the two articles repeating opinions which conflicted with
the CDF's declaration *Dominus Iesus* and its subsequent 'notification'
on Dupuis's *Toward a Christian Theology of Religious Pluralism*. Ratzinger
asked the Jesuit General 'with all the authority which belongs to
you', to require Dupuis to refrain in the future from repeating views
incompatible with the CDF's two documents. The Cardinal added
that, were Dupuis not to do so, 'the opportuneness' of his continuing
as director of the *Gregorianum* 'would have to be reconsidered'.

With William Burrows and Jacques Dupuis, late 2002

A four-page document, evidently written by Angelo Amato, accompanied the Cardinal's letter and listed 'ambiguous formulations and erroneous opinions' which, even after the CDF's two documents, Dupuis repeated in the two recent articles. Dupuis shared with me the four pages of criticisms, some of which struck me as hardly reconcilable with the doctrine of the early councils of the Church. I shared my astonishment in letters to Fr Kolvenbach and the rector of the Gregorian. The idea of 'the divine activity of the eternal Logos being "eclipsed" or "circumscribed"' left me astonished. It seemed to 'sweep aside the teaching of the Third Council of Constantinople about the divine "energies and operations" of the eternal Son of God not being lost or suppressed in and through the incarnation'. That Council 'speaks not merely of the two wills but of all the operations' of both the divine and human natures being 'maintained' in the incarnation. Another statement caught my eye in those pages of attack on Dupuis's articles: 'the Word as such is the Word incarnate.' This ignored the fact that from all eternity the Word existed as such 'before' being incarnated. I had 'very serious difficulties about the orthodoxy' of this statement. Should one change the opening of John's Gospel and make it read 'in the beginning was the Word incarnate'? This would make the incarnation a sham, the mere unveiling of an eternal state of affairs (the Son of God actually equipped with a human nature from 'the beginning').

In the letters to my superiors, I pointed out how in Amato's text 'Dupuis is not always accurately represented. Appropriate sentences are quoted from him, but then his words are twisted or not precisely exegeted.' It seems that 'something bigger' than issues between two theologians 'is at stake. What Dupuis writes about the activity of Christ and his Spirit in and for "others" seems to me to parallel teaching and practice that has come from the Holy Father himself.'

By a curious coincidence it happened that three days after Dupuis received the latest bombshell from Cardinal Ratzinger, the CDF concluded its biennial plenary meeting at an audience with John Paul II. The Cardinal reported that during the previous two years 'important notifications had positively concluded dialogues with three theologians who represent different areas of theology (dogmatic, moral and liturgical)'. The Cardinal mentioned the names, with Dupuis being the dogmatic theologian in question, and continued: 'The modalities of these dialogues and above all their conclusion have been exemplary as to how a fruitful collaboration between the magisterium of the Church and theologians can be developed nowadays.' Some of the nuances in the Pope's response were not lost on its hearers and readers. He recommended to the members of the CDF more reflection on the 'dynamic of the means of mass communication' (a reference to the reactions to *Dominus Iesus*), respect for theologians and people of culture, the value of 'mutual listening', and the 'centrality of the love of Christ in our existence'. Unlike his speech to the CDF's plenary session two years earlier in 2000, one heard this time much more of the deep concerns of John Paul II to proclaim effectively the good news of Christian and Catholic faith.[40]

Right at the time that this further strike arrived from the CDF, Dupuis was booked to participate in (but not deliver a lecture at) a meeting on Muslim-Christian relations to take place at Lambeth Palace, London, 17-18 January. It had been organized by the Archbishop of Canterbury and funded by the British government. George Carey and the Prime Minister, Tony Blair, wanted to do their best for interreligious dialogue in the aftermath of the destruction of the Twin Towers. Superiors thought it more prudent for Dupuis to cancel that London trip, as well as a visit to Lisbon where he was

---

40 For further analysis see the London *Tablet* for 26 January 2002, p. 27.

to deliver a lecture on 6 February. (In the event, that lecture, the text of which Dupuis had sent in advance, was read in his absence.) But by mid-February, through meetings with Cardinal Ratzinger and with Dupuis himself, Fr Kolvenbach encouraged Dupuis to keep up his theological activity. As Dupuis summarized the new situation, while 'saying and writing what he believed open to theological discussion', he was obliged, where he did not fully agree with some theological assertions of the declaration *Dominus Iesus* and the 'notification', to inform his audience about this clearly and to propose his own opinions with modesty and in full submission to the Church's magisterium or official teaching.

The situation was cleared up, and Dupuis was back on the road or, more often in the air, to deliver lectures in Italy and abroad. This activity continued after the summer holidays of 2002, when from 1 October he finished his eighteen-year stint as editor of the *Gregorianum*. He was not happy about all the circumstances in which he passed the baton to a younger editor. But on 5 December he celebrated his 79th birthday, and it was time to give up the heavy work of directing an academic quarterly. With his commitments lightened, he began writing a memoir (*Do Not Stifle the Spirit*) and continued accepting invitations to attend conferences and deliver lectures. From the end of 2002 and through 2003 these invitations were to take him to Belgium, France, Holland, India, Mexico, Poland, Portugal, Switzerland, Thailand, and the United States, as well as to various cities within Italy. A bit reluctantly he came to recognize that 'the measures taken' by the CDF, besides bringing him 'to the notice of theologians the world over and eliciting much sympathy', also massively boosted the sales of *Toward a Christian Theology of Religious Pluralism* in five languages. Dupuis added in his unpublished memoir: 'Someone suggested with a grain of humour that I ought to be thankful to Cardinal Ratzinger for the fame acquired and the publicity received.' Apropos of the latter, in September 2002 I drew Dupuis' attention to something the Cardinal said to a group of 120 newly ordained bishops who were attending a course in Rome: 'When a theologian appears to stray from a truth of the Catholic faith, his bishop must react with prudence, attempt to read the theologian's work in a positive light, and spend time personally discussing the issues with him.'

To celebrate the eightieth birthday of Dupuis (5 December 2003), Dan Kendall and I prepared a volume in his honour, *In Many and Diverse Ways* (Orbis Books) and invited eighteen scholars to write essays for the book. They included two cardinals (Avery Dulles and Franz König) and two archbishops (Henry D'Souza and Michael Fitzgerald). We added a 38-page bibliography of writings by Dupuis (1960-2003) and an eleven-page bibliography of publications (especially reviews) concerned with the book which the CDF had challenged, *Toward a Christian Theology of Religious Pluralism*. Well before the date of Dupuis' birthday, I went to see Fr Kolvenbach. He gave his official blessing to presenting in the Aula Magna of the Gregorian University our volume in honour of Dupuis.

After several speeches (by myself, the publisher and others), some testimonials to the work of Dupuis were read. He concluded the proceedings with an account of his vocation as a theologian. The audience was deeply moved when Dupuis declared that Jesus Christ had been 'the one passion' of his life. He ended by saying: 'I trust that the Lord who reads the secrets of hearts will know my intention in writing what I have written and saying what I have said has only been to express to the best of my ability my deep faith in him and my total dedication to him.'

By December 2003, I felt glad to have done something for

Dupuis. He was grateful for two articles I had published that year in his support.[41] The celebration and volume in his honour ended the year on a cheerful note. I hoped that the sufferings which Dupuis had endured were now over. But the last year of his life turned very painful, not least because of a further challenge coming from the CDF.

On 11 October 2003 Dupuis had delivered a lecture ('Interreligious Dialogue, a Challenge to Christian Identity') at an international congress in Fatima (Portugal) — a country where not only the Cardinal Patriarch of Lisbon but also the bishop of Fatima were committed to inter-faith dialogue. When he received the provisional programme for the congress, Dupuis saw that he was scheduled to be the second-to-last speaker and that Cardinal Ratzinger was to deliver the final paper. At the congress itself Dupuis found that the Cardinal was no longer listed and that someone else was to give the final lecture. The Patriarch of Lisbon, a number of bishops, and many theologians attended the congress, and, seemingly, found Dupuis' lecture acceptable and helpful. After the proceedings were published in mid-2004, I read Dupuis' chapter and was astonished to learn that Fr Kolvenbach had received complaints from the CDF that this chapter, along with a similar talk Dupuis had given in New York (in early 2004), undermined the uniqueness of Jesus Christ.

On 10 November 2004 I wrote a long letter to Fr Kolvenbach and a few days later summarized what I took to be the CDF's three main concerns. (1) First, they worried over Dupuis's view of what is 'absolute'. At the Fatima congress he had said: 'We must insist on the unsuitability of using the terms 'absolute'...for Christianity as an historic religion and indeed for the historic humanity of Jesus. While

---

41 'Christ and the Religions', *Gregorianum* 84 (2003), pp. 347–62; 'Jacques Dupuis's Contribution to Interreligious Dialogue', *Theological Studies* 64 (2003), pp. 388-97.

the humanity of Jesus is the personal human being of the Son of God, it remains by its very nature created, limited, and contingent. God alone is the Absolute.' In support of this version of 'absolute', one can cite the authority of St Thomas Aquinas, other classical authors, and Pope Paul VI.[42] In its classical sense, 'absolute' means a) simply necessary and totally independent in its existence, b) free from any limitations, c) unconditioned, and d) not open to change. As regards a), the incarnation of the Son of God was a free act of divine love. Hence the coming into being of the created humanity of Christ cannot be called 'simply necessary'. After the incarnation, the humanity of Christ as such was not and is not totally independent. As regards b), the human being of Christ was that of a first-century, Jewish male, and hence limited by time, culture and sex — not to mention other limitations. As regards c), the humanity of Christ was conditioned by various historical, cultural and religious factors. As regards d), the humanity of Christ was open to change: e.g. the growth to adulthood (Luke 2: 52) and, at the end, the change of death. In short, to use 'absolute' for the historic humanity of Christ (and even more for Christianity as an historic religion) is careless, dangerous and even doctrinally false talk, and hence rightly excluded by Dupuis.

(2) Second, the CDF challenged Dupuis' position about the human nature of Christ being and remaining 'created, limited and contingent'. Yet Dupuis had two councils on his side, even if he did not explicitly appeal to them in his Fatima lecture: the Council of Chalcedon (451) and the Third Council of Constantinople (680/81). Chalcedon taught that 'proper character of the two natures' of Christ 'are preserved as they come together in one person'. Constantinople III drew on Chalcedon to teach that 'the operations' of the two natures were neither separated

---

42 In his 1976 apostolic exhortation *Evangelii nuntiandi*, Paul VI wrote that only God is 'absolute' (art. 27).

nor blended together. Now 'the proper character' of a human nature is to be created, limited and contingent. To allege that the human nature of Christ is uncreated, unlimited and necessary would be incompatible with the teaching of those two councils about 'the proper character' of Christ's humanity and its operations.

(3) A third concern of the CDF bore on the claim by Dupuis that 'through the experience and testimony of the others, they [Christians] will be able to discover at greater depth certain aspects, certain dimensions of the Divine Mystery that they had perceived less clearly and that have been communicated less clearly by Christian tradition'. This position presupposes the teaching of the Second Vatican Council (1962–65). In its Constitution on Divine Revelation, *Dei Verbum* (the Word of God), the Council taught that the self-revelation of God has reached a 'fullness' in Christ (art. 2); he 'completes and perfects' revelation at his death and resurrection, along with the coming of the Holy Spirit (art. 4). But *Dei Verbum* did not so emphasize the 'fullness' as to forget what is still to come, 'the glorious manifestation of the Lord' at the end of history (art. 4). The constitution did *not* claim that our present knowledge of God as revealed in Christ is definitive or absolute. That would have ignored the way in which, as we saw above, the language of divine revelation in the New Testament is strongly angled towards the future (e.g. 1 Cor 13: 12; 1 John 3: 2). John Paul II taught the same thing in his 1998 encyclical *Fides et Ratio*; he quoted St Paul's language about our seeing now 'through a glass darkly' and not yet 'face to face'.

In the light of this teaching from the New Testament, Vatican II, and John Paul II, one should agree with Dupuis and refuse to say that through revelation Christians now perceive with total clarity and at full depth all aspects and dimensions of the Divine Mystery. Hence, while not communicating *new truths* about God that are not found in the revelation completed by Christ (something Dupuis never alleged), members of other religions, through prayerful dialogue, might be the means used by the Holy Spirit to help Christians grasp a little more clearly and at greater depth aspects of the Divine Mystery already revealed to Christians but previously perceived by them less clearly.

For two reasons, one might expect the enrichment Dupuis mentioned in his Fatima lecture. One is the 'seeing-through-a-glass-darkly' character of the present knowledge Christians have received from divine revelation. The second reason is the universal presence and activity of the Holy Spirit expounded in various documents by John Paul II. Dupuis was firmly in line with that teaching when he said in his lecture: 'the principal agent of interreligious dialogue is the Spirit of God who animates people'. It would not be surprising that through sincere and prayerful dialogue with 'others', Christians could find themselves helped by the Holy Spirit to perceive more clearly and at greater depth certain aspects of the Divine Mystery, which they already 'know' but only 'notionally'.

When we talked over the CDF's latest challenge to his work and I shared my criticisms of them, I told Dupuis: 'Jim, Amato is so concerned to show that you are wrong that he is now mounting arguments that are incompatible with Catholic doctrine.' But Dupuis felt sick at heart over the renewed attack and was ready to let Fr Kolvenbach arrange for me to meet Amato (now Archbishop Amato) and discuss the new assault on Dupuis. That meeting was to take place in early 2005. But by that time Dupuis had died and so I never had the chance of returning to the CDF on his behalf.

In October 2004 Dupuis spoke in London before flying across the Atlantic to lecture in Washington, DC. This trip was to take him also to the University of Notre Dame (Indiana) but was cut short when he fainted and had to spend some days in the infirmary at Georgetown

University. He returned to Rome and in November celebrated the fiftieth anniversary of his ordination to the priesthood. On 26 December at supper with him in the refectory of the Gregorian University, I put out an arm to catch him when he rose from table and nearly fell to the floor. A day later he did fall and suffered (or had already suffered) a cerebral hemorrhage. The following day he died in hospital.

Visitors, including Archbishop Michael Fitzgerald (from the Pontifical Council for Interreligious Dialogue), helped to fill the community chapel at the Gregorian for the funeral Mass. Afterwards I went out to the cemetery to lead the prayers when we buried Dupuis in the mausoleum for Jesuits who die in Rome. A young Indian priest burned some incense and sang a hymn in Malayalam, the language of Kerala (southern India), before the metal coffin was placed in its niche.

Many papers and journals carried obituaries: *The Boston Globe* (11 January 2005); *The Guardian* (15 January 2005); *The Independent* (1 January 2005); *Nouvelle Revue Théologique* 127(2005), pp. 177-79; *Rassegna di teologia* 46 (2005), pp. 123-31; *The Tidings* of Los Angeles (21 January 2005); *The Times* of London (12 January 2005).[43] In *The National Catholic Reporter* John Allen wrote warmly of Dupuis and so too did Gerard O'Connell in a number of Asian papers. My obituary of Dupuis appeared in the London *Tablet* (8 January 2005) and ended by saying: 'Because of his fidelity to Christ and the Church, Dupuis found the accusations against him so disconcerting. May the Lord heal those wounds and take Jacques to himself in everlasting light'. The librarian at the Gregorian University made many photocopies of that obituary for any who wished to take one. She left them in the

---

43 In my letter published on 15 January 2005, *The Times* carried a few corrections that needed to be made in their obituary.

library alongside the chair where Dupuis would sit each Wednesday when he came to check recently published journals and books.

The challenge Dupuis took up when he wrote his major work remains. For him and the CDF alike, the central question is the same: how to profess faith in Jesus Christ as the one redeemer of all human beings, while simultaneously following Pope John Paul II in recognizing the Holy Spirit at work in the religions and cultures of the world. Perhaps we cannot do much more than explore the foothills of God's majestic providence for all humanity and the created cosmos. When sharing in that exploring, I am still happy to hang onto Jacques Dupuis and glad that, after doing something for him during his lifetime, I can continue his work after his death.[44]

---

44 A chapter ('Jacques Dupuis' Contribution to Interreligiouos Dialogue') is dedicated to Dupuis in my *The Second Vatican Council on Other Religions* (Oxford: Oxford University Press, 2013), 182-96; see also my 'Jacques Dupuis: The Ongoing Debate,' *Theological Studies* 76 (2013).

9

Summers and Travels

If all roads lead to Rome, they also lead away. My first rector at the Gregorian University, Father Hervé Carrier, encouraged me to leave Rome in the summer and take off for distant parts of the world. He valued such travel for the contacts it maintained with alumni of the University and leaders of the Catholic Church, who often turned out to be alumni. I also found my travels to be a rewarding way of learning from the audiences and picking up new ideas. With the exception of the summer of 1986 when I visited South America, the summer travel was well and truly paid for by the universities or other institutions that had invited me. Since the Gregorian had regularly to find half of its annual budget from gifts and the earnings of the Jesuit staff, it pleased me to be able to return to the University with a handsome cheque or two for the bursar. The summer teaching could be extremely exciting and was also a way of putting a final polish on typescripts I was preparing for publishers. From the start of my life at the Gregorian, travel entered my bloodstream never to depart.

Outside Italy

The summer of 1975 took me to New Zealand and Australia, and started with a week of lectures in Burlington, Vermont. For twenty-five years (1966-1990) an energetic Sister of Mercy, Miriam Ward, brought together four or five lecturers to present the best Catholic, Protestant, and Jewish scriptural scholarship for an average audience of well over 150 participants attending the annual Trinity College biblical institute. Her list of sixty-three faculty members reads like a Who's Who of the biblical world: from John Bright, Raymond Brown and Reginald Fuller, through Bruce Metzger, Roland Murphy, Carolyn Osiek and Pheme Perkins, to Donald Senior and George Ernest Wright. Like many others lecturers I returned for several summers. The bewitching beauty of Vermont, the cheerful interest of the audience, and the smooth organization of those weeks make them linger happily in my memory.

I remember a particularly pleasant week in 1981 when the other speakers included Theodor Gaster of Columbia University, New York. Then in his late 70s, Gaster had been born in London, where his father was the rabbi for a Spanish and Portuguese congregation. Gaster had known everybody: from Sigmund Freud to the poet A. E. Housman, the novelist Thomas Mann, and the Oxford classical scholar Gilbert Murray. Gaster peppered his lectures with wonderful asides: 'I was in Rome twice when they elected a pope and both times they passed me over'; 'we should have taken the scrolls out of the Qumran caves and put the scholars in'; 'there are forty Isaiahs and thirty of them lived in Leipzig.' (Prior to the Second World War, Leipzig had been a centre for biblical studies and extravagant speculations about biblical authors.) When I told Gaster that I had a niece who worked as a New York lawyer, he urged me: 'Either get her to leave the city, or pray for her night and day.' One of the 1981 participants was a haematologist who was delighted to hear me talk about blood in the Old Testament and the blood of Jesus, but was indignant that in his Bible the translation of Colossians 1:20 had replaced 'blood' with 'the sacrificial death of Jesus'.

On my 1975 trip I travelled on from Vermont to New Zealand to teach at Holy Cross Seminary in the South Island town of Mosgiel about ten miles out of Dunedin. The homestead, around which the town grew, had previously belonged to a great nephew of the poet Robert Burns and took its name from Burns's Scottish farm, 'Mossgiel'. Somehow the second 's' got lost on the journey out from Scotland. On July 20 I wrote to my mother in Australia:

Time is whistling by here in the South Island. Unkind critics (noting the drift to the North Island which set in when the gold-rush days ended) remark: 'Will the last person out of the South Island please switch off the lights.' That's as bad as the story of the pilot telling his passengers: 'You are now approaching Auckland, New Zealand. Please put your watches back thirty years.' All very unfair. People have been extraordinarily hospitable to me, and I appreciate the sense of dialogue which seems to operate at all levels...

Theologians seem to swarm regularly in New Zealand. The great Brazilian archbishop, Helder Camara, is expected shortly and the Jerusalem Dominican, Jerry Murphy-O'Connor, is already here. I am due to meet Monsignor Ralph Brown from London's Westminster archdiocese who refused to give me an imprimatur for my dogma book last year. He is in New Zealand lecturing on marriage tribunals. What do you say to a man who refused you an imprimatur? He seemed a pleasant person from his letters but stuck with a highly conservative cardinal and archdiocese.

There are about thirty seminarians at Holy Cross, many of them with good Protestant-sounding names like Wynn-Williams and Hay-McKenzie. One of the staff explained that this was because the girls stuck to their Catholic faith and passed it on to their sons although they had sometimes married Protestants. On his mother's side Wynn-Williams is related to Father Damien of Molokai [a nineteenth-century missionary to lepers on an island near Hawaii, who has since been canonized as Saint Joseph de Veuster].

On my way back to Rome from New Zealand and Australia, I stopped in Port Moresby to share in the ceremonies with which Australian rule ended on 15 September and Papua New Guinea became an independent country. At the flag-raising ceremony Imelda Marcos, representing her husband, the President of the Philippines, stole the show. From the grandstand she waved to the crowd and then lent forward to be kissed by the tall Australian Prime Minister, Gough Whitlam. She had arrived that morning on a private jet, paid $2,000 (US) cash for hotel facilities during the day, and flew out towards midnight. The speeches, prayers, and pledges were frankly Christian and seemed to set on edge the secular nerves of Whitlam.

In 1976 I continued my summer travels and the highlight was the Eucharistic Congress in Philadelphia. On the plane out of Rome I had the great good fortune to find myself next to Mother Teresa of Calcutta, who was also en route to the Congress. We chatted about various things, including the good effect she had on Malcolm Muggeridge, whose latest book confirmed the fact that he had come to full faith in Christ. In Philadelphia I found myself in the same hotel as Mother Teresa, and the other guests included Archbishop Helder Camara, the American theologian Avery (later Cardinal) Dulles, Prince Rainier and Princess Grace of Monaco, and other speakers. A bellhop asked me: 'Where's that nun? I want to shake her hand before they canonize her.' Mother Teresa smiled, shook his hand, and wrote on a piece of paper for him: 'Let us love one another, as Jesus has loved us.'

The hotel had just been the headquarters for a July meeting of the American Legion, a very large association made up of veterans of World War I, World War II and the Korean War. Twenty-six people, almost all Legionaires, caught a mysterious new disease and died. News was beginning to come through about the deaths, and the connection with the 'Bellevue Stratford', the hotel in which we had all been staying. I secretly thought: 'If the disease had struck during the Eucharistic Congress, I might have slipped into heaven behind Mother Teresa and the former Grace Kelly, now Princess Grace of Monaco!'

When Archbishop Helder Camara, the saintly Brazilian campaigner for the hungry and the miserable, who always seemed to me like a cheerful leprechaun, finished his major speech, Mother Teresa sprang up from her seat on the platform and embraced him. The straitlaced Archbishop Giovanni Benelli, soon to leave the Vatican to become Archbishop of Florence, was the third figure on the platform; he looked startled. But in front of an audience of several thousand people, he had no choice; he had to get up himself and embrace Archbishop Camara and Mother Teresa.

In the early 1980s Father Theodore Hesburgh of the University of Notre Dame pressed me to take a fulltime post there. I suggested the compromise of teaching summer courses and from 1985 did so on ten other occasions (down to 2005). It was only when he retired after thirty-five years as President of Notre Dame that I could bring myself to move onto first-name terms with this extraordinarily great academic leader. Calling Father Hesburgh 'Ted' seemed tantamount to addressing God by a nickname.

There were also summer visits to India and South America. From Mangalore in Southern India I wrote on 8 September 1979 to my sister Dympna: 'The Indians really lay on a warm welcome. When I celebrated Mass for a local congregation, the Bethany Sisters, three novices wearing saris danced a welcome. The superior said they felt they were receiving Jesus, as Martha and Mary did long ago in the original Bethany! I replied that I felt more like Lazarus coming back to his sisters from the dead.'

One evening Fr. George Oliapuram, an Indian priest who had done his thesis with me in Rome, took me out to supper at his parents' home. A cake with 'Welcome Gerry' on it stood in the middle of the table. We had dish after dish: pork, mutton, black fish, beef, onions

In Japan, 1980

('pungent' and 'non-pungent' as the Indians say), soup, chicken, fruit, and, of course, rice. No meal in Kerala is a real meal without rice. I was very touched by their kindness and gave George's sixty-seven-year-old father a great hug when I left. I had certainly needed the mega-meal after a day of lecturing.

One late afternoon eleven sisters, George Oliapuram, the Indian driver, and myself piled into a hospital ambulance and drove to the birthplace of the holy philosopher Sankara (A.D. 700-50) at Kalary, singing charismatic hymns on the way. The inside wall of a winding staircase in the circular temple carry scenes in cement from the life of Sankara: the power of his prayer saving him from a crocodile; Sankara refusing to follow his mother's wishes and marry; Sankara confounding the old by his youthful wisdom, setting off to find his guru, crossing a river on a pathway of lotus leaves, dividing the waters to get his old mother across, sending her off to heaven in a kind of assumption scene, making his great discovery (non-dualistic theism), and finally reaching a kind of apotheosis — apparently in Nepal. From the top of the temple we looked out across neat paddy (rice) fields stretching away in the sunset and bordered everywhere by coconut palms. I was surprised to find how deeply I was affected by this trip to India. Although I had made two previous visits, this one remained with me.

From George's home in Kothamangalam I flew north to Bangalore, India's so-called 'air-conditioned city' because of its altitude, and another strenuous round of lectures. The orchards, vineyards, and cow pastures of the Salesian college delighted me. In a letter to my sister Moira and her husband in Australia I was able to recommend something they might like to use on their farm: 'Here, as in many other places, they use Gober gas, cooking gas produced from fresh cow dung. You simply dump the fresh manure into a container each day; the central tank fills up with gas; and what is left over can be used as fertiliser.'

Never having set foot in Latin America, I decided to remedy the deficiency in 1986 with a visit to Brazil, Argentina, Chile, and Columbia. At this point I had served as dean of the theology faculty for a year and thought it well worthwhile to visit some of our alumni, meet bishops and other Church leaders, and get a sense of the centres which fed us with Latin American students. Starting with Brazil, I went to pray beside the gigantic statue of Christ the Redeemer and couldn't help reflecting that his arms needed to spread wide in order to embrace, forgive, and redeem so much of what I was seeing in Rio de Janeiro. The terrifying contrast between the affluent and the hundreds of thousands who lived in the *favelas* or slums struck me hard — not least when I called upon the cardinal archbishop in his luxurious, air-conditioned chancery overlooking a hillside covered with the shacks of the poor. To make matters worse, my arrival coincided with the opening night of Sylvester Stallone's 'Cobra', a film that featured or even celebrated paramilitary death squads.

It was a relief to meet the bishop in charge of a section of São Paulo, Dom Luciano Mendes de Almeida, who welcomed all alike with a lovely smile and the kindest manner. The very simple building that served as both his chancery office and his home faced onto a noisy square. I met there both the destitute and the rich. A tall, stylishly dressed man told me: 'I don't attend worship anymore. The priests talk politics. My only contact with the Church is my old friend Dom Luciano.' A young lawyer turned up who belonged to the 'best' clubs and had travelled the world. A religious conversion had now led him to seek ordination to the priesthood, and that involved his studying in Rome. 'Please do look after Roberto when he comes,' Dom Luciano asked me. What none of us then knew was that the young man was

HIV positive and would die after completing his studies in Rome and just before being ordained to the priesthood.

When I moved on to Argentina, it surprised me to find very few police in evidence. In Brazil smartly dressed and heavily armed police had been present everywhere, not to mention private vigilantes. The Argentinians, however, were still coping with the collapse of their military regime. Some of those whom I met held very right-wing and militaristic views, even some of the clergy. The wife of a judge complained to me about the existence of slums and the huge number of political slogans written on walls: 'The military would never have let this happen.' Several bishops were currently protesting against a giant mural in the National University of the North-East (in Resistencia) as 'unjust and malicious'. The mural recalled events from 1976, the year of the military coup headed by General Jorge Videla, and depicted a Catholic priest assisting at a scene of torture. The artist was a professor of fine arts and the mother of one of the 'desaparecidos', those abducted by the military and never seen again.

When I flew on to Chile, I visited the place in Santiago where the military had poured gasoline on two young people: the boy, Rodrigo, died but the girl, Carmen Gloria, had survived horribly disfigured. She would be embraced by John Paul II when he visited Chile in 1987. I drove past the house of the Chilean dictator, General Augusto Pinochet, a low, concrete building that resembled a bunker. Over lunch in his own home, Cardinal Raul Silva Henriquez, the retired Archbishop of Santiago, commented on Pinochet: 'An animal is most dangerous when it is wounded and cornered.' The old Cardinal had visited the disfigured Carmen Gloria in hospital; he spoke of her recovery as a symbol of the resurrection of the people. The bishops of Chile had just published a pastoral letter detailing their hopes and plans for the next few years: the finest such pastoral I have ever read.

Its leitmotif was life — true human and Christian life at all levels of society. The priests, religious, and lay leaders I met in Santiago were inspiring.

From Chile I flew to Bogotá, the capital of Colombia, to be the guest of Cardinal Lopez Trujillo, the Archbishop of Medellín. He had just returned from Philadelphia and Washington. I made the mistake of trying to lift his two suitcases. They weighed a ton and must have been stuffed with books. His opposition to liberation theology and difficult relations with many of his flock made him a *bête noire* for liberal minded Catholics. Eventually, in 1990, John Paul II called him to Rome to head the Pontifical Council for the Family. I found him most hospitable, enormously energetic, and quite charming. We went for a rapid lunch at the permanent secretariat for the Colombian bishops. The Cardinal then drove a hire car back to the airport, and caught the shuttle flight to Medellín with five minutes to spare. At Medellín someone was waiting with Lopez Trujillo's Japanese land rover. The Cardinal took the wheel and drove through heavy traffic to the seminary on the far side of the city. He proved easily the best driver I was with in South America, and we Italians had high standards!

On the hour's run to the Medellín seminary the Cardinal regaled me with his views on the Latin American situation: 'The hierarchy here in Colombia is united, unlike Peru and Brazil. We have quantity in the Latin American Church. But do we have quality, a real Catholic identity? History will prove who is right.' Contrary to what some people seemed to be thinking, he argued: 'you don't have to be an extremely radical to work with and for the poor.' He didn't like the word 'ideology', and so I refrained from using it. I found myself in broad agreement with Lopez Trujillo's concern for orthodox faith alongside social justice. Experience shows that Catholics who are truly orthodox work with greater passion and purpose for the poor and the disadvantaged.[45] I discovered that he had read my *Fundamental Theology*, and wondered how he had reacted to my advocacy of an experiential approach. But he did not consider that it posed any threat to orthodoxy, and so we were in agreement. At the seminary I lectured to the staff in the presence of the Cardinal and finished off my month in South America by lecturing in my best Spanish at the Bolivarian University, also in Medellín.

In Europe some prelates still have big, smart cars. In Medellín the 'pecking order' seemed to be the Cardinal Archbishop in a land rover and priests in jeeps. One of the jeeps took me back to the airport over a mountain road which an ordinary car could never have coped with. On the flight back to Rome I felt hugely grateful over the opportunity I had been given of seeing a little of the Latin American reality, with its grinding poverty, terrifying violence, and wonderful faith.

Two years later I was back in Bogotá to deliver to sixty bishops of Colombia five lectures (in Spanish) on the state of theology and, in particular, on Christology or the doctrine of Christ. I repeated the same lectures to a group of 240 priests, before giving the same lectures in two other cities, Pereira and Medellín.

What struck me on this visit in July 1988 was the constant presence of violence. The bishops were holding their two-week updating course in a large seminary on the outskirts of Bogotá. A few hundred yards away were the headquarters of CELAM (Conference of Latin American Bishops), which had been seized by a group of guerillas a month earlier. The danger was that the army would burst into the building and kill not only the guerillas but also the twenty or thirty hostages. The bishop-president of CELAM, incidentally, was not one of them. He happened to be away in Moscow, celebrating a thousand

---

45 In the London *Tablet* for 9 August 1986, I had just argued that very point against Bishop David Jenkins of Durham.

years of Christianity in Russia. A group of religious men and women staged a demonstration outside the CELAM building, and helped convince both the army and the guerillas to reach a compromise. No one was hurt and two buses took the guerillas off to a university campus, where they disappeared among the crowds of students.

Violence had grown in Colombia, with well over three hundred people now being killed each month. The night before I arrived, 40% of Bogotá was blacked out when two pylons carrying high tension wires were blown up. That same day a farmer who had been wounded five days earlier (in an attack that left his mother and two brothers dead) was finished off by gunmen on the sixth floor of a hospital — in front of a some terrified nuns and a doctor. A daily paper carried a comment from a man who said: 'I don't believe in anyone or anything any more. I tried to help people by giving them work on my farm, and then this is what has happened.' 'This' meant that in less than two years, of his four sons, two had been murdered, one wounded very badly, and one had been kidnapped.

Against this background, it was not surprising to find a heavy army presence around the seminary when I lectured to the bishops. I wrote to a friend: 'I have never lectured before while soldiers carrying submachine guns patrolled outside the windows.' On the second day a bishop explained to me why the two Colombian cardinals were missing: 'They are downtown at a meeting with the representatives of the three political parties to see what the Church can do in helping towards a peaceful and just settlement of social problems.' In the letter to my friend I added: 'Incidentally, three Spanish priests are on "service" with the guerillas in Colombia, one of them leading a particular group of guerillas.'

I was hardly acclimatized to the violence of Colombia before I flew back to Europe for a month doing some priestly work in

Nuremberg and its environs. That included immersing myself in the peace of Heldmannsberg, a village about twenty-five miles south-east of Nuremberg. The village was surrounded by forests, valleys, and fields of maize, sugar-beet, barley, wheat, and potatoes. The farmers liked to be woken up at 5.30 by the bells from the tower of the small church.

On 15 August, the Feast of the Blessed Virgin's Assumption, with another priest I went down the road around 9.30 with cross, banners, brass band, altar boys, and altar girls to welcome 150 pilgrims who had walked for over two hours from a neighbouring village, with their perspiring parish-priest at the head of the procession. The pilgrims provided a vigorous choir, which sang away in church at every possible chance. By 11.30, the Mass, a rousing sermon and extra blessings (for

With Cardinal František Tomášek in Prague, 1990

the crops) were over. The crowd dispersed for lunch to the local pub and to a barbecue on some lawns. Around 2 p.m. devotions in the church got the pilgrims ready for the walk home through the fields and forests.

Peace was writ large in Heldmannsberg, and I was glad to return there in the summers of 1990, 1992 and 1994; and on those visits I preached myself at the celebration of 15 August. I could find only so much to say about the belief Catholics share with Orthodox and some other Christians: that at the end of her earthly life Mary was taken up body and soul into eternal, heavenly glory. In 1990 and 1992 I exhausted all that I could think of preaching about the assumption into glory of the Virgin Mary. But I was aware also that, since the farmers of Heldmannsberg had tenacious memories, I could not simply repeat a sermon preached four, still less two, years earlier. So in August 1994 I adapted and simplified as best I could a sermon on the assumption by the great German theologian Karl Rahner, who had died exactly ten years earlier. 'A good sermon, but a bit above our heads', commented one of the farmers.

Those summers in Germany made me think often about the suffering and terrible evil that can afflict the human condition. In Nuremberg itself a modern bronze statue of Job helped to focus my reflection. Naked and hunched up, he sat near the door of a late Gothic church, right alongside the main street which cuts across the city from the railway station. Handsome, well-fed people moved briskly past Job on their way to sales in those temples of consumer society, huge department stores. Foreign and local tourists came off the intercity trains to see the paintings and engravings of Albrecht Dürer and the late medieval sculptures which make Nuremberg an artistic mecca. Other people hurried by to buy their tickets for *the* musical event of the year, Placido Domingo's outdoor concert that was to fill the old marketplace. I turned away from the busy street to look at Job and think about my question: who are we?

His gaunt shoulders showed how pain had got the better of him. Yet something about his face slipped beyond mere resignation to hint at real human hope. The thought came to me: 'Job expresses the truth of our common humanity. Each one of us suffers and hopes. We are all beings who suffer and hope — the shoppers, the tourists, and the concert-goers, no less than the lonely soldiers and derelicts who drift around the railway station.'

After I contemplated Job, I went across the city to say Mass in an old people's home. Over breakfast the matron told me of her two years in a Russian prison-of-war camp. 'It was a very hard time, but I learned much from that experience.' She paused and then went on: 'What still seems utterly meaningless, though, was the death of my twelve year old brother. Soldiers beat him to death.'

One Sunday in Nuremberg I took part in a silent march to the place where fifty years earlier the first of the city's two synagogues was torn down. Twenty or thirty Jews stood in front of the monument. Their cantor sang a lamentation in memory of the millions of his brothers and sisters systematically wiped out by hatred. Jewish people, Job, and that matron in Nuremberg confronted me with the death, meaninglessness, and brutal indifference that shape our history. But there was hope and faith as well. After the lamentation a leading Protestant pastor of the city prayed:

Lord, our God, full of shame we think of what happened here fifty years ago and we pray to you. Fill us all with your Spirit, so that finally we recognize in one another our brothers and sisters, so that — with all prejudices overcome — love instead of hate may rule the hearts of human beings and peace may bind us all together. Grant that in our city and land people may never again be persecuted and their places of worship destroyed. Lead us into a future in which each person helps and takes responsibility for the other and in which each person is on hand for the other, just as you, our God, are there on hand for us all.

But Nuremberg raised more questions for me. On a summer afternoon I went through one of the medieval gates on the west side of the city, walked under the trees along the River Pegnitz, and came to the cemetery of St John. Dürer and other famous Christians are buried there. Many of the old tombs belonging to great families of the city carry messages of warning and hope. One is told, 'Keep on the watch, for you know not the day nor the hour', but one also reads: 'Blessed are the dead who die in the Lord.' Some of the tombs go back to the late Middle Ages. For most of the year the whole cemetery is ablaze with flowers.

On the left towards the river you find the tomb of Ludwig Feuerbach. The gray stone covering his grave bears his profile in bronze and the dates, 'Born 1804, died 1872'. He had already delivered his message through his writings: the Christian God is nothing else than the projection of human wishes and needs. Men and women should be liberated from this illusion. Was Feuerbach right? Is the all-powerful, all-knowing, and perfectly good God of the Jewish-Christian tradition merely a product of our needs and imagination? Or is there an omnipresent, infinitely caring personal Power who envelops our lives and to whom we owe our deepest allegiance?

Several years earlier Gerald Priestland, an outstanding Quaker and media personality, had interviewed me for his radio programme *The Case Against God*. In his book which has the same title he mentions that while we sat together, the lights failed and 'it gave us a pretty picture of two men talking about God in the dark'. What struck me even more was what Priestland suggested after concluding the interview: 'Let us wrap our conversation in silence and prayer.' I cannot think of any better advice to give anyone who approaches the question of God: 'Let your search take you into silence and prayer. See what signs of God's presence that experience brings you.' In silent prayer, believers experience the way faith keeps our existence in working order. It provides the vision by which they can live, find meaning, experience love given and received, and cope with suffering.

Feuerbach and his various successors encouraged 'modern' people to dispense with the God-hypothesis and get on with building a better human society. For many decades secular humanism, Marxism, atheistic schools of psychology, Nietzsche's vision of super-men, and hopes engendered by theories about human evolution exerted an extraordinary grip upon the imaginations and aspirations of millions. But the brave new world has not come. Communism is not the only god that has failed.

Feuerbach's ideas helped to shape Nietzsche, who assured us that 'the Christian concept of God is sick, corrupt, the contradiction of life'. Nietzsche's own ideas flowed into Adolf Hitler's National Socialism, a thoroughly sick, corrupt, and life-destructive system if ever there was one. In Nuremberg I sometimes crossed the railway tracks to the parade grounds where I sat for lunch in the crumbling stands. Over a beer and a sandwich I looked down on the place where Hitler staged his monster rallies and fuelled the support that brought death and suffering to millions.

Visits to the Holy Land (1984) and to Croatia (1993) also made me think deeply about evil, suffering and faith. It was after sunset when I reached Tantur, the Ecumenical Institute for Theological Research which sits on a rise south of Jerusalem. Down the road the lights of

Bethlehem shone at me through the warm August darkness. High above the town the evening star glittered in the sky.

Next morning the muezzin from a nearby mosque woke me just after 4 a.m. I slept again but fitfully until the bells from Christian churches announced the dawn. Then the sun came up over the hills of Moab to show me Bethlehem. I lifted my eyes across the olives and cypresses to the towers and spires of David's 'royal city'. In the left distance a flat-topped cone drew my attention. It was the Herodion, the hill where Herod the Great (d. 4 BC) built a citadel and where they later brought his body for burial. To the right a new Israeli settlement, Gilo, crowned another hill like a latter-day crusader castle.

After breakfast I sat on my tiny balcony to face Bethlehem and say the divine office. To my delight I found that the Office of Readings began: 'But you, Bethlehem Ephrathah, the least of the clans of Judah, out of you will be born for me the One who is to rule over Israel. He will stand and feed his flock with the power of the Lord.' The sight of the city itself charged Micah's prophecy with fresh meaning.

The sun had swung across the sky to the west before our meetings ended at Tantur and I was free to go down to Bethlehem. Along the road I passed two shepherds. Several goats were mixed up with the flock of sheep. Until I looked closely at their heads and tails, I could not tell the goats from the sheep. I pressed on past Rachel's Tomb, where some young Israeli couples still came to seek her blessing on their marriages.

I hurried on to Manger Square and into the Basilica of the Nativity. Distant organ music followed me down into the cave. A young man and woman squatted in prayer. Their silent devotion filled the place. The thought shook me and brought tears to my eyes: the Son of God really took flesh among us. Other pilgrims drifted in. Some closed their eyes and prayed. Some read the story of Jesus' birth and sang a Christmas carol. Others stood there and wept.

I climbed out of the cave, slipped through the church, crossed the square, and walked back along Star Street. A pregnant woman passed me. A little later another young mother came along leading a tiny, open-faced boy. I laughed for the joy of these reminders. Then I remembered how Bethlehem means 'house of bread'. I stopped to buy a fragrant roll. It sustained me on the climb back up the road to Tantur.

From the roof of the institute my gaze drifted across the stony landscape. Fifteen miles or so to the southeast, three packs of leopards still roamed the Judean wilderness. They lived off ibex and other animals. Away to the north, storks, eagles, and other birds of prey were to gather in their thousands when the shorter days drove them south from central and eastern Europe. They would soar to great heights on the warm air currents and glide past Tantur on their way down to Africa. They would all have gone south by the time Christmas came round again.

Up on the terrace of Tantur some fearful questions played on my mind: What can we expect from a world that is so good at doing evil? Will we continue to hunt each other in our tribal and national packs? Or will be simply glide away from situations that have become difficult and seemingly unbearable?

The light drained out of the sky. The evening star came into view again over Bethlehem. It dreamt up the vision of a peasant woman and her tiny Son. His presence can always bring us peace. That peace does not mean the survival of the fittest but bread in the hands of the hungry.

Nine years later a visit to Croatia (to inspect a theological institute affiliated with the Gregorian University) pushed some of the same questions at me. 'It's always Good Friday, sometimes a little of Holy Saturday, but never Easter Sunday.' The comment came from the pastor of a parish on the edge of Karlovac, a city of about sixty thousand that was less than an hour's drive from Zagreb. Since the Serbs started shelling and shooting in September 1991, nearly fifty of his parishioners had been killed. The front-line cut his parish in half. Two thousand of his parishioners had fled into Karlovac itself. They lived there with thirteen thousand other refugees. In November 1993 I watched some of them shuffling forward in lines to receive their daily handout of bread and apples.

We drove out towards a wrecked village just short of the front-line, ducked behind a hill, and pulled up next to a chapel. Its roof had been blown off and the stone walls gaped with huge holes. Up the slope was a cemetery. 'I can't use that cemetery', the parish priest explained. 'Just eight days ago, on All Saints' Day, it was hit again — this time with four shells. My second cemetery is occupied by the enemy, just like my parish church.' He shook his head in disbelief: 'Fancy shelling one cemetery and occupying another!' What happened to the chapel?, I asked. 'A tank came over the hill and started firing at the chapel', he said. 'A couple of our soldiers crept up through the trees, hit the tank, and killed the four Chetniks in it. You can see the remains of the tank up there on the top of the rise.'

I thought of those four young Serbs dying as they made a cemetery chapel their target. I thought too of what the parish priest had told me about his young parishioners, who asked incessantly: 'Where is God? What is God doing?' It sent me back to a cry from another cross: 'My God, my God, why have you forsaken me?' (Mark 15: 34). There was no immediate answer. The choice was and remains between anger at our suffering or joining Christ with the cross that comes our way. The outcome of that acceptance will be a transforming resurrection.

My parish priest from Karlovac did not find an Easter Sunday in his situation. But he did bring to mind the truth, 'those who laugh last laugh best.' The autumn weather was turning cold when we stood next to the ruins of his cemetery chapel. A member of a religious congregation, he had laid aside his gleaming white habit and put on a sweater and shabby trousers before driving me out to the front. 'I don't always go round here in my habit', he explained. 'It turns me into a very good target.' Then he grinned: 'But when the snow comes, I wear the habit. It makes for good camouflage.' He showed me once again that belief in Jesus' death and resurrection does set us free — for a little joy and laughter.

Inside Italy

Within Italy a workable train service up and down the peninsula made it easy to accept invitations to give lectures or teach mini-courses which could be fitted in between duties at the Gregorian itself. Thus in August 1984 I gave a paper ('The Resurrection: Mystery of Love') for a convention held at the Sanctuary of Divine Love, a huge and remarkable house of prayer fifty miles north of Rome. Nuns served at the bar, peacocks strutted in the grounds, and dozens of people prayed constantly at the tomb of the foundress. The centre owes its existence to an utterly uneducated and extraordinarily holy Spanish nun, Madre Speranza (Mother Hope), who died in 1983. The closest town, Todi, crowns a nearly hill and has preserved three sets of walls: the Etruscan, the Roman, and the medieval.

Not long before she died, Madre Speranza looked up the valley one evening at the lights of Todi and remarked: 'How beautiful!' She paused and then said: 'But behind every light there is a cross.'

She made me think of the greatest citizen of that charming town, Jacopone da Todi (1230–1307). His dissolute life changed in 1268 when his wife was killed in a tragic accident. From his years as a Franciscan lay brother, Jacopone has left us many devotional poems, including the exquisite *Stabat Mater* (known in English as 'At the cross her station keeping'). He accepted his suffering and did not curse God because of it. During Lent and Holy Week many Catholics and some other Christians sing Jacopone's *Stabat Mater*, a hymn which praises the Virgin Mary for the way she said 'yes' to the terrible pain and death of her Son's passion and death.

A few years later I was much further north, in Cremona, just before All Souls' Day. Two friends from Cremona drove me west across the Lombardy plain to Mantua. Before leaving town they pointed out the school where the greatest Latin poet had studied. 'Virgil was born near Mantua, but went to school in Cremona', they proudly announced. We stopped to see an exhibition of photographs showing how ugly apartment blocks had been steadily engulfing the agricultural land and old farmhouses that still ringed Cremona.

A gray sky hung low over the fields. At the end of particularly warm October the temperature had suddenly dropped. The leaves were starting to fall from the trees that lined the road. Shortly before Mantua heavy traffic outside a huge cemetery slowed us down. Along the road florists were doing a brisk trade selling pots of bright chrysanthemums. The licence plates on the cars showed just how many people had come from distant cities to grieve, pray, and leave flowers at the graves of their dear departed.

In Mantua we spent hours being guided around the faded magnificence of the endless Gonzaga palace. After the terrible sack of 1630, the city never recovered its former grandeur. In 1708 the last duke died in exile. The family had come to power and wealth in the fourteenth century. The name 'Gonzaga' did not even appear in Mantua's telephone book. It was almost as if the Gonzagas had never been. The dukes, artists, cardinals, and St Aloysius Gonzaga were little more than figments of our historical imagination, mere flotsam swept away on the racing water of time.

On the way back to Cremona I quoted Virgil's melancholy summary of our human condition: 'Sunt lacrimae rerum et mentem mortalia tangunt' (which one can roughly translate as 'there are tears at the core of things, and our mortal condition touches the heart'). 'But there's bread under the snow', commented Mimma. 'What do you mean by that?', I asked. 'It's a proverb from the farming community', she explained. 'They work the fields and sow the seed now — before the feast of St Martin on 11 November. The earth keeps its basic heat. The snow isn't violent. The seed germinates. When the blanket of snow disappears in the spring, up pop the green sprouts.'

That day in Lombardy set me thinking about Christ's radical solidarity with human beings. He stands with us not only through having a body and sufferings but also through the place where bodily suffering eventually takes us all, death itself. The sights on the road between Cremona and Mantua vividly imaged for me our common mortality. The grain and grapes had been harvested. The days were shortening, the leaves were falling, and there was a feel of snow in the air. Life was closing down. The only flowers within sight were those the Italians generally reserve for their cemeteries and their dead. But it is not enough simply to take winter, pain, and death for granted. There is bread under the snow and new life rising from the tomb. Jesus descended to the dead, but he also rose to full and final glory. Ultimately it is his resurrection that can answer Virgil's mournful lines.

Some of the trips up and down Italy wedded academic work with the delights of tourism. One of the international conferences held in

1990 to mark a century since the death of John Henry Newman was staged in Leonforte, the small town in Sicily where he nearly died of typhus in 1833. 'On day one', I wrote to my sister Maev, 'we visitors were bussed around to see Roman mosaics, fed to the teeth, and looked after splendidly by a bunch of uniformed young people. Day two was dedicated to the lectures, a Mass which featured a vigorous sermon by Cardinal Pappalardo of Palermo, and more trips to the table. I have rarely been forced to eat as much in my life. The organizers liked my lecture on Newman's midlife journey being associated with or even triggered by his Sicilian experience.' Leonforte was still in my mind when I wrote to my sister-in-law Posey a month later:

The typhus he [Newman] brought from Naples flared up at Leonforte and he almost died. He recovered, of course, and headed home to England and the Oxford Movement, writing on the way 'Lead, kindly light', a poem about his self-discovery in Sicily. Apart from its foundation around 1600 by Prince Branciforti, Newman's illness, and a visit from Garibaldi (who is supposed to have said there for the first time, 'Rome or death'), nothing much has ever happened at Leonforte. Incidentally, it is the first time I have ever heard of, let alone participated in, an international symposium on someone's nearly fatal illness. What I never realized before was that, while Newman was on his voyage of self-discovery in Sicily, Charles Darwin was on his world-voyage to find out where we all come from.

At Leonforte they killed us with kindness, sightseeing and meals, especially the golden young men and women who are trying to build a better Sicily. Maybe Newman's recovery from a serious illness symbolizes the future of a sick Sicily that will recover and set its rich humanity at the service of the world. Sicily is featuring an offensive of cultural and academic initiatives. A way of undercutting the Mafia? Shortly before the Newman symposium, group of seismologists met somewhere in Sicily. One of them warned: 'We are a dangerous lot. Wherever we meet, often enough the region is shortly thereafter hit by an earthquake.'

What I failed to mention in my letter about the Newman symposium was the approach of Cardinal Pappalardo. He began his sermon by recalling the little that he knew about Newman: 'He was a great English gentleman, and would never have approved of the Mafia.' That allowed the Cardinal to launch into his real theme, a long denunciation of the Mafia.

In February 1992 I flew over Sicily to give three lectures for the University of Malta and one for the clergy of Gozo. During my visit I stayed in the national seminary, occupying the apartment used by John Paul II during his Malta experience of May 1990. Five nights in the papal bed did not do anything much for me. The last night I dreamt of an eight-year-old girl, a child actress, who wanted me to join her on the stage. When I shared this dream over breakfast the following morning, the resident shrink commented: 'The Pope was/is an actor, after all. Something was coming through there.' I thought it best not to share with the psychologist my full stream of consciousness when occupying the papal 'throne', shaving in the papal mirror, and using other pieces of equipment in the bathroom.

Into the Third Millennium

From his election in 1978, John Paul II proved himself a world evangelist. Inevitably I found his travels to the ends of the earth inspiring. Even if I never visited nearly as many countries, his example encouraged me to accept invitations to teach and preach around the world through the nineties and into the third millennium.

January 2002 was a typical month on the road or, rather, in the air. It began with a week in Washington, DC, preaching at St Patrick's

Church in downtown Washington. The week finished at the Feast of the Epiphany, with a mega-Mass for the John Carroll Society, who included lawyers, doctors, judges, one or two members of President George Bush's administration, and others.[46] I preached, and tall, gaunt Cardinal Avery Dulles, who had come down from New York, celebrated the Mass and spoke to four hundred people at the brunch. Over the meal, Avery and I were presented with John Carroll Society Medals — a lovely gesture, which I had not anticipated. I wrote to my brother Jim and his wife Posey:

> Uncle Avery is as sharp as ever at 83, but needed the excellent permanent deacon at his elbow to make sure that he didn't trip on any steps. Among other things, I mentioned in my sermon the habit still practised in various Northern European countries of writing with chalk over the main entrance to your house on 6 January: 'CMB 2002'. The number refers, of course, to the year which has just begun; CMB refers to Caspar, Melchior, and Balthasar, and/or means 'Christus mansionem benedicat (may Christ bless his house).' In the vestibule of the church I left two boxes of chalk for those who wanted to do the same.

They were very busy days in Washington, and included an overnight trip to New York to visit a niece (Joanna Peters) and her children and see the horrendous, Dante-like hole which was Ground Zero. On the flight out of Dulles Airport (called after Avery's father, John Foster Dulles, secretary of state under President Eisenhower), I found myself next to the nicest young couple imaginable: half

---

46 John Carroll, S.J. (1735–1815), Archbishop of Baltimore, was the first Catholic bishop in the United States and founder (in 1786) of Georgetown University, the oldest Catholic institution of higher education in the United States.

English and half French, he had been at Downside School with my Roman friend Jonathan Doria; she, American, blondly beautiful, and utterly sweet, was expecting a baby, their first. They simply needed someone with whom to share the wonderful news. And who better than a priest, especially with her very, very spiritual attitude to her baby and motherhood?

I was hardly back in Rome before I flew off to preach in Belfast and Armagh during the week of prayer for Christian Unity (18–25 January). My Anglican, Catholic, and Presbyterian hosts were a delight. But I wondered and worried about others, especially the small crowd of demonstrators outside St Anne's Cathedral (Church of Ireland) who held up placards ('What has Christ to do with Belial?') and harassed a delightful Salvation Army couple when they entered for the service. I felt like crying out: 'Please leave the Salvos alone!'

The night before I arrived almost the whole population of Northern Ireland seemed to have watched on TV 'Bloody Sunday'. Someone had taped it, and I was able to see part of it. The portrayal of Ivan Cooper, a 1972 Protestant civil rights leader in Derry and the central figure in the film, was gripping. But the most astonishing thing for me, on my first visit to Northern Ireland since 1965, was the total invisibility of any security forces. Apart from one or two police I saw at the airport, I never caught sight of any police in Belfast, Armagh, Portadown, or along the roads. The only soldier I saw was the Anglican chaplain to the troops hidden away in the barracks of Armagh. He had studied at my Cambridge College (Pembroke), and so we had many friends to talk about.

The year 2002 came and went. And I needed to repeat what I had written in a circular letter to friends on 1 January 1987: 'At the end, all I can do is pray, "Have mercy, Lord, for I have travelled far. Yet all knowledge is as nothing".'

(Honorary) Doctorate at the University of San Francisco, 1991

10

A Dreamlike Adventure

Surrounded by bright and brilliant treasures, I grew older in Rome. Nothing can ever repay the goodness, love, and loyalty of those whom I was privileged to call my friends during my Roman years. I share W. B. Yeats' feelings about his life. In 'The Municipal Gallery Revisited' he wrote: 'say my glory was I had such friends.' Everything began and ended with them.

Missing Meetings

When I arrived in August 1974, I knew hardly anyone in Rome. I phoned Martin Molyneux, a slim, dignified ex-Anglican whom I had first met in Oxford. Of Norman descent, Martin told me that his cautious ancestors had arrived in England from Normandy some months after the Battle of Hastings in 1066. 'They wanted to see how things went before committing themselves!' Martin had come to Rome to teach at the Beda College. I asked if we could have a pizza together. Martin happily agreed and suggested that he bring another priest from the Beda, Richard ('Dixie' to all his friends) Taylor. The evening was a great success and we began meeting every month or six weeks to talk over some book or article, before moving on to a local pizzeria. Others joined us: Redemptorists, Dominicans (both priests and nuns), Jesuits, and in the end we were twelve or so. People came and went; Martin and several others from our circle died. By 2006, only the irrepressible Dixie and myself remained in Rome from the founding members of the autumn of 1974.

My secret hope was that the circle might come to resemble the Inklings, those legendary Oxford dons who met to discuss the latest article or chapter from C.S. Lewis (1898-1963), J.R.R. Tolkien (1892-1973) and other members of the group. But we almost always seemed to be talking about classic texts (such as works from Dante, Descartes, Goethe, and Shakespeare), or some recent official church document.

Occasionally I persuaded the others to read and respond to some article I had drafted. Their feedback was always sharp and constructive. I realize now with regret how rarely I looked for such feedback over the years. I did not regularly present my latest work before audiences that included my academic peers, and I failed to attend the annual meetings of any learned, theological society between 1972 and 2010 — largely because such meetings often take place during the summer break and I cherished too deeply the opportunity of lecturing around the world. I can excuse myself with the thought that I was meeting professional colleagues when I visited their departments, faculties, or seminaries. But such contacts were no substitute for the hard give and take which follows a formal presentation to fellow theologians.

Sometimes (as I mentioned in Chapter 2) theological peers turned up in Rome or elsewhere in Italy. In April 1980, for instance, I took part in a round-table discussion of the latest work by Wolfhart Pannenberg (b. 1928), a six-hundred-page book on the human condition. We met in the faded magnificence of an old hall in Naples and sat on a platform backed by richly carved wooden panels. After praising the book for its vast erudition, I noted a certain lack of attention to such themes as suffering, injustice, and war, which continue to characterize the human situation. In reply Pannenberg argued that he had dealt with the roots of evil; in any case it was an illusion to think we could rid the world of war and injustice, not least because no consensus existed about justice itself. As his remarks closed the proceedings, I had no chance to point out that the 1948 declaration of human rights by the United Nations showed some consensus about matters of justice, even if the interpretation and application of those principles had often been deficient. After the symposium four Italian professors, including one heavy-set man who wore dark glasses and kept the money flowing into his institute from the regional government, took Pannenberg, his wife, and myself out to a fish dinner down by the Bay of Naples. We drank white wine from Ischia, and Pannenberg spoke of his respect for Karl Rahner, 'the greatest theologian of the twentieth century and a truly holy man'. As we ranged over many academic topics, I kept thinking of how we had debated the human condition in the city of the Camorra (the Neapolitan version of the Mafia) and only a few hundred yards from the Mount Calvary Centre for drug addicts. The question ran through my mind: 'Why did we avoid talking about the scourge of heroin, organized crime, the arms trade, and the whole shadow side of life in our Western world?'

Occasionally editors and publishers provided me with critical response to my writing. I remember with gratitude the precise criticisms which I received when I submitted my first draft of the entry on 'Salvation' to the *Anchor Bible Dictionary* (published 1992), my first draft of the entry on 'Jesus' to the *Encyclopedia of Religion* (edited by Mircea Eliade and published in 1987), and other examples of editorial expertise.

My lifelong concern with the resurrection began in 1967 when I was at Pembroke College, Cambridge, and doing my research for a doctorate. I received an urgent telephone call from Henry Hart, the dean of Queens' College, Cambridge, who was looking for someone to deliver a lecture to his college theological society at two days notice. He didn't mind what I spoke about, and on the spur of the moment the only subject I could come up with was the resurrection of Jesus. That eleventh-hour invitation from Henry Hart has kept me thinking, teaching, and writing about the resurrection for well over forty years, and resulted in eight books, numerous articles, chapters in books, and several dictionary entries. While I obviously retraced ground already trodden by others, I believe that I have been able to contribute additional insights: for instance, concerning the role of Peter as Easter witness, the nature of the first encounters with the risen Jesus, and the justification of faith in Jesus as gloriously risen from the dead.

It was encouraging to learn in 1987 that my reflections on these and other resurrection themes in *Jesus Risen* (published that year in English, a year later in Spanish, and two years later in Italian) had won the Malipiero Prize for theological research, an award equivalent to around 2,500 euros given every year by a Venetian family with a booming publishing house in Bologna. Centuries ago the Malipieros had supplied two doges for the Venetian Republic. They had lost their political power, but worked together as a close-knit family that did well economically.

As regards my three themes, interpreting Peter primarily (but not exclusively) as Easter witness has been dismissed by some commentators as Catholic apologetic. They have ignored the fact that throughout the twentieth century it was almost exclusively German Protestant scholars who proved willing to look at the special importance of Peter in announcing the resurrection. Some feminists dismiss the thesis because they take it as a denigration of Mary Magdalene. But I have persistently championed the Gospel traditions which report that women were present at the empty tomb, a tradition which stands or falls with the presence of Mary Magdalene.[47] Can we not honour both Mary Magdalene and Peter among the original Easter witnesses?

As regards the work I have done on the nature of the first encounters with the risen Jesus and the validation of our resurrection faith, I received valuable feedback from Dr Peter Carnley, the Anglican Archbishop of Perth (Western Australia) and the American theologian Francis Schüssler Fiorenza at a New York meeting: the Easter Summit in 1996. Carnley, in particular, prompted me to give much more thought to the possibilities *and limits* of analogies between the appearances of the risen Jesus and the documented experiences of contact between, for example, between widows or widowers and their beloved spouses. The discussion with Carnley motivated a contribution to a February 1998 meeting on the resurrection held at the Roehampton Institute London and, eventually, an appendix to my *Believing in the Resurrection*.[48]

When I was working on my Ph.D. for Cambridge University, 'The Theology of Revelation in Some Recent Discussion', I found myself obliged to think through such issues as the relationship between (a) God's self-revelation which reached its high point with the coming of Jesus, and (b) the living presence of that revelation as history unfolds and people are called, in one generation after another, to accept in faith the divine self-manifestation which was completed with Jesus and his first disciples. I called (a) foundational revelation and (b)

---

47 This criticism also normally ignored what Dan Kendall and I wrote about Mary Magdalene as Easter witness in a 1987 article in *Theological Studies*, reprinted with another chapter about female witnesses to the resurrection in my *Interpreting the Resurrection* (New York: Paulist Press, 1988).

48 'The Risen Jesus: Analogies and Presence', in S. E. Porter *et al.* (eds.), *Resurrection* (Sheffield: Sheffield Academic Press, 1999), pp. 195-217; *Believing in the Resurrection: The Meaning and Promise of the Risen Jesus* (Mahwah, NJ: Paulist Press, 2012), pp. 175-91.

dependent revelation, insisting always that, while (b) added no new content or hitherto unknown truth, it involved the constant renewing of God's revealing word to people now. In *Has Dogma a Future?* (1975) I queried the usefulness of lumping together as 'dogmas' the essential content of foundational revelation, which Church teaching had elucidated over the centuries. In *Fundamental Theology* (1981) I proposed using experience as the leitmotif for interpreting revelation and its transmission in the great tradition and the inspired scriptures. I was helped me to develop an experiential approach to these basic themes by an English theological teacher Nicholas Lash and a German doctoral student Alfred Singer.

Back in the 1970s Nicholas Lash, soon to become the Norris-Hulse Professor of Divinity at Cambridge University, remarked that I needed more system. It occurred to me that the theme of experience would help me to organize the major themes in fundamental theology. About the same time I took on the stimulating task of acting as dissertation director to the brilliant German priest, Alfred Singer, whose research involved him deeply in the theme of experience. I read much of what philosophers had written about experience, and learnt a great deal from Alfred himself. Alas, he proved to be a perfectionist rather than a realist. Despite writing well over a thousand pages, he remained dissatisfied and never submitted his thesis.

Among leading protagonists in the discipline of fundamental or foundational theology, my proposals received little attention. The distinction between foundational and dependent revelation shaped the thinking of some Gregorian graduate students, and may have rubbed off on readers of *Fundamental Theology* (which in English, Italian, Korean, Portuguese, and Vietnamese sold well over 25,000 copies). But that was about all. As far as I am aware no prominent teacher of fundamental theology outside the Gregorian ever discussed *either* the distinction between foundational and dependent revelation or the feasibility of experience as the leitmotif for our discipline. In the bulletin on fundamental theology which he published every now and then in the *Revue Thomiste*, Jean-Pierre Torrell once or twice called his readers' attention to my proposal about experience. But that was it.

I failed to argue for any of these ideas at meetings of specialists in fundamental theology. One evening in the late eighties, when the former dean of our theology faculty, René Latourelle, came to my room and proposed convening an international conference of fundamental theologians, I countered with the suggestion of a dictionary of fundamental theology, which he accepted. Latourelle produced the *Dictionary of Fundamental Theology*, which he edited with Father (now Archbishop) Rino Fisichella, and it appeared in English, French, Italian, Portuguese, and Spanish. When Fisichella, after Latourelle's return to Canada, put together an international meeting on fundamental theology at the Gregorian in September 1995, I attended some sessions but was too taken up with other projects to present any paper myself.

An interest in religious experience fuelled my desire to write in the area of spirituality and to do so for general, non-specialist readers. From the 1970s into the early 1980s, Father James Walsh, the founding editor of the British journal of spirituality *The Way*, regularly asked me to contribute. A concern about spiritual experience also lay behind many of the articles I have written for the London *Tablet* and *America* magazine, as well as prompting me to publish *The Second Journey* (1978), *A Month with Jesus* (1978), *Finding Jesus* (1983), *Experiencing Jesus* (1994), *All Things New* (1998), *Following the Way* (1999), *Reflections for Busy People* (2009), and *Pause for Thought* (2011).

After I had written on the theme of hope in the late 1960s, the themes of love and hatred drew my attention to the area of redemption, or the salvation offered by Christ and his Spirit to a world constantly wounded by the forces of hatred. It surprised me that twentieth-century theologians had paid so little attention to love as *the* clue to the whole drama of creation and redemption and no attention at all to hatred, the opposite of love. Yet Christianity offers a uniquely rich tradition of reflection upon love. Once again, however, I limited myself to the exploration of redemptive love with students at the Gregorian and in other universities, dedicating chapters of books to that theme as well as publishing some work on hatred. I never brought my thesis up for debate with professional theologians.

In the Open

Friends helped to push me out into a wider theological world: an American priest Bernard McGarty, a New York couple Eugene and Maureen McCarthy, a great expert in early Christianity Henry Chadwick, and others. Though I never expected greater things after the end of the eighties, the best was yet to come. In late 1990 the Catholic Biblical Association of Great Britain invited me to address them at St Mary's College, Strawberry Hill (London) on the occasion of their golden anniversary. That led me to try out on this critical audience some reflections about interpreting the Bible in the light of Vatican II's Constitution on Divine Revelation, *Dei Verbum* ('The Word of God'). The lecture was to become part of a chapter in *Retrieving Fundamental Theology* (1993).

About that time I received an invitation to lecture from a priest of La Crosse, Wisconsin. Father McGarty was working with a team of Catholics, Episcopalians, and Lutherans in planning an international conference on St Augustine of Hippo to be held in the fall of 1991 at the University of Wisconsin, Madison. For my lecture I gathered and evaluated some themes from Augustine's thought on the resurrection.

A bonus from that meeting was the chance of spending time with Professor Henry Chadwick, who gave a vintage lecture on Augustine which concluded the conference. For me and many others Henry always epitomized scrupulous scholarship elegantly presented.

From the Madison meeting I went straight to spend a sabbatical semester at Pembroke College, Cambridge and lived close to Henry's home, the Master's Lodge of Peterhouse. Gene and Maureen McCarthy not only funded my sabbatical but also encouraged me to present the results of my research to professional audiences. I ended the sabbatical by trying out a paper on the faith of Jesus before audiences at Durham University and at New College (Edinburgh). Meantime Henry had gently urged me to write for Oxford University Press. I set to work on a study of Jesus Christ, which appeared in 1995 as *Christology: A Biblical, Historical and Systematic Study of Jesus*. Before publication, Oxford University Press submitted the manuscript to seven different readers. All of them helped to improve the final product, not least the one who sent several pages of extremely negative evaluation. I used the theme of presence to tie together my views on the person and redemptive mission of Jesus. Feedback from some reviewers has prompted me to develop that theme further, not least in a 2012 article in the *Irish Theological Quarterly*.

A quietly spoken scholar who attended the 1991 Madison conference on Augustine turned out to be Dr Patrick Carey, the head of the theology department at Marquette University, Milwaukee. He and others at Marquette pressed me to visit: first to give the Père Marquette lecture of 1993 (on current debates about Christ's resurrection) and then to become the Wade Distinguished Professor for the fall semesters of 1994/95, 1998/99 and 2006/07. The appointment to that chair in 1994 involved teaching one graduate course, on the use of the Bible in theology, and delivering a single public lecture, on John Hick's interpretation of Christ as being merely one of the world's great gurus. Following the advice from the McCarthys, I repeated that public lecture to audiences in Boston College and in Claremont (California), which helped to polish the text. It finally appeared in the *Gregorianum* and subsequently in a book I co-authored with my Jesuit friend at the University of San Francisco Dan Kendall, *Focus on Jesus* (1996). The course at Marquette fed into a summer conference at the University of Notre Dame and, eventually, into a book I published also with Dan Kendall, *The Bible for Theology* (1997).

The friendliness and the sound scholarship of the Jesuits and others at Marquette made the autumn of 1994 both peaceful and productive. A new and precious friend at Claremont, Professor Stephen Davis, agreed to organize with me an interdisciplinary conference to be held in St Joseph's Seminary, Yonkers (New York) at Easter 1996, the 'Resurrection Summit'. Dan Kendall joined us as the production manager for the book that emerged, *The Resurrection: An Interdisciplinary Symposium on the Resurrection of Jesus* (Oxford University Press, 1997).

Most of the reviews of *The Resurrection* proved encouragingly positive, referring to the book as 'particularly welcome', 'Christian theology at its best', and so forth.[49] Steve, Dan and I had worked hard to encourage those presenting papers to circulate them months ahead of time to all the participants. Some good feedback came in long before we met in April 1996, and almost all the adjustments to the texts encouraged by debate at the Resurrection Summit and by the readers for Oxford University Press could be attended to quickly. We wanted the book out by Easter 1997; it appeared in June. We shared

---

49 I responded to the reviews in 'The Resurrection of Jesus: the Debate Continued', *Gregorianum* 83 (2000), pp. 589-98.

the conviction that symposia which appear in print three or four years after the meeting in question have usually been forgotten by the public; even the participants themselves may well have lost interest. All the momentum has died away — not to mention footnotes and bibliographies failing to include the most recent scholarship.

The Easter 1996 number of *Newsweek*, with Kenneth Woodward's cover story on the resurrection, not only sold extraordinarily well but also encouraged the press and television networks to cover our meeting. ABC, CNN, and NBC could not have done more for us. When I flew out of Kennedy airport at the close of the Summit, there was a close up of Steve Davis on the evening news assuring everyone that 'unless Jesus is risen from the dead, none of us has any hope'.

Luciano Pavarotti provided the only disappointment of the Resurrection Summit. He had agreed to sing without a fee at a sacred concert in St. Patrick's Cathedral, New York. Then television screens and newspapers were filled with the news that he had left his wife and found a new love. Cardinal John O'Connor of New York had to disinvite him, explaining to me: 'He now needs us more than we need him.' The affair had become so blatantly publicised that the Cardinal could not look the other way — as Catholic leaders have so often done for great artists and geniuses. At the last minute the Cardinal then tried to secure the services of the tenor I had first suggested, Placido Domingo. But it was too late. In the event the Resurrection Summit Commemorative Concert took place on 10 April, with the cathedral orchestra, the cathedral choir and two guest artists from the Metropolitan Opera, but it failed to draw a large audience.

In 1996 I had not intended that the Resurrection Summit should be repeated. But its success meant that Eugene and Maureen McCarthy, Cardinal O'Connor, Steve Davis, and others more or less insisted on a repetition. I thought of proposing the Holy Spirit as the theme. But it struck me that the general public might misunderstand our meeting to be a convention of Pentecostal or Charismatic Christians. Steve agreed that the theme should be reflection on all three divine persons, and so we made the subject of our Easter 1998 meeting 'the Trinity Summit', again held at St Joseph's Seminary in Yonkers, New York. In the event, after Ken Woodward had prepared for the Easter 1998 issue of *Newsweek* a cover story on the Trinity, his editors decided that the Holy Spirit and Pentecostal movements were more interesting for their readership. Ken's story on the Trinity and our meeting was thus limited to a couple of pages at the heart of a Pentecostal piece which he had to write at the last minute. Then a further episode in the personal adventures of President Bill Clinton put his face on the cover of *Newsweek* in Europe and that of the special prosecutor Ken Starr on the cover in the United States. The Holy Spirit could no longer be the cover story but had to be content with a brief reference on the top corner of the front cover.

With a somewhat different group, we returned to Yonkers a second time at Easter 1998 for the Trinity Summit. 'A Trinity Summit! How high can you go?', quipped Cardinal O'Connor. The proceedings began with biblical papers. While not suggesting that Jesus anticipated the language of a later age and went around announcing himself as the second person of the Trinity, Craig Evans, of Trinity Western University (British Columbia), explored the high implications of Jesus' self-designation as Son of Man.

Others looked to the gospel stories. The fact that Jesus forgave sins and authoritatively changed the law formed an implicit claim to divine status. Here we have a first foothold for Christians who were to recognize subsequently that Jesus is divine and so personally belongs to the Godhead. Gordon Fee, the author of *God's Empowering Presence* (1994), argued that in Paul's letters the term 'Spirit' is central and should often be read personally, with an initial capital letter, and not in lower case as though referring to a vague kind of divine graciousness. As he put it, 'The Spirit is not seen as a third something but a third Someone.'

The fourth-century Cappadocian writers (Sts Basil, Gregory of Nazianzus, and Gregory of Nyssa) have had a lasting input into trinitarian theology: God as one divine nature or substance and three persons. Sarah Coakley then at Harvard University warned against putting in the centre of the picture Gregory of Nyssa's comparison between three men and the three persons of the Trinity. Gregory employs other analogies, such as the rainbow, and the spring from which water gushes forth in a continuous stream, and these may be more significant. Joseph Lienhard, of Fordham University (New York), was at pains to stress the flexibility and tentative nature of the thought of the Cappadocians. 'They were feeling their way. Their trinitarian language was not something they learned in first-year theology and could look up'. Another paper, by Michel Barnes of Marquette University, considered the early trinitarian thought of St Augustine, who used the enduring analogy of the tripersonal God as Lover, Beloved, and mutual Love.

The Trinity Summit struggled with the classic challenge. If you save the threeness of God, will you lose the divine unity? If you save the unity, will you lose a sense of the divine threeness? And yet the divine Trinity must not be reduced to the model of a loving family or a very united committee. Such human comparisons fall short. Unlike the Trinity, two parents with their only child do not share in one individual divine being or nature. The three divine Persons must not be misrepresented as three individual people; the communion within the tripersonal God is infinitely closer than the community that can exist between three human persons. In a brilliant retrieval of

the trinitarian thought of St Thomas Aquinas, Brian Leftow then at
Fordham University in New York stressed that in God there are no
separate centres of consciousness and decision-making.

The Summit ended with a sobering report from Marguerite Shuster
of Fuller Theological Seminary, Pasadena (California) on the fact that
few preachers present faith in the Trinity at all well or even attend to
it. Out of a sample of well over three thousand sermons, she found
only twenty that dwelt on the Trinity. Even those twenty frequently
did so through appeals to experience that implied false versions of
this utterly central doctrine.

Once again the symposiasts at the 1998 Summit were looked after
most expertly by Father Gerard Rafferty, a professor of scripture
on the staff at St Joseph's Seminary, Yonkers. At Easter 1996 and
again at Easter 1998 he never missed a detail. My advice to anyone
organizing a meeting of scholars from different parts of the world is:
'Get yourself a Rafferty, someone who takes responsibility for all the
practical details, so that nothing is missed.'

Over Easter 2000, Rafferty once more coordinated expertly matters
for the Incarnation Summit. A few months earlier, in late 1999, Oxford
University Press had published *The Trinity*, the proceedings from our
1998 meeting.[50] For the 2000 'Summit', I joined twenty-two Anglican,
Catholic, Jewish and Protestant scholars to reflect on Christian faith
in the incarnation — namely, the belief that the Son of God fully
took on our human condition and visibly came among us. We faced
questions galore. What background, if any, does the doctrine of the
incarnation have in Jewish beliefs? When did Christians first articulate
their belief in the incarnation of the Son of God? Only towards the
end of the first century A.D. at the appearance of the Gospel of

---

50 I responded to the reviews in 'The Holy Trinity: the Debate Continued', *Gregorianum*
81 (2002), pp. 363-70.

John, or much earlier? Does this belief have roots in the words and actions of the earthly Jesus himself? How well does later teaching and theology about the incarnation stand up today? Is belief in the incarnation successfully expressed in contemporary preaching, art, and literature?

The Incarnation Summit concluded with a slide lecture on Christ in twentieth-century art at the Metropolitan Museum in New York. The English theologian David Brown of Durham University expertly took his audience of over seven hundred invited guests through what we can glean about Christ's humanity and/or divinity from Francis Bacon, Marc Chagall, Jacob Epstein, Georges Rouault, Andy Warhol, and other painters and sculptors. Brown concluded that the 'religious impulse in art during the twentieth-century has been healthier than commonly supposed'. After the lecture the guests enjoyed a charming reception around the pool of the Egyptian Temple at one end of the Metropolitan. Cardinal O'Connor was dying, but his office organized the evening and a Jewish friend of his paid the bill.

Before we met again in New York, Steve Davis and Dan Kendall surprised me with a delightful gift for my seventieth birthday (2 June 2001). They organized and edited a collection of essays written in my honour by twenty-one scholars, who included Brendan Byrne, James Dunn, Jacques Dupuis, Cardinal Avery Dulles, John Fuellenbach, Michael Paul Gallagher, William Henn, John O'Donnell, Janet Martin Soskice, Frank Sullivan, and Jared Wicks. The essays focused on four areas in which I had lectured and written: New Testament studies; Vatican I, Vatican II, and Catholic theology; fundamental theology and spirituality; the resurrection and christology. The Archbishop of Canterbury, George Carey, wrote the foreword, and the book, *The Convergence of Theology* (Paulist Press, 2001), ended with a complete bibliography of my published writings down to the year 2000.

Dr Carey, with his wife Eileen and some of his family, flew to Rome for the celebration, as did various relatives and other friends of mine from Australia, England, South Africa, and the United States. In the late afternoon the book was presented in the *aula magna* of the Gregorian, and a group from the English College sang a motet to open the proceedings. At the end of the launch party Archbishop Carey and Cardinal Edward Cassidy of the Pontifical Council for Promoting Christian Unity gave a joint blessing to those attending. Then a group from the Mexican College sang some Latin American songs to put us all in the mood for the reception which followed in the atrium of the Gregorian. My brother Jim and his wife Posey hosted a dinner at a restaurant for the Carey family, Cardinal Cassidy, and other close friends and relatives.

The next day, 2 June, was my actual birthday. The British Ambassador to the Holy See, Mark Pellew, and his wife Jill offered a celebratory brunch at their residence near the Catacombs. With its lovely English garden, bordered by part of the Aurelian Wall which dates back to the Roman Empire, the house was the envy of all. It happened to be the Italian Republic's national day, and during the brunch military jets roared overhead, filling the sky with the red, white, and blue of the Italian flag. 'It's the only country I have ever lived in', I told the guests, 'which knows how to celebrate my birthday in style.'

In 2002, Oxford University Press published the proceedings of our Incarnation Summit, *The Incarnation*. By then Steve, Dan, and I had launched ourselves into the preparations for the Redemption Summit which took place over Easter 2003 and again at St Joseph's Seminary, Yonkers. With the publication of its proceedings, *The Redemption* (Oxford University Press, 2004), we concluded our summit meetings on the core Christian beliefs: the resurrection, the Trinity, the incarnation, and the redemption.

The End of It All

With the end of my Roman years in sight, some friends (mainly Anglican), led by John Batt, proposed my name to the Australian government. In January 2006, I was created a Companion of the General Division of the Order of Australia (AC), the highest civil honour granted through the Australian government. In that list of honours the only other Australian living abroad who received an AC was Nicole Kidman. When colleagues at the Gregorian University celebrated my AC, they could not refrain from quips about 'her' beauty and 'your' brains.

Back in 1956 John Batt and I had shared the exhibition in comparative philology at the University of Melbourne. In 1957 I just pipped him for the final prize in classics. He went on to become a QC and then a judge of the Supreme Court of Victoria. Over the decades our friendship grew stronger, and I regularly met John and his wife Margaret on trips home to Australia. They both visited Rome to share my birthday in June 2006, notably the dinner hosted by my sister Maev in the Abruzzi restaurant and presided over by 'the prince of darkness (il principe delle tenebre)', an swarthy and expert Italian waiter.

George Carey (now Lord Carey of Clifton) and Eileen Carey joined us that evening, as did Mary Venturini, Desmond O'Grady, the Princess Gesine Doria Pamphilj, her husband Massimiliano Floridi, and other friends. A few days earlier Gesine and Massimiliano had invited me and twenty or so other guests to a dazzling dinner in the Doria Gallery. On another evening Mary Venturini, along with her colleague Maggie Mason (with whom she founded the paper *Wanted in Rome)*, offered me another memorable farewell, a reception at the Irish College.

I had buried Maggie's husband in the Protestant Cemetery in Rome, and had earlier done the funeral for the wife of Desmond, a doyen of foreign journalists in Rome For the London *Tablet*, I had written the obituaries of Gesine's parents, Don Frank and Donna Orietta. In life and death so much bound me to these and other old friends in Rome.

But I had done my teaching; after 32 years it was time to pack and leave behind all the glittering beauty of Rome. The Gregorian University's *Liber Annualis* or yearbook has kept a precise tally of my professional activities during the closing decades of the second millennium and beyond. But where was I personally in all that? What were my regrets, and what was I happiest about?

I wish that over the years I had done more for the poor and needy. At the crossroads of the world, Rome does not lack for those who cry out for help. I wish too that I had lived a life of more persistent prayer. Rome has been the permanent home of countless saints, heroically holy men and women, some of whom have been officially recognized for their sanctity. One feels the living presence of all those holy people who have gone before us to God. Their invisible presence and the visible presence of innumerable wonderful churches make it easy to pray. But the sheer busyness of our life at the Gregorian sometimes allowed me to drift away from that courageous closeness to God which was at the heart of everything for the saints.

As the time came to leave Rome, I prayed for a night of rain and that happened. I went up onto our roof in the bright sunlight of the early morning before the smog gathered again. Far above the great doors of the Gregorian and cheerful tourists crossing the square en route for the Trevi Fountain, I looked straight ahead at St Peter's. Encouraged once again by the majestic beauty of Michelangelo's masterpiece, I simply said to our ever-loving God: 'Thank you for all you gave me here in Rome.'

Downstairs a dark-haired, Irish Jesuit, Tom Casey, was waiting for me. He came to teach philosophy at the Gregorian during my final years, and was a personification of cheerful kindness. One evening he had come with his guitar to sing when a smart bookstore right at the Trevi Fountain launched the Italian translation of one of my books, *Incarnation* (2002). Now Tom wanted to drive me to the airport. Naturally, my stuffed suitcases put me well over the allowance for the flight to London and beyond. But Attila at the BA counter accepted all the luggage, issued a boarding pass, and waved me on.

Postscript. From late 2006, St Mary's University College (Twickenham) provided me with the post of research professor. After 'doing' the wedding for two friends at the Farm Street church in Mayfair, I returned to Australia in September 2009, and became a writer in residence and spiritual animator at the Jesuit Theological College, Parkville. The Australian Catholic University had already made me an adjunct professor; the MCD University of Divinity made me an honorary fellow. On 11 February 2013, I had just walked home from a dinner in Newman College (University of Melbourne) when a colleague walked into my room to say: 'Pope Benedict has resigned.'

Index of Names

Venturini, Mary, journalist 198-99, 297

Vergil, poet 274-75

Victor Emmanuel I, king 87

Videla, Jorge, general 261

Von Galli, Mario, journalist 158

Wainwright, Geoffrey, theologian 31, 183, 188 fn. 25

Walsh, Grace, religious superior 138

Walsh, James, editor 287

Walsh, Milton, writer 78-79

Ward, Miriam, scripture scholar 253-59

Wardrobe, Bevan, priest 44-45

Ware, Metropolitan Kallistos, theologian 31, 188 fn. 25

Warhol, Andy, painter 295

Wayne, John, actor 60

Wellington, Arthur Wellsley, duke 126

West, Susan, theologian 188 fn. 25

Whitlam, Gough, prime minister 256

Wicks, Jared, theologian 33, 78, 295

Wilken, Robert, historian 31, 188 fn. 25

Willebrands, Jan, cardinal 47, 182

Willey, David, journalist 200

Wilson, William, ambassador 79

Wojtyla, Karol (see John Paul II)

Wolf, Markus, spy chief 212

Woodward, Kenneth, journalist 113, 291-92

Wright, George Ernest, scripture scholar 254

Wright, John Joseph, cardinal 186-87

Wright, Tom, bishop 32, 188 fn. 25

Yallop, David, fiction writer 57-59

Yeats, W.B., poet 42, 281

Young, Guilford, archbishop 51

Young, Norman, theologian 183

Zeffirelli, Franco, film director 122

Zizioulas, John, bishop 31

Zolli, Eugenio, rabbi 7

Lightning Source UK Ltd.
Milton Keynes UK
UKOW05f0021190814

237104UK00001B/53/P